East Asia and Iran Sanctions

Shirzad Azad

East Asia and Iran Sanctions

Assistance, Abandonment, and Everything in Between

Shirzad Azad
Tehran, Iran

ISBN 978-3-030-97426-8   ISBN 978-3-030-97427-5   (eBook)
https://doi.org/10.1007/978-3-030-97427-5

© The Editor(s) (if applicable) and The Author(s), under exclusive licence to Springer Nature Switzerland AG 2022
This work is subject to copyright. All rights are solely and exclusively licensed by the Publisher, whether the whole or part of the material is concerned, specifically the rights of translation, reprinting, reuse of illustrations, recitation, broadcasting, reproduction on microfilms or in any other physical way, and transmission or information storage and retrieval, electronic adaptation, computer software, or by similar or dissimilar methodology now known or hereafter developed.
The use of general descriptive names, registered names, trademarks, service marks, etc. in this publication does not imply, even in the absence of a specific statement, that such names are exempt from the relevant protective laws and regulations and therefore free for general use. The publisher, the authors and the editors are safe to assume that the advice and information in this book are believed to be true and accurate at the date of publication. Neither the publisher nor the authors or the editors give a warranty, expressed or implied, with respect to the material contained herein or for any errors or omissions that may have been made. The publisher remains neutral with regard to jurisdictional claims in published maps and institutional affiliations.

This Palgrave Macmillan imprint is published by the registered company Springer Nature Switzerland AG.
The registered company address is: Gewerbestrasse 11, 6330 Cham, Switzerland

PREFACE

Sanctions, especially international sanctions politics, function as a powerful tool for social engineering internally and national engineering externally. Domestically, sanctions most often harm innocent and susceptible segments of society but benefit the guilty party or the very people that sanctions vow to target in the first place. Internationally, opportunities that are taken from a sanctioned country are given to other nations which ride on the coattails of sanctions to improve their lot, sometimes undeservedly. When last for a long time, moreover, sanctions rearrange foreign interactions of a penalized country, and vicissitudes of relationship between a sanctioned country and its external partners in different areas are also greatly influenced by the relevant international penalties and restrictions. The present study concentrates largely on the latter implication, probing how international sanctions reshaped the contours of East Asia's relationship with Iran.

Almost all East Asian political entities, from the industrialized and developed nations of Japan and South Korea to the communist and developing countries of China and North Korea, turned out to become major international partners of Iran over the past several decades. As a consequence of international sanctions levied against the Persian Gulf country, even the arbitrarily marginalized yet industrialized Taiwan could get its cameo appearance at some point, while the "white glove" role of Hong Kong was adequately noticeable to be ignored in total. More important, East Asian states were, by and large, thought to be among the leading foreign beneficiaries of Iran sanctions, and the overall impacts of sanctions in transforming both the scope and size of their rather multifaceted

v

connections to the Middle Eastern country happened to be truly consequential.

Despite its significance, however, so far academic studies about this topic has, for the most part, remained sparse and scattered. Not only East Asia's relationship with Iran, and generally the greater Middle East region, is an understudied subject, few research projects concerning contemporary interactions between both sides have made a serious attempt to examine such critical connections primarily in terms of sanctions and their repercussions. More broadly, scholars of international sanctions across various academic disciplines are yet to pay sufficient attention to Iran sanctions and what sundry international penalties virtually brought about for Iranians over a course of more than four decades. Since academic studies about manifold international ramifications of Iran sanctions are equally sketchy, it is thereby no coincidence to come across the poverty of research and investigation about the repercussions of sanctions on East Asian–Iranian transactions.

This book, therefore, aims to partially fill out that research lacuna by surveying all relevant information and data available in the archives of several languages which, in alphabetical order, include Chinese, English, Japanese, Korean, and Persian. Often several versions of accessible resources about a particular issue or development were consulted in order to better shed light on how international sanctions could effectively determine certain aspects of bilateral relationship involving an East Asian country and Iran. Given the nature and scope of the present study, appropriate and reliable data were sometimes hard to come by particularly when an issue at hand required some statistics and mathematical calculations. In such cases, the accessible data and statistics which turned out to be very dissimilar or contradictory had to be utilized with meticulous care or be simply ignored.

While the study also strives to cover as much as possible the entire sanctions period (i.e., from 1979 until the present day), most of the analysis focuses on the past one and a half decades when Iran came under the severest sets of international sanctions. It was during this particular time period when international quandary over the Iranian nuclear program led to a slew of far-reaching penalties and stringent restrictions levied against Iranians by the United Nations and the United States. These recent waves of international sanctions and limitations transformed substantially many quintessential characteristics of East Asia's interactions with Iran almost in every area favorable to both sides. Such sanctions-induced critical developments and changes, moreover, are bound to play an instrumental role in the direction and volume of exchanges between East Asian countries and the Mideast country in the coming years and decades.

Structurally, the book is divided into fourteen chapters. Excluding Chap. 14 which deals with the research conclusions, the other thirteen chapters each takes on a particular yet significant aspect of East Asian–Iranian connections to find out why and how the matter under discussion was to be influenced by Iran sanctions. Organized under several subheadings, every formative chapter for the most part puts the spotlights on those East Asian stakeholders whose interactions with Iran in that area were to be affected considerably by the way sanctions worked or did not work. As a corollary, China is well represented in almost every chapter, North Korea and particularly Taiwan are remotely discussed in some chapters, and Japan and South Korea occupy the middle ground. Iran, and generally Iran sanctions, as the causal variable, is also omnipresent throughout the inquiry.

Finally, sanctions are pain, and writing a book about sanctions is hardly a pain-free endeavor. Much of the agonizing and nerve-racking experience has to do with the scatological realities of sanctions politics which the author encounters ineluctably throughout the long process of researching and writing. For all its subtle innuendo, however, I did my utmost not to let such self-realization interfere with my academic impartiality and personal mores. More surprisingly, this work turned out to be truly rewarding, both intellectually and morally, from the very moment the idea crept into my mind and I jotted it down on a small piece of paper. At that fleeting instant, I had no clue how such celestial spark could give me a sense of mission and duty, galvanizing me into action throughout the long period required to carry out this research project. Having said that, any mistakes and shortcomings in this book are only mine.

Tehran, Iran   Shirzad Azad

CONTENTS

1 The Sweep of Iran Sanctions: Its Essence and Eastern Entanglement   1

2 Sanctions Reverberate: Stoking up Political Allegiance   21

3 Targeting the Lifeline: Oil and Energy Security in Trouble   43

4 In Other Party's Terms: Frozen Oil Funds   71

5 Clogged Up: The World of Non-oil Banking and Credit Matters   93

6 The Minefield for Moneymakers: Investments in a Fluctuating Land   105

7 Tipped to Profit: The Non-stop Gravy Train of Trade   123

8 Not Impervious to Pressure: Teetering Technology Transfer   139

9 Arms Embargoes: Military and Security Adjustment   151

10 Cracks in the Ivory Tower: Academic and Cultural Repercussions — 169

11 Looking East or Looking Elsewhere: Fault Lines of International Orientation — 181

12 The Empire Strikes Back: Circumventing Sanctions — 199

13 The West and the East on the Lookout: Tracking a Tangled Web of Sanctions-Busting — 215

14 East Asia and Iran in Retrospective and Prospective: The Staying Power of Sanctions — 231

Bibliography — 243

Index — 253

About the Author

Shirzad Azad is an independent scholar possessing a doctorate in International Relations. He studied and taught in the East Asian countries of Japan, South Korea (ROK), and China for roughly one decade (2005–2015). This is his eighth scholarly book. His previous titles include *East Asia's Strategic Advantage in the Middle East* (2021), *Iran and China: A New Approach to Their Bilateral Relations* (2017, 2020), *Koreans in the Persian Gulf: Policies and International Relations* (2015, 2019), and several other academic studies with a special focus on East Asia–Middle East relations.

CHAPTER 1

The Sweep of Iran Sanctions: Its Essence and Eastern Entanglement

SANCTIONS IN THEORY

The practice of levying sanctions against states is arguably as old as the institution of the state itself. From the ancient strategy of laying siege to castles and cities to the modern means of imposing economic and technological restrictions deleterious to a target country's normal functions and overall prosperity, sanctions have virtually been an integral component of international politics throughout history. As varied circumstances of time and space dictated, sanctions differed in form and frequency, but they continued to remain part and parcel of international statecraft for thousands of years.[1] Such continuity has actually had a lot to do with this perception that sanctions application could eventually achieve whatever which was at stake, ranging from starry-eyed political and ideological aspirations to solid economic and technological expectations. The sanctioner or the coercer wishes to fulfill its core objective by essentially depriving the target state or the receiver from certain benefits or advantages denial of which would probably cause some sort of setback or discomfort.[2]

The philosophy of sanctions is, therefore, to cause pain and hardship by rendering psychological effects upon the target country or the receiver. After all, sanctions are a penalty, and sometimes a very harsh punishment, which is meted out for the target state's perceived misbehavior or its unwillingness to fully cooperate with the sanctioner or the sender. Without producing punitive results or even short of having coercive impact,

© The Author(s), under exclusive license to Springer Nature
Switzerland AG 2022
S. Azad, *East Asia and Iran Sanctions*,
https://doi.org/10.1007/978-3-030-97427-5_1

1

sanctions would have likely had little chance to be continuously applied both in ancient and modern times. Pain is simply the sine qua non for successful sanctions because they aim to hurt, for the most part, by depriving a target country of certain material benefits and thereby creating hardship and suffering for its normally hapless citizens. Whether or not material deprivation would ultimately lead to accomplishing what certain punitive measures are principally carve out for, a great number of people are often undergo unpleasant and distressing conditions as an inevitable consequence of that particular sanctions policy. To cap it all, any set of sanctions and pernicious prohibitions would bring about a whole host of collateral damages which are relatively hard to size up.[3]

Because of their retributive repercussions, sanctions have historically been used as a major instrument of foreign policy in order to force a target state to reappraise certain elements of its domestic or foreign policies, if not both.[4] By serving such intention, sanctions come to occupy a middle ground between gentle diplomacy and cataclysmic military conflict. Even when sanctions are considered to be a form of coercive diplomacy, they are still a far less costly approach to wield pressure on the target state in comparison to what a shooting war would require.[5] Through making recourse to all non-military resources at its disposable, the sanctioner often intends to take advantage of sanctions as a powerful tool of leverage vis-à-vis the target country without shedding blood or losing lives in a brutal conflict. As a corollary to that function, this *modus vivendi* of foreign policy lies between the two extremes; unrestricted interactions which would benefit the target state one way or the other, and calamitous military campaign which may finally deal a knock-out blow to the sanctioner's overall capabilities.[6]

In spite of the foregoing characteristics, sanctions may still be regarded as an alternative form of war even when they are considered as an alternative to war. That is a reason why sanctions are sometimes called "economic warfare" or "war by other means," because they are applied primarily through economic and financial devices. In this way, referring to sanctions as a "quiet combat" is hardly an exaggeration when they generate various ruinous results similar to what a shooting war would give rise to.[7] The difference is that commercial constraints are used in lieu of military weapons, and the macroeconomic policy of withdrawing economic and financial interactions replaces military campaign. For sure, the sanctioner needs to forego, sometimes quite substantially, economic interests by resorting to export controls related to particular goods and services which the target state desperately requires, but this economic orientation of exercising power and wielding pressures still dwarfs the military approach in terms of all unintended consequences triggered by a bloody war.[8]

When sanctions are intended to induce economic distress, therefore, the goal is most probably about scoring some political gains. This is based on the supposition that once a target country was denied access to certain economic benefits and commercial rewards, its government or ruling elites would ultimately come into compliance, fully or partially, with any set of conditions put forward by a sanctioner or a group of countries which initiated sanctions. In fact, the desired political end result would come about as a consequence of a significant change in the mindset and mood of the target state's citizens.[9] It all happens because economic sanctions and financial blockades would deprive the targeted political system to fund its ongoing programs and policies successfully, causing frustration and anger among its population. Under such lamentable circumstances, the target country's government would, as many proponents of economic sanctions often argue, opt for political concessions in favor of the sanctioner or further jeopardize its legitimacy, if not its very survival.[10]

In order to expedite that process and make the implemented economic measures more effective, the proponents also assert that sanctions are better to be imposed multilaterally and in coordinated ways.[11] Without the participation of several countries, especially the more powerful and resourceful ones, the target state may easily recourse to various methods to get rid of those pesky impediments forced upon it by any set of economic and financial sanctions. Besides the issue of effectiveness and success, multilateralism and extensive international collaboration would probably give more legitimacy to certain sanctions diktats which can potentially pose a threat to a more number of ordinary citizens in the target country.[12] Even when the issue at hand has something to do with international peace and security, unilateralism and heavy-handed approaches to sanctions may hardly appear sufficiently legal and justifiable compared to the time when those punitive measures involve a relatively big number of influential great powers and international organizations across the world.[13]

For all the philosophy and imperative matters, two additional factors contributed to the frequency of sanctions application over the past several decades. The first element has been economic globalization and increasing interdependence among countries, making it possible to easily single out and then draw a bead on a target country's vital sources of generating incomes and foreign currency. It has also made international coordination more attainable and less faltering, at least among a powerful sanctioner's close allies and partners, by agreeing to punish the target country economically and financially in exchange for some quid pro quo arrangements beneficial to the senders or the coercers of sanctions.[14] The other factor has been about rapid advances in technology and new ways of doing international business and communications, providing a powerful and resourceful sanctioner with more additional tools and authoritative mechanisms to enforce its sanctions.[15] No matter if all the technical progress and innovative instruments still failed to stave off any act of sanctions cheating, the sanctioner now turned out to be in a better position to quickly find it out and take corresponding measures.[16]

CONVENTIONAL SANCTIONS THEORY AND IRAN: FROM TARGETED TO COMPREHENSIVE SANCTIONS

Despite the fact that a relatively large number of theories have been developed about international sanctions over the past several decades, however, sanctions theory is still an evolving theme as there is no one-size-fits-all theory to apply to myriad forms of far-reaching and supranational penalties and restrictions levied against certain countries such as Iran. Since the prime objective of the present research is not to formulate a new theoretical framework on international sanctions but to provide as much as possible an in-depth analysis concerning some particular implications of Iran sanctions in light of a hypothetical portmanteau thought up by conventional sanctions theory, it would be essentially futile to allocate a great deal of the study arguing why some premises of this or that meta theory of sanctions do not really fit squarely into the Iranian case. The core arguments contended by conventional sanctions theory form the backbone of this study throughout the ensuing chapters, though the work also benefits from a rather large body of relevant seminal texts produced by sanctions scholars. But what is conventional sanctions theory, and what does it assert principally?

Since 1967 when the journal of *World Politics* published Johan Galtung's case study about "the effects of international economic sanctions" on Rhodesia (Zimbabwe), conventional sanctions theory has been based on this rather firm assumption that imposing external penalties and restrictions, primarily through economic and financial means, would bring about internal political changes.[17] This traditional or classical conviction, which has served as the sinews of sanctions in all forms in modern history, takes it for granted that once the target country's citizens were afflicted with economic pain and financial deprivation, they would eventually rise up against their political system, peacefully or violently, and demand some or sweeping changes in its policies and behaviors. Even when external pressures function as a hindrance to political change rather than as a catalyst for change in certain political systems, still conventional sanctions theory puts a blind faith in the trickle-up power of international restrictions in turning economic pain into political gain in a rather mechanical way.[18]

Because of their perceived effectiveness, moreover, sanctions have long been prescribed as a foreign policy tool especially in the hands of resourceful and domineering powers of international system to force a target country to reconsider its objectionable regional and international policies and behaviors. This function makes sanctions an instrument of upholding international norms and standards by inflicting reputational damage as well as economic and financial loss upon those recalcitrant and unruly players which might be tempted to disregard their international obligations and pose as a potential threat to the world's peace and security.[19] The mere threat of using international sanctions by a powerful coercer or a group of coercers may just intimidate the target to observe its external commitments and obligations. More precisely, the senders may not need to bother with carrying out their warnings and threats because they can use, or actually disabuse, sanctions as a symbolic message of sorts to virtually browbeat the receiver into taking a particular course of action desired by the coercers.[20]

Whether for generating domestic political changes or shoring up international rules and principles, therefore, sanctions needed to be painful and unsympathetic in order to achieve their intended objectives. In fact, international sanctions and penalties had a higher chance of success if they managed to inflict as much as economic and financial ruins as possible in a target state so that even food sanctions could function virtually "as a good catalyst for political change."[21] Besides having a much wider reach, sanctions had to be designed in a way to shut down all the loopholes left open in the receiver's regional and international interactions so that its socio-economic systems were affected immediately and substantially in the wake of limited or no access to the outside world. Generally known as comprehensive sanctions, a set of such all-embracing international restrictions and punitive measures, somehow similar to the practice of sieges in ancient times, had to hurt indiscriminately a bigger number of the target country's citizens because they were supposed to get annoyed sooner or later and turn against their political leaders who had triggered those sanctions in the first place.[22]

Like embargoes, comprehensive sanctions forbid almost all types of normal economic interactions between a target country and other sovereign nations. The goal is to impose a blanket ban on the receiver's accessibility to external markets in all economic, financial, technological, and service sectors, though some exceptions may still be made on humanitarian grounds. To reach their declared objectives, moreover, comprehensive sanctions require an active and undisguised participation of nearly all international players in both the public and private sectors. Since some stakeholders may ignore certain sanctions diktats and engage the receiver, either formally or informally, for politico-ideological or economic reasons, comprehensive sanctions would additionally entail their own set of rules and regulations with regard to the punishment of those players which help the target country to go around sanctions, one way or the other. This feature inevitably makes comprehensive sanctions more complicated, though they could be more instrumental in materializing what conventional sanctions theory is all about.[23]

For all their applicability and effectiveness, however, comprehensive sanctions have long been fraught with serious negative consequences. Such all-inclusive international penalties and limitations are usually ignored and bypassed by some major stakeholders at home and abroad, while they provide ample opportunities for the ruling elites and their close associates to reap enormous benefits.[24] More important, comprehensive sanctions almost always inflict tremendous pain and suffering upon the target country's innocent population and vulnerable citizens. To rectify part of such flaws, targeted sanctions or smart sanctions have received more attention among interested scholars, politicians, and pundits since the 1990s, though this type of international punishment had long been practiced in various forms either separately or in conjunction with other sanctions and threats.[25] Aiming to primarily harm the individuals and organizations that are believed to be responsible for what a set of smart penalties are designed and implemented, targeted sanctions by and large include selective import and export restrictions, aid suspensions, arms embargoes and terminated military cooperation, asset freeze, and travel ban. Instead of being pervasive, targeted or smart sanctions are essentially partial and get a bead on a limited range of commodities and services conducive or favorable to the elites in power.[26]

In spite of their higher objective of minimizing the hardship and misery of the most susceptible and hapless segments of the populace, targeted sanctions have had their own weak points and limitations. Such sanctions are really hard to carve out since their enactment requires much broader and deeper knowledge about how the target country and its politico-economic systems function. Their implementation is equally problematic because both the ruling elites as well as their foreign partners would, in all likelihood, find new ways to evade them.[27] On top of that, ordinary and innocent citizens are often among the biggest casualties of smart sanctions since the ruling elites are simply willing to exploit their civilians as a shield through passing on sanctions tax to them and using any sort of under-handed strategies and tactics in order to mislead the coercers. As a corollary, targeted sanctions are not generally more successful than other types of international penalties and restrictions in achieving their goals, and that is a reason why the sender or a group of coercers are tempted to make recourse to comprehensive sanctions as happened in the case of Iran sanctions.[28]

In essence, Iran has been a testing ground for conventional sanctions theory over a course of more than four decades, experiencing comprehensive sanctions as well as targeted sanctions. The United States, which spearheaded a slew of unilateral and multilateral punitive measures against the Middle Eastern country, kept arguing that it wanted to force the regime of the Islamic Republic to abandon some of its domestic and foreign policies by heaping it with both types of comprehensive and smart sanctions.[29] Unlike some other targeted nations in contemporary history, however, Iranians first had to bear with targeted sanctions fraught with significant collateral damages before their country was hit with heavy-handed international penalties or comprehensive sanctions over the nuclear controversy roughly from 2010 onward. As championed by conventional sanctions theory, the declared and undeclared objective was always the same under both clusters of international punitive measures: the deprived and downtrodden citizens of Iran were expected to ultimately rebel against their theocratic political system and compel its top leaders to do away with their objectionable policies and behavior at home and abroad.[30]

The Panorama of Iran Sanctions

Over the past three decades, the literature on international sanctions has truly mushroomed. Among a relatively large collection of academic and non-academic works dealing with sanctions, the case of Iran sanctions has turned out to be a prime example. Apart from many case studies which have exclusively concentrated on some aspects of Iran sanctions, hardly other sanctions-related scholarly books, articles, and journalistic works have missed the Iranian story. In fact, the Internet is now overwhelmed with the size and scope of data and information which can be retrieved handily from a simple Google search about the term "Iran sanctions." Part of this phenomenon had to do with an obsession in the global media and top policy circles around the world regarding Iran sanctions and their possible *casus belli*. That is no coincidence why the US Departments of State and Treasury have each produced their own relevant "encyclopedia" of Iran sanctions, covering all the laws, regulations, interpretations, and guidelines concerning the Iranian predicament.[31]

It would be no exaggeration, therefore, to argue that Iran sanctions emerged virtually as the most high-profile case of international coercion through which the Middle Eastern country came under some of the most draconian diktats of far-reaching punishment over a course of more than four decades. Of course, Iraq for some 13 years (1991–2003) was subject to some of the harshest and unprecedented forms of international sanctions, and the communists countries of Cuba and North Korea have undergone various crippling practices of penalty for more than 60 and 70 years, respectively, but each of those three model examples came to pale in comparison in terms of what the rigorous regime of Iran sanctions entailed in practice.[32] The Iranian case ineluctably became a one stop shop of international sanctions and an embodiment of universal arm-twisting in the whole history of contemporary world politics simply because no any other sanctions regime in the past had obsessed so many countries and people around the globe in addition to what the long-lasting punitive measures did to the Persian Gulf country itself.

On top of that, the commencement of Iran sanctions in the late 1970s paved the way for a long series of notorious cases initiated and pushed unilaterally outside the framework of the United Nations (UN). Even if only a few international players were really capable of making constant recourse to sanctions, the genesis of the Iranian case triggered a new wave of non-military disciplinary measures which international politics had never witnessed in the past. The whole practice soon became something of a cottage industry, bringing into the world over time various categories of sanctions and punitive policy practices. Since the country moved to retain its dubious position as the archetype for all formal penalties and coercive initiatives, the internationalization of Iran sanctions during more than four decades came to play an important role in the promotion, if not say in the production, of certain relevant terminology and discourse such as unilateral sanctions, multilateral sanctions, individual sanctions, comprehensive sanctions, smart sanctions, secondary sanctions, precision-guided sanctions, and so on.[33]

Although the international coalition which was behind that bureaucratic juggernaut of Iran sanction included different groups with different interests, however, the United States dominated the whole business from start to finish, turning supranational bodies like the UN or close allies such as European Union (EU) and Canada virtually into junior partners in the process. In the United States itself, Iran sanctions involved many powerful players, ranging from the White House to the media and from the Congress to the Jewish and gun lobbies. For instance, the American Congress emerged unprecedentedly as a prominent force, enacting myriad sanctions acts which came to subsequently require an army of lawyers and experts to explore and interpret for all those that had something at stake.[34] In the same way, eight American commanders in chief ruled, one after another, to allocate a good number of their presidential privilege of Executive Order (EO) issuing separate decrees over years to either proscribe or prescribe how or when other nations could actually engage the Iranians.

A major reason was that the Americans could almost always find new justifications under which a fresh round of sanctions had to be added to the Iranian dossier from one decade to another. It all started with the mysterious incident of seizing the US embassy in Tehran in 1979 and taking American diplomats hostage for 444 days. The subsequent serious of sanctions were to be levied against Iran largely on the charges of terrorism and the Islamic Republic's support for some terrorist and extremists groups across the Middle East region and beyond. The Islamic regime in Tehran was to be then charged with other issues such as human rights, and even narcotic-trafficking, providing new grounds for Washington and its close allies to impose other biting sanctions against the pitiable Iranian citizens. Still, none of those allegations and their related sanctions diktats came close to the nuclear controversy for which the country had to undergo the most biting punitive measures over the past two decades when the relevant US campaign effectively led to anti-Iran sanctions throughout the world.[35]

The nuclear charges, therefore, encouraged Washington to shackle Iran with several sets of harshest sanctions which turned out to be, in the words of a top US official, "unprecedented in scope in modern American history." With their increasing severity, these new sanctions were to affect practically a vast range of different issues and areas. As a matter of fact, the nuclear-related measures which were initiated mostly unilaterally by the United State and then pushed internationally came to be a stringent regime of comprehensive sanctions, covering almost all political, diplomatic, military, economic, financial, technological, and even cultural areas, though none of these domains had already remained safe from other sanctions which had previously been imposed on Iran under non-nuclear charges. Thanks to its resources and global prominence, the United States was in a position to rather comfortably use the Iranian nuclear file for consensus-building and coalition-making through which to further isolate and punish the rowdy regime of the Islamic Republic.[36]

Despite the existence of a fat body of literature, the real implications of Iran sanctions on all of those areas are yet to be investigated fully and properly. Due to a whole host of political and bureaucratic impediments, few ground-breaking field works have so far been conducted inside Iran to find out the depth and scope of all those sanctions measures which have been imposed against the Mideast country over the course of more than four decades. Real data and statistics are not often easy to come by, leaving many interested scholars and pundits dependent on the available pool of materials some of which should be taken with a pinch of salt. Additionally, some implications of Iran sanctions, like the topic which the present work is dealing with, are among the most critical aspects of the punitive measures forced upon the Iranians, but they are poorly understood and rarely well-explored in part because of those obstacles. More research needs to be conducted in order to partially fill out the yawning gap in the current literature concerning the vast and multifarious outcomes of Iran sanctions.

Rampant Domestic and International Implications

Estimating the real size and scope of what sanctions bring about is really a hard business. A bulk of the literature on sanctions is also obsessed with the question of effectiveness, asking whether or not certain punitive measures against a given country could actually achieve their clear-cut goals.[37] Even when it was not difficult to distinguish between undeclared and declared objectives of a set of sanctions, the task of discerning their intended and unintended consequences would still be rather complicated and demanding. The crux of the problem is that almost all sanctions turn out to have lots of collateral damages not foreseen by the sanctioner or the coalition of the nations which initiate and enforce them. On top of that, a sanctioned country may end up paying heavily for some types of sanctions several generations after those crippling measures are actually lifted. Human affairs are complex enough, and the intricacies of socio-economic issues make it almost impossible to assess precisely both the current and the future ramifications of particularly broad-based sanctions.[38]

For their part, the scholars of sanctions are largely biased into thinking that sanctions ultimately do not work. They essentially argue that sanctions are ineffective tools of pressure because their primarily intended goals are hard to achieve. Without giving a second thought about a possible existence of undeclared objectives or sizing up a whole host of unintended implications, this line of reasoning highlights the futility of sanctions in failing to eventually achieve their declared aims.[39] Interestingly, many top politicians and pundits from sanctions-stricken countries are used to put a spotlight on the failure of sanctions in comparison to what they intend to accomplish. This approach is definitely a propaganda tactic to mostly dissuade the sanctioners to further pursue their goals, and to mobilize the populace around the sanctioned state and its policies at home and abroad.[40] Deep down, what both groups share in common is that sanctions are principally inefficient since they rarely manage to swiftly bring down the political system of the target country or bludgeon its cloistered leaders into accepting all conditions for which a set of punitive measures are carved out in the first place.

Meanwhile, there are various other scholars and experts who assertively defend the effectiveness of sanctions by stressing their various negative and corrosive results for the target country in short and long terms. They argue in favor of sanctions application because the sanctioned nation will "deservedly" suffer its consequences, one way or the other.[41] Likewise, many moralists and political activists usually give prominence to the caustic nature of sanctions in terms of how much they do serious harm to the wrong people.[42] In their views, sanctions are inherently painful, and any sanctions which fell short of causing pain would not be called sanctions at all.[43] Comparing modern sanctions to the siege warfare in the past history, this group of people denounce sanctions as "a genocidal tool" and a "weapon of mass destruction" which wreak havoc on the lives of mostly innocent civilians without punishing those who truly deserve them. These two clusters of opinions obviously accept that sanctions actually work, though each of them argues from a totally different point of view.[44]

Regarding Iran sanctions, there is a lot to say that they could not achieve a great deal of their declared objectives. For more than four decades, the US-led West ostensibly drew a bead on the Islamic Republic by constantly adding new rounds of punitive measures on the citizens the theocratic regime was representing in order to force it to change some of its contentious policies at home and abroad. Various sets of sanctions were put in place for different reasons, ranging from supporting terrorism to pursuing nuclear weapon charges; however, they failed to weaken the Islamic Republic systematically or compel it to reappraise fundamentally its disputed behaviors in the region and beyond. And in sharp contrast to the sanguine view among some Western policymakers and Iranian opposition forces who thought that maintaining extensive international pressures through economic sanctions and non-military methods was going to ultimately topple the Islamist regime in Tehran, the Islamic Republic actually survived to adhere steadfastly to its controversial rhetoric and plans one decade after another.[45]

When taking into account the bigger picture of what sanctions could do with the Middle Eastern country as a whole, nevertheless, there is plenty of persuasive evidence to prove that the regime of Iran sanctions could achieve far beyond what they were intended to have. For a resourceful and ambitious country that was once going to crawl out of the twentieth century as one of the world's top great powers, it was only a badge of shame for most of Iranian nationals when in the early twenty-first century the name of their proud fatherland still had to be part of some all-purpose portmanteau categories into which the names of several tinpot states and insignificant players had been listed.[46] In fact, sanctions had hurt Iran badly during the final two decades of the twentieth century, but things were to only get worse in the initial two decades of the twenty-first century as more severe bouts of sanctions were levied against the country for its alleged policy of working hard to edge toward a nuclear threshold.[47] All those sanctions and penalties were to shape profoundly the direction of affairs both in domestic and foreign fronts.

Domestically, the country underwent seismic changes after being subject to an omnifarious array of international sanctions and restrictions over a course of more than four decades. Those limitations and obstacles were to have a malign effect on almost every aspect of life in Iran, ranging from birth rate to employment and from inflation to migration. By and large, the Iranians managed to survive those difficult decades thanks to their own tough-mindedness and whatever benefit their resourceful country could offer. But international sanctions were not the only problem which the Iranian citizens had to grapple with; their political system had created enough troubles for them because of its incompetence, mismanagement, and unbridled corrupt practices. Sanctions and punitive measures imposed externally were to only exacerbate all those misfortunes caused by the way the Islamic Republic used to manage the state of affairs in Iran. Similarly, the Islamic Republic's style of governance was to add fuel to the flames of sanctions, causing more harms to an already suffering population.[48]

Internationally, sanctions were to have a lasting impact on the Islamic Republic's orientation toward the outside world since the early 1979. Iran's political and diplomatic relations with the West, and the United States in particular, remained frosty and antagonistic, while the economic and technological interactions between the two sides were to almost always follow all the twists and turns of political developments involving the Iranians and their Western counterparts.[49] In sharp contrast to the West, however, the East emerged as a major stakeholder in Iran's international relations. The more the West imposed sanctions on Tehran, the larger the role and influence of the East grew in Iran one decade after another. Of course, Iran's friendly and often accessible partners in the East happened to include a rather large coalition of different countries with different interests, but the political entities of the Northeast Asian region (henceforth East Asia), including China (along with Taiwan, Hong Kong, and Macao), Japan, South Korea, and North Korea all turned out to play a major role throughout the decades when Tehran was struggling to curb the hurting impacts of sanctions.[50]

East Asians Get Involved

Sanctions are a great tool of redistributing power and wealth, creating winners as well as losers both in domestic and international fronts. Almost in every sanctioned state, certain groups and businesses find propitious opportunities and accessible resources to thrive largely at the cost of other unlucky social forces and professions.[51] Internationally, sanctions are not about a target country and its leading sanctioner or sanctioning nations alone; they have an impact on third parties sometimes very seriously. After all, sanctions can change significantly the balance of power, politically or economically, if not both, between major foreign partners of a target country.[52] Iran sanctions turned out to have such a significant outcome in relations between Tehran and its East Asian stakeholders. It would be really hard to imagine how the scope and size of Iran's interactions with East Asia could undergo so much critical developments by any single factor other than the sanctions which the US-led West imposed on the Persian Gulf country over a course of more than four decades.

Essentially, East Asia was among the first geographical regions which the post-Pahlavi regime of the Islamic Republic approached in order to counter partially the problems caused by sanctions. At that time, Iran made overtures to East Asia to acquire a rather large quantity of arms and military equipment to fight its ongoing war with the neighboring country, Iraq. Although China and North Korea supplied lots of weapons to Iran then, other East Asian players such as South Korea and Taiwan also had a role to play in that sensitive business both overtly and covertly. As time went by, some aspects of military and defense cooperation between Iran and a number of its East Asian partners remained intact, while the Middle Eastern country moved forward to increasingly rely on East Asia for a great deal of its growing economic and technological needs which were denied largely by the sanctions regimes levied by the West. In the same way, sanctions were really instrumental in turning East Asia over time into a top destination for the Iranian exports of energy products and non-oil goods.

During the past several decades, therefore, Iran and its East Asian partners fostered rather multifaceted connections a large part of which was a direct result of sanctions. The very dynamics of interactions between the two parties in different areas had to be influenced ineluctably by the number and severity of punitive measures carved out and implemented against Iran. The all-out relationship was not to imply that every East Asian state had an equal share in Tehran's engagement with the region, and some countries in East Asia emerged to play a bigger role in the Iranian looking-East orientation to counter the corrosive impacts of sanctions. Still, they all managed to maintain a semblance of bilateral interactions in other areas even when their ongoing ties had to be constrained merely to one or two fields. As a case in point, Iran used to develop better political and military relations with North Korea at a time when Tehran was courting South

Korea primarily for economic and technological purposes without forego-ing its foreign policy objectives in Pyongyang and Seoul in other areas.[53]

Consequently, sanctions made it possible for all those East Asian coun-tries to gradually position themselves as Iran's top partners in politico-diplomatic and military as well as in economic and technological fields. Even when Iran's other Eastern partners like Russia could make up, par-tially or wholly, for what China and North Korea were willing to give Tehran politically and militarily, hardly any other Eastern and Middle Eastern country was in a good position to provide Iran with a bulk of the economic and technological requirements which Japan and South Korea were supplying.[54] Additionally, the Persian Gulf country happened to count on East Asia significantly for selling crude oil as its main source of earning foreign currency. A main reason was that sanctions forced a big number of Western countries out of Iran's oil market, while a developing and industrializing East Asia was given a better chance to expand its increasingly rising energy stakes in the Mideast country long before the Trump administration moved to virtually bring the Iranian exports of oil to nil.

In spite of their powerful role in promoting high volumes of exchanges between Iran and its East Asian partners, however, sanctions spawned plenty of troubles between the two sides. The East Asian countries were not always prepared to meet Iran's expectations in terms of providing Tehran with any kind of support and assistance it desperately needed to overcome some pesky problems caused by sanctions. In many cases, the rich and resourceful states of East Asia shunned away from committing themselves to long-term cooperation with Iran especially on certain proj-ects which demanded a great deal of financial capital and technical know-how. The examples were also abound concerning large projects and business deals which many East Asian companies and contractors aban-doned in Iran by excusing sanctions and international restrictions. The worse was that sanctions were sometimes given as a convenient justifica-tion and threadbare excuse for countless cases of betrayal, cheating, duplicity, and denial of service in a welter of deals and agreements involv-ing Iranians and their counterparts from East Asia.

The crux of the problem was that the partnership between Iran and its East Asian counterparts was not always on an equal footing. Sanctions cre-ated a whole host of limitations and troubles for Iran, forcing the Middle Eastern country to rely on the support and assistance provided by its for-eign partners in East Asia and other regions. A good number of deals and accords between the two sides were often agreed not under quite normal circumstances but under tense pressure of sanctions and international isolation, making it easier for the East Asian party to sometimes walk away from its promises and commitments unscathed. Misfortunes and setbacks of such genre were not constrained only to the realm of business and commercial interactions as political and other nonmaterial affairs between Iran and an East Asian country could be affected gravely by the stumbling block of sanctions. Iran was often the weaker party in the game, and if things went awry because of international penalties, it would be the Iranian underdog which had to give up its ambition and expectation.[55]

Besides influencing the dynamics of Iranian–East Asian connections, moreover, sanctions gave rise to a multitude of headaches regarding the relationship between most of East Asian countries and their Western partners, the United States in particular. The US-led West levied sanctions against Iran, but it also did its utmost constantly to make sure that other regions, including East Asia, was implementing those crippling measures targeting the Mideast country.[56] While the East Asian governments and businesses were after maximizing their benefits from cooperating with a sanctioned and isolated Iran, they were striving simultaneously to minimize various potential perils of pursuing a dual-approach in their relations with the West. The policy of attempting to please the two antagonistic parties was not always an easy task, and when push came to shove, Iran needed to be sacrificed inescapably in favor of much larger stakes which the East Asians had to secure in the West. This scenario was to be repeated for the umpteenth time nearly in every area which Iran put faith in its East Asian partners in order to reverse or at least reduce the aching impacts of sanctions.

NOTES

1. Stephen C. Neff, "Boycott and the Law of Nations: Economic Warfare and Modern International law in Historical Perspective," in Ian Brownlie and D. W. Bowett, eds., *The British Yearbook of International Law,* 1988 (Oxford: Oxford University Press, 1989), pp. 135–145.
2. David A. Baldwin, "The Sanctions Debate and the Logic of Choice," *International Security,* Vol. 24, No. 3 (1999), pp. 80–107.
3. Antonios Tzanakopoulos, *Disobeying the Security Council: Countermeasures against Wrongful Sanctions* (New York: Oxford University Press, 2011), p. 82; and Daniel W. Drezner, "The Complex Causation of Sanction

Outcomes," in Steve Chan and A. Cooper Drury, eds., *Sanctions as Economic Statecraft: Theory and Practice* (New York: Palgrave, 2000), pp. 212–230.

4. James Barber, "Economic Sanctions as a Policy Instrument," *International Affairs*, Vol. 55, No. 3 (1979), pp. 367–384.

5. Thomas G. Weiss, "Sanctions as a Foreign Policy Tool: Weighing Humanitarian Impulses," *Journal of Peace Research*, Vol. 36, No. 5 (1999), pp. 499–510.

6. Zane H. Spindler, "The Public Choice of Superior Sanctions," *Public Choice*, Vol. 85, No. 3/4 (1995), pp. 205–226; and Tzanakopoulos, p. 76.

7. Marjorie M. Farrar, *Conflict and Compromise: The Strategy, Politics and Diplomacy of the French Blockade, 1914–1918* (The Hague, Netherlands: Martinus Nijhoff, 1974), p. 2.

8. Makio Miyagawa, *Do Economic Sanctions Work?* (London and New York: Palgrave Macmillan, 1992), p. 204.

9. Margaret P. Doxey, *Economic Sanctions and International Enforcement*, 2nd Edition (London: Macmillan for the Royal Institute of International Affairs, 1980), pp. 9–10.

10. Robert Eyler, *Economic Sanctions: International Policy and Political Economy at Work* (New York: Palgrave Macmillan, 2007), p. 33.

11. Klaus Knorr, *The Power of Nations: The Political Economy of International Relations.* (New York: Basic Books, 1975), p. 160.

12. William H. Kaempfer and Anton D. Lowenberg, "Unilateral Versus Multilateral International Sanctions: A Public Choice Perspective," *International Studies Quarterly*, Vol. 43, No. 1 (1999), pp. 37–58.

13. Kern Alexander, *Economic Sanctions: Law and Public Policy* (New York: Palgrave Macmillan, 2009), p. 11.

14. Alan P. Dobson, *US Economic Statecraft for Survival 1933–1991: Of Sanctions, Embargoes and Economic Warfare* (London and New York: Routledge, 2002), p. 261.

15. For more information concerning this aspect of American power in imposing sanctions, see: Juan C. Zarate, *Treasury's War: The Unleashing of a New Era of Financial Warfare* (New York: Public Affairs, 2013).

16. Richard Nephew, *The Art of Sanctions: A View from the Field* (New York: Columbia University Press, 2018), p. 44.

17. Johan Galtung, "On the Effects of International Economic Sanctions, With Examples from the Case of Rhodesia," *World Politics*, Vol. 19, No. 3 (April 1967), pp. 378–416.

18. Dursun Peksen, "When Do Imposed Economic Sanctions Work? A Critical Review of the Sanctions Effectiveness Literature," *Defence and Peace Economics*, Vol. 30, No. 6 (May 2019), pp. 635–647.

19. Nicholas L. Miller, "The Secret Success of Nonproliferation Sanctions," *International Organization*, Vol. 68, No. 4 (fall 2014), pp. 913–944.
20. Dean Lacy and Emerson M. S. Niou, "A Theory of Economic Sanctions and Issue Linkage: The Roles of Preferences, Information, and Threats," *The Journal of Politics*, Vol. 66, No. 1 (February 2004), pp. 25–42.
21. Margaret P. Doxey, *International Sanctions in Contemporary Perspective*, 2nd Edition (London: Macmillan Press LTD, 1996), p. 108.
22. Clara Portela, *European Union Sanctions and Foreign Policy: When and Why Do They Work?* (Abingdon and New York: Routledge, 2010), p. 5.
23. Thomas G. Weiss, David Cortright, George A. Lopez, and Larry Minear, "Toward a Framework for Analysis," in David Cortright, George A. Lopez, Thomas G. Weiss, and Larry Minear, eds., *Political Gain and Civilian Pain: Humanitarian Impacts of Economic Sanctions* (Lanham, MD: Rowman & Littlefield, 1997), pp. 35–53.
24. Drew Christiansen and Gerard F. Powers, "Economic Sanctions and the Just-War Doctrine," in David Cortright and George A. Lopez, eds., *Economic Sanctions: Panacea or Peacebuilding in a Post-Cold War World?* (Boulder, CO: Westview Press, 1995), pp. 97–117.
25. Joy Gordon, "Smart Sanctions Revisited," *Ethics & International Affairs*, Vol. 25, No. 3 (fall 2011), pp. 315–335.
26. Alexander Orakhelashvili, *Collective Security* (New York: Oxford University Press, 2011), p. 212.
27. William H. Kaempfer and Anton D. Lowenberg, "The Theory of International Economic Sanctions: A Public Choice Approach." *American Economic Review*, Vol. 78, No. 4 (September 1988), pp. 786–793.
28. Oliver Borszik, "International Sanctions against Iran and Tehran's Responses: Political Effects on the Targeted Regime," *Contemporary Politics*, Vol. 22, No. 1 (2016), pp. 20–39.
29. Stephen Tankel, *With Us and Against Us: How America's Partners Help and Hinder the War on Terror* (Cambridge, MA: Columbia University Press, 2018), pp. 86–89.
30. Gilles Carbonnier, *Humanitarian Economics: War, Disaster and the Global Aid Market* (New York: Oxford University Press, 2015), p. 115.
31. The Department of State's inclusive information on Iran sanctions is available at: https://www.state.gov/iran-sanctions/. The Treasury Department's relevant data and instructions can be reached at: https://home.treasury.gov/policy-issues/financial-sanctions/sanctions-programs-and-country-information/iran-sanctions.
32. Geoff Simons, *Imposing Economic Sanctions: Legal Remedy or Genocidal Tool?* (London and Sterling, VA: Pluto Press, 1999), pp. 4–5.
33. Meghan L. O'Sullivan, *Shrewd Sanctions: Statecraft and State Sponsors of Terrorism* (Washington, D.C.: Brookings Institution Press, 2003), p. 48.

34. Kimberly A. Elliott, "Trends in Economic Sanctions Policy: Challenges to Conventional Wisdom," in Peter Wallensteen and Carina Staibano, eds., *International Sanctions: Between Words and Wars in the Global System* (Abingdon and New York: Routledge, 2005), pp. 3–14.
35. Kimberly A. Elliott, "The Sanctions Glass: Half Full or Completely Empty," *International Security*, Vol. 23, No. 1 (summer 1998), pp. 50–65; and Gary Clyde Hufbauer, Jeffrey J. Schott, Kimberly A. Elliott, and Barbara Oegg, *Economic Sanctions Reconsidered*, 3rd Edition (Washington, D.C.: Peterson Institute for International Economics, 2007), pp. 144–145.
36. O'Sullivan, p. 49.
37. A. Cooper Drury, *Economic Sanctions and Presidential Decisions: Models of Political Rationality* (New York: Palgrave Macmillan, 2005), p. 30.
38. Drury, 56.
39. Robert A. Pape, "Why Economic Sanctions Still Do Not Work," *International Security*, Vol. 23, No. 1 (summer, 1998), pp. 66–77.
40. Margaret P. Doxey, "International Sanctions: Trials of Strength or Tests of Weakness?" *Millennium: Journal of International Studies*, Vol. 12, No. 1 (March 1983), pp. 79–87; and Valerie L. Schwebach, "Sanctions as Signals: A Line in the Sand or a Lack of Resolve?" in Steve Chan and A. Cooper Drury, eds., *Sanctions as Economic Statecraft: Theory and Practice* (New York: Palgrave, 2000), pp. 187–211.
41. David A. Baldwin, "The Power of Positive Sanctions," *World Politics*, Vol. 24, No. 1 (October 1971), pp. 19–38; and David A. Baldwin and Robert A. Pape, "Evaluating Economic Sanctions," *International Security*, Vol. 23, No. 2 (fall 1998), pp. 189–198.
42. Michael Walzer, *Just and Unjust Wars: A Moral Argument with Historical Illustrations* (New York: Basic Books, 1977), pp. 170–172; and Dursun Peksen, "Political Effectiveness, Negative Externalities, and the Ethics of Economic Sanctions," *Ethics & International Affairs*, Vol. 33, No. 3 (2019), pp. 279–289.
43. John R. Bolton, *Surrender is not an Option: Defending America at the United Nations and Abroad* (New York: Threshold Editions, 2007), p. 431.
44. Simons, p. 7.
45. Eyler, p. 32–33.
46. Lee Jones, *Societies Under Siege: Exploring How International Economic Sanctions (Do Not) Work* (Oxford and New York: Oxford University Press, 2015), p. 3.
47. Nephew, p. 3.
48. Eyler, p. 76.
49. O'Sullivan, p. 88.
50. Miyagawa, p. 213.

51. David W.H. Palgrave, *Western Trade Pressure on the Soviet Union: An Interdependence Perspective on Sanctions* (New York: Palgrave Macmillan, 1991), p. 43.
52. Steve Chan and A. Cooper Drury, "Sanctions as Economic Statecraft: An Overview," in Steve Chan and A. Cooper Drury, eds., *Sanctions as Economic Statecraft: Theory and Practice* (New York: Palgrave, 2000), pp. 1–16.
53. Shirzad Azad, *Looking East: A Changing Middle East Realigns with a Rising Asia* (New York: Algora Publishing, 2020), pp. 12–13.
54. Alexander, p. 47.
55. Azad, p. 11.
56. Brendan Taylor, "Chapter Three: Sanctioning Iran," *The Adelphi Papers*, Vol. 49, No. 411 (2009), pp. 59–100.

CHAPTER 2

Sanctions Reverberate: Stoking up Political Allegiance

The Saga: A Long and Curved Road to "the Strongest Sanctions in History"

Although the application of sanctions is almost as old as the history of foreign policymaking in the United States, the frequency and scope of resorting to this "policy tool of choice" in contemporary history turned out to be far beyond what the liberal-minded Woodrow Wilson once expected.[1] In the post-Cold War era, more importantly, the United States put sanctions at the core of its foreign policy to serve as a critical component of Washington's regional strategies. From 1993 until 1996 alone, for instance, the United States levied sanctions on 35 nations around the world, raising the rhetoric of unilateralism another notch.[2] The American policymakers were not even afraid to often find themselves at odds with many of their important allies and partners here and there over the extraterritorial nature of various sanctions and punitive measures which they were carving out persistently and implementing enthusiastically.[3] Aside from paying very little attention to the issue of national sovereignty and international law, some American policymakers across the political spectrum were really hell-bent on sanctions application regardless of the fact that such a unilateral approach could sometimes jeopardize, one way or the other, the prestigious global status of their dollar.[4]

Among all the countries which became the target of American sanctions during the past several decades, however, no country could rival Iran

© The Author(s), under exclusive license to Springer Nature Switzerland AG 2022
S. Azad, *East Asia and Iran Sanctions*,
https://doi.org/10.1007/978-3-030-97427-5_2

21

in terms of number and severity of the penalties enforced by Washington and its close allies and partners around the world. Turning the country into an object of both benign and malign aspects of its contemporary foreign policy and double standards practices, the United States ran the gamut, regarding Iran as a "forward defense" country in the early Cold War and designating it as the "enemy of the year" once the Cold War climate was irrelevant.[5] With respect to sanctions obsession, the Middle Eastern country became an archetype of the international victims hit by the United States over a course of more than four decades as many leading American politicians were never short of finding a new excuse to incessantly heap the Islamic Republic with a new round of sanctions, though most of the insiders and informed experts knew full well that mostly innocent and ordinary Iranians were going to bear the brunt of those punitive measures, one way or the other.

It all started with the seizure of the US embassy in Tehran and the follow-up hostage crisis of 1979–1981 during which Washington responded steadfastly by a series of retaliatory steps, targeting a significant part of the Iranian assets and properties in the West in addition to imposing certain economic and military embargoes against the Persian Gulf country. In 1983 when a deadly suicide attack by Hezbollah, a proxy militia apparently supported and financed by the Islamic Republic and its state apparatus, against American marine barracks in Lebanon killed more than two hundred American forces stationed there, the United States upped the ante by putting Iran on its Department of State's terrorism list. The accusation for that incident and more other terrorism charges, which were never lifted, gave the United States a strong reason to levy time and again a whole host of sanctions and punitive measures against Tehran in the years and decades to come. Just designating the Islamic Republic the world's "most active state sponsor of terrorism" and the world's "central bank for international terrorism" was thereby sufficient enough to renew regularly almost all Iran-related sanctions and restrictions in addition to prohibiting the country and an overwhelming majority of its citizens from a wide range of benefits and rewards flowing from normal international interactions in various areas with the outside world.[6]

Meanwhile, from the 1990s onward the United States linked terrorism charges against Iran to its broader foreign policy priorities in the Middle East. In particular, the "dual containment" policy carved out by the Clinton administration made Iran, along with Iraq, subject to a whole array of stringent sanctions and hindrances. The Saddam-controlled Iraq had already been clobbered and weakened substantially by the US-led Operation Desert Storm in 1991, but the Islamic Republic was to be still regarded as a serious menace to some crucial American interests in the region, ranging from a safe and sustainable supply of crude oil from the strategic Straits of Hormuz to the ongoing peace negotiations between the Arabs and the Israelis.[7] Soon after the White House under Clinton pressed for a blanket ban on practically any type of consequential economic relationship between the United States and Iran in May 1995, the American Congress enacted the famous Iran–Libya Sanctions Act (ILSA) in August 1996, harassing any foreign company which dared to invest upwards of $20 million in the Iranian oil and gas industry as the mainstay of the country's international commerce.[8]

In comparison to the costly charges of terrorism, however, the accusation of pursuing a nuclear bomb and other types of weapons of mass destruction (WMD) by the regime of the Islamic Republic provided a better ground for imposing the harshest and augmented types of sanctions Iran had ever seen. In 2005, when it was discovered that Iran had resumed its uranium enrichment program, the country was swiftly referred to the UN's Security Council to face a torrent of punitive measures buttressed by many nations other than the familiar Western countries. From 2006 onward, the nuclear controversy condemned Iran to four rounds of UN sanctions culminating in Resolution 1929 on June 9, 2010, authorizing a series of swingeing universal sanctions against Iran in addition to further isolating the country diplomatically.[9] The UN resolutions gave the United States a powerful mandate to put in the crosshairs a number of critical sectors of Iranian economy by compelling a large crowd of rich and resourceful companies around the world to choose between investing in Iran and doing business with the Americans.[10]

In 2014, when the Obama administration started in earnest to negotiate with Iran over a period of 18 months, therefore, the Mideast country was under collective UN sanctions apart from all other punitive measures levied against Tehran separately by the United States and its allies in the EU, Britain, Canada, and so on.[11] Once the nuclear negotiations between Iran and the sextet (the United States, France, Britain, Germany, China, and Russia) led to a dodgy document entitled the Joint Comprehensive Plan of Action (JCPOA) in June 2015, the country could not still get rid of various other non-nuclear sanctions such as those imposed on Tehran for terrorism and human rights charges. Despite being endorsed by the UN Security Council Resolution 2231 on July 20, 2015, the JCPOA was also a hard sell for the Obama administration domestically as a majority of American lawmakers in both houses of Congress eventually refused to give their *nihil obstat* to an accomplishment which some dubbed Obama's "singular foreign-policy initiative." On top of that, the euphoria in Iran and many other countries around the world over the JCPOA and "crumbling the foundation of Iran sanctions" proved to be premature because it only needed the triumph of Donald Trump in the American presidential election in November 2016 to soon undo what the Obama administration required to jump through hoops and hurdles to pull off.[12]

The ascendancy of Donald Trump turned out to be the harbinger of the darkest period of Iran sanctions. In his determination and restlessness to put the final kibosh on the JCPOA, Trump went against some key members of his cabinet, including Secretary of State Rex Tillerson, Secretary of Defense James Mattis, and National Security Advisor H.R. McMaster, all of whom advised the president to stay in the deal and refrain from taking a dangerous decision which an anonymous White House source had called "World War III levels."[13] On May 8, 2018, the Trump administration ultimately withdrew the United States from the JCPOA, paving the way for the "most biting sanctions ever" imposed on Iran. From now on until the very last day of his one-term presidency on January 20, 2021, Trump left no stone unturned in an effort to hurt Iran by loading it with additional doses of sanctions and international restrictions.[14] The utterly crippling measures which the United States under Trump executed to meet his pledge for pushing "the strongest sanctions in history" were to include the imposition of sanctions on more than 700 Iranian entities and individuals, ranging from the Central Bank of Iran (CBI) to the National Iranian Oil Corporation (NIOC) and from tourism to the health sector.[15]

ALLIES MOBILIZED: THE UNITED STATES AND ITS PARTNERS

By dint of its strategic location and internal developments, Iran in the post-Pahlavi era emerged increasingly as a serious menace to various American interests across the Middle East region. Since certain foreign policy behaviors of the Islamic Republic or its contentious domestic policies such as the nuclear energy program could put into jeopardy Washington's rising stakes in the region and beyond, the United States needed to build up a coalition of fairly like-minded nations and willing partners in order to confront the perceived Iranian threat.[16] Despite being tempted seriously on several occasions to resort to force and military means to neutralize the Iranian nuisance, however, the Americans capitalized almost always on their politico-diplomatic power and economic might to pressure Tehran by forming an international coalition of mostly Western countries and some close allies from East Asia and the Middle East. As it turned out, the decades-long Iran policy of this large and influential international alliance was to be united, and sometimes disunited, by Washington's conventional *modus operandi*: sanctions.

As a two-part process, sanctions required both political inclination and economic obligation. Most of the American allies on Iran sanctions were often prepared to throw their staunch support behind the United States politically and publically, but they were twice cautious when their action demanded certain economic and financial sacrifices. Even when the United States and its partners seemed to be in unison in public with regard to any punitive measure levied against Iran by Washington, sanctions could still cause significant diplomatic rifts among them behind the scenes. In fact, such a conflict of interests existed right from the moment the Carter administration imposed some economic restrictions on the Islamic Republic in the wake of the hostage crisis, but sanctions caused more disputes between the Americans and their allies from the Clinton presidency onward when various unilateral and extraterritorial measures by Washington created a lot of Iran-related economic and financial troubles for its allies.[17] At the end of the day, there happened to be more agreement among the US close friends and partners with regard to Iran sanction, while those countries rarely found themselves on the same wavelength with Washington in terms of carving out and implementing another round of economic penalty against Tehran.

Of all major allies of the United States, Western European countries, especially Britain, France, and Germany, were almost always critical of any American sanctions policy toward Iran. Long before the EU came into existence as a rather unified bloc in international politics or decades before the Brexit became a reality, however, European countries often differed with Washington on how to deal with Iran. Their brewing tensions with the United States eventually burst into the open in August 2020 when Britain, France and Germany, along with an overwhelming majority of other US allies, voted against a resolution pushed by the Trump administration at the UN to extend the expiring arms embargoes against Tehran.[18] For many decades, the Europeans preferred to follow a "dual-track" orientation of sorts regarding Iran by applying material pressures in the form of economic and technological sanctions, and at the same time engaging the Iranians in order to better influence their behaviors at home and abroad.[19] This European approach was usually in sharp contrast to the American policy which focused for the most part on stick without offering any actual carrot.

Besides the major Western European countries, Japan was among the few close US allies with a large stake in Iran. For some time, the Japanese were the biggest customer of Iranian crude, importing a large quantity of both oil and non-oil products Iran had to sell. Even when Japan was relegated to a secondary and third position concerning its overall share of the Iranian exports, the energy-dependent East Asian power still remained instrumental in generating a lot of hard currency which the Byzantine bureaucracy of the Islamic Republic required unremittingly to make ends meet. In the same way, Japan used to occupy an important place in terms of providing Iran with lots of advanced goods and technological products a great deal of which had been sanctioned by the United States and its European partners. As a corollary, the American policymakers really needed to convince their Japanese counterparts to equally put pressures on Tehran by limiting significantly the size and scope of their vital economic and technological cooperation with the Iranians.[20]

But a big problem was that the Japanese policy toward Iran often shared much in common with Europe than the United States. Like their European counterparts, the Japanese believed that applying pressures along with opening the lines of communication with Iran would assist various moderate forces inside the Islamic Republic to win over other conservative and extremists groups within the political establishment in Tehran.[21] More important, the Japanese did not want to lose their sedimented interests in Iran by following exactly what Washington wished. As a major source of energy and a bankable market for various Japanese products, Iran was simply too dear to lose for nothing. Another bugbear was that Japan's East Asian rivals were increasingly and assertively expanding their interests in Iran, making it clear that Tokyo would have a tough time to reclaim its rather envious position in the Iranian market once it decided to scale back its bilateral interactions with Tehran in lockstep with what various diktats of American sanctions and restrictions called for.[22]

Compared to Japan, South Korea came out as the dark horse of all US allies in Iran since its accomplishment and success in the Middle Eastern country turned out to be far more than expected. The Koreans were more stubborn than the Japanese were in maintaining their robust commercial relationship with the Iranians without doing anything in public to contradict what the United States often advocated regarding the regime of the

Islamic Republic. By and large, the Republic of Korea (ROK) cared very little which party was right or wrong in the topsy-turvy world of Iranian politics as long as the governing elites in Tehran were inclined to ship as much as crude oil Seoul asked for and then return back a bulk of the revenues in the form of importing Korean products of every type into their insatiable markets. Even when the ROK was to be forewarned by the Americans about "a minefield of reputational risk" if the East Asian ally refused to toe the line, the Koreans could still appeal to Washington to take care of some 2000 Korean companies doing business with Iran by granting a sanctions waiver to South Korea in every possible way.[23]

The South Korean display of understanding the US policy of Iran sanctions or its reluctant implementation of those punitive measures against Tehran were, therefore, more symbolic rather than substantive as the ROK was always far more worried than Japan about losing its crucial interests in Iran to a rising China and other rivals from the developing world.[24] Seoul's gesture of submission to Washington in punishing Iran was particularly connected to the North Korean nuclear issue since the United States had conventionally made critical linkages between various potential perils stemming from the nuclear policy of Pyongyang and Tehran.[25] Just in case a ruling political party in Seoul desired to improve inter-Korean relations in addition to calming down the nuclear controversy, it would be more convincing for South Korea to at least show it in public that the ROK took the matter of Iran sanctions very seriously.[26] That is no coincidence why the liberal Moon Jae-in turned out to be more willing than his conservative predecessors, Park Geun-hye and Lee Myung-bak, in cooperating with the Trump administration to impose the highest level of sanctions against Iran during the past several years.[27]

A Rank Outsider in Search of Companionship

Throughout its turbulent yet covetable history, Iran has rarely been loved genuinely by all the countries and nations surrounding the Iranian plateau. In the same way, distant powers or jealous rivals from the neighboring regions hardly proved to be more devoted and dependable in the long run in their sporadic and self-serving offers of friendship and cooperation with any classic or modern political system governing the Iranians. As a lion puts faith in its paws to survive and thrive, geographic advantages and natural resources almost always turned out to be Iran's greatest assets, making it quite obvious that the country needed to primarily rely on its internal capabilities than outside sympathy and support. Acknowledging of and bowing to the fiat of geopolitics destiny, therefore, successive Iranian political establishments both in ancient and modern times have had little options but to concentrate, to a large extent, on exploiting the country's own advantages and resources to make ends meet even when they still required to get along with the notoriously fickle world of regional and international alliances.[28]

Despite their ineptitude and lack of sufficient knowledge for modern and efficient governance, the neophyte officials who acceded to power in Iran in early 1979 largely attached to that cardinal principle. "Neither the East, nor the West" was their ear-splitting political rhetoric, signifying that the visionary rulers of the Islamic Republic were going to manage the affairs of the state by depending predominantly on the country's domestic potentials. This was the approach the country took to fight the bloody eight-year long war with Iraq which left close to one million Iranians dead and wounded in addition to other enormously economic and social repercussions the internecine conflict brought about. During and particularly after the brutal war with Iran, the Islamic Republic embraced a rather similar approach to neutralize various distressing implications of sanctions by passing on the pain to the citizenry. Stipulated by the idea of "resistance economy," sanctions and international restrictions against Iran needed to be fought back primarily through mobilizing internal resources and undergoing economic and financial austerity.[29]

As the United States, regardless of its hegemonic power, was in need of foreign allies and partners in order to intensify the aching impact of Iran sanctions and make those punitive measures appear more legitimized and acceptable internationally, however, the pariah leaders of the Islamic Republic for all their penchant for autarky and self-reliance equally required some rather like-minded friends and supporters around the world to counterbalance what the sanctions against Tehran aimed to ultimately achieve. Iran had to look for those foreign partners and sympathizers which could help preventing the imposition of the US-led sanctions in the first place.[30] Besides this small group of typically great powers, the Middle Eastern country had to also court other agreeable yet resourceful nations which were in a relatively good position to lend a helping hand to Tehran to offset the hurting impact of sanctions. At least association and cooperation with such countries could give a modicum of legitimacy to various counter-sanctions measures sought by the Islamic Republic's rulers who generally expected their subjects to bear the brunt of sanctions for the most part.[31]

In the neighboring regions, only the Soviet Union and later the Russian Federation happened to possess a more number of those useful qualifications. In fact, from the time of the hostage crisis when the Soviet Union dared to veto a draft resolution proposed by Washington to impose sanctions on the Persian Gulf country, the Russians emerged as a potential friend and partner of the Islamic Republic in spite of Tehran's fierce anti-communist campaign at home and abroad then.[32] More than two decades later when Moscow prioritized its own national interests and voted in favor of some UN resolutions authorizing sanctions against Iran, the Russian power was still very instrumental and valuable in watering down the original contents of those US-drafted punitive measures targeting the Iranians. Over the past several decades, therefore, many times when the US-led West was planning to levy new sanctions against Iran through some influential international bodies, especially the UN Security Council, the Russian veto power had to be won over as the first stumbling block to punish Tehran.[33]

Although the Russians were not very privileged economically and technologically in assisting Iran to prevail over the sanctions, there was still one area which happened to be Russia's true métier: the armaments industry. From the early 1980s until the end of the Iran–Iraq War in 1988, overt and covert access to the Soviet Union's arms markets proved to be precious for Iran at a crucial time when the Middle Eastern country had encountered serious impediments to get its military requirements from the West. The ensuing international arms embargoes against Tehran only made things worse, deepening Iran's dependency on Russia for a great deal of its military demands. As a consequence, Russia became the largest supplier of various conventional weapons which Iran needed to import, though Moscow still managed to maintain its rather unique position in helping the Iranians to either develop or improve some of their capabilities in the realm of unconventional weaponry. The Russians were also destined to become a major player in the Iranian nuclear program from the moment many Western stakeholders abandoned the ambitious project after the Pahlavi monarchy fell from power.[34]

As time went by, it became an important policy of Russia to drive a wedge between Iran and the West. The Russians simply did not want Iran to get closer to the West so that Moscow could often take advantage of the ongoing antagonism between the two parties as a bargaining chip in its relationship with powerful Western countries, the United States in particular. Even when some top Russian officials accepted in private meetings with their Western counterparts that "Iran was a security threat to Russia," they pretended quite to the contrary in public by finding fault with the West and rooting for the legitimate rights of Iranians to advance their nuclear energy program.[35] From the second administration of Barack Obama onward when an assertive Russia came under several rounds of Western sanctions, moreover, Moscow appeared more alluring to some conservative and dominant forces within the Islamic Republic, temping them to increasingly capitalize on Putin's Russia in order to nip in the bud a number of initiatives taken by other reform-minded circles within the political establishment in Tehran to chip away at a number of key sticking points, such as the nuclear controversy, which had long prevented normal relationship between Iran and the West.[36]

Besides the Russians, East Asia was probably the only region which the Islamic Republic made overtures to, initially, for the sake of sanctions-busting. Still in East Asia, South Korea and Taiwan were too small and too dependent on the United States to cater to all demands put forward by Tehran, though both Seoul and Taipei could be of great help to certain economic and technological, and even military, restrictions which Iran encountered in the years and decades to come.[37] In comparison, the Democratic People's Republic of Korea (DPRK) seemed to share more in common with the Weltanschauung of the Islamic Republic, but all Pyongyang could offer to Tehran subsequently was to be constrained largely to the realms of politics and military because North Korea happened to lag far behind its East Asian rivals in terms of economic and technological accomplishments.[38] That left Iran more dependent on Japan and especially the communist China both of which possessed more political influence and material resources in the face of their contrasting world views and alliance-making.

SHARED VISIONS: IRAN AND CHINA TEAM UP

In the early 1980s when the newly established Islamic Republic approached Beijing, China was very weak and its international clout could hardly rival that of the Soviet Union. It was only a few years earlier when the communist Chinese had launched their "reform and opening-up" (*gaige kaifang*) program, and they were still unqualified to be a major purveyor of various economic and technological services most of which Iran used to

2 SANCTIONS REVERBERATE: STOKING UP POLITICAL ALLEGIANCE 31

get from the West by the late 1970s. Of course, the communist leaders of China and the Islamist officials in Tehran shared a lot in common politically, and Beijing could also supply a great deal of the arms and munitions which Iran desperately needed in order to fight a well-equipped Iraq. But Beijing's international diplomatic and political support for Tehran at that critical period was at best armchair quarterbacking, while the Chinese were twice cautious to openly supply armaments to Iran, using their communist comrades in North Korea as an intermediary for some time before they could muster the courage to engage directly in arms trade with the Iranians.[39]

By the late 1990s, however, the ambitious and hardworking Chinese had already achieved significant progress in various economic and technological areas, turning the rising East Asian giant into a global powerhouse and a strong contender for an increasingly multipolar world order. From now on, more and more influential people and opinion-makers in the Unites States and some other Western countries urged China strongly to be a "responsible stakeholder" in international politics by scaling back, instead of doubling down, on its expanding multifaceted ties with isolated and problematic political regimes such as the Islamic Republic.[40] Beijing was also asked to prioritize sensibly its swiftly deepening relationship with Washington now that various crucial interests of the two great powers at the global level as well as in the greater Middle East region largely conversed as far as Iran was concerned.[41] In the following decades, therefore, many Americans and their close allies and friends kept at "the spinach treatment" of China with regard to Beijing's sedimented interests in Iran, and generally the Middle East and some other parts of the world.[42]

Across the Middle region itself, China gradually yet uninterruptedly encountered many disgruntled voices which warned Beijing not to put all of its eggs in the Iranian basket. From giving priority to stability in the region to contributing to the ongoing peace process between the Arabs and the Israelis, the Chinese were thereby pressed to behave prudently in the Middle East by at least maintaining a semblance of balance between their vested interests in Iran and other Middle Eastern nations. Arguments and advices of such genre appeared to be more convincing and persuasive once the share of China's economic relations with the Arab countries surpassed the total volume of bilateral commercial interactions involving Beijing and Tehran.[43] On top of that, not only the Chinese needed to foster over time closer connections with some advanced military and technological industries in Israel, the rather powerful "Jewish lobby" in the

West, especially in the United States, happened to be a major factor influencing the way China was going to act toward Tehran and other important political capitals in the region.

For all those expectations and propositions, however, from the beginning the Chinese mapped out and implemented their Iran policy principally based on their own understanding and evaluation of Iran's rather unique status in the Middle East. As a strategic country straddling a number of regions and territories very vital to China's long-term interests and ambitions, Iran had simply turned out to be a crucial factor in Beijing's calculations toward the greater Middle East region and beyond.[44] No matter what type of political system was calling the shots in Tehran, the Persian Gulf country's overall significance and its regional role had to be factored in within the corridors of power in Zhongnanhai. After all, the starry-eyed regime of the Islamic Republic proved to be in sync with the communist China's vested interests to such an extent that the continuation of antagonistic relations between Iran and the Western countries, the United States in particular, made the ruling Mullahs in Tehran look nothing less than manna from heaven for Beijing's regional and global power projection.[45]

Economically, China's impression of Iran was equally and strikingly seductive. By the time Xi Jinping managed to pull the strings in Beijing, the two-way commercial relationship between China and the sanctions-stricken economy of Iran ratcheted up to more than $50 billion, encouraging the two countries to soon talk about the prospect of reaching a $600 billion trade turnover within a short period of time after sanctions were removed.[46] It was based on such sanguine anticipations that by March 2021 Iran and China could finalize myriad details of the widely discussed 25-year agreement which commits China to, among other things, invest at least $400 billion in myriad energy and infrastructure projects in the Middle Eastern country.[47] That is no coincidence why energy, especially an uninterrupted and affordable supply of crude oil, had become a key factor in the Chinese foreign policymaking toward Iran right from 1993 onward when China had been turned into a net importer of oil after years of industrialization and economic development at breakneck speed.[48]

Combined nearly all elements of political and military as well as economic and technological power, therefore, China by the time of Xi Jinping's ascendancy to power came to mesmerize many top officials of the Islamic Republic, motivating them to more than ever prioritize Beijing in their decades-long policy of looking-East. In fact, the rising East Asian giant could make up for a great deal of Iran's economic and technological requirements which the Russians were not able to provide. Additionally, the Chinese along with the Russians were widely expected in Tehran to stand up to various excessive demands of the US-led West by forcing Washington not to impose any new sanctions on Iran or at least water down certain parts of the sanctions resolutions which the American policymakers used to draft.[49] Still, there happened to be in the Islamic Republic some staunch anti-West forces calling for a sort of ad hoc alliance between the three sanctioned-countries of Iran, Russia, and China so that the aggregated size and power of this discontented nexus of continental powers would ultimately deal a devastating blow to the United States' hegemonic position and privileges in the Middle East and beyond.[50]

As time elapsed, nevertheless, it seemed that some top Iranian officials had recognized a subtle difference between the position taken by Russia and China concerning Iran sanctions. The Russians had condemned, sometimes in the strongest terms, the sanctions imposed on Iran and had called repeatedly and publicly for their abolition, while in reality they had never wished the Iranians be let off the hook through a normalization of political and economic ties between Tehran and the West. The Chinese were also much louder in their frequent call for the removal of Iran sanctions, but they appeared to be more genuine in their demands because a sanctions-free Iran was predicted by many Chinese experts and pundits to offer a whole host of lucrative opportunities for Chinese businesses.[51] In that sense, China suddenly came into view as a force for good and progress in the eyes of many liberal and reform-minded Iranian officials, while the Russian historical image in Iran had to be further tarnished because of Moscow's tacit alliance with and connections to certain conservative and backward-looking forces within the political and security establishment of the Islamic Republic.

Excelsior with Iran: A Special Role for Japan

Over the past several decades, Japan has maintained rather amicable connections to Iran in spite of its close alliance with the United States. In an interview with an Iranian newspaper in February 2019, the Japanese ambassador to Tehran, Mitsucho Saito, made it clear that his country has actually never left Iran regardless of the approach taken by many of Japan's allies and friends in the West. In his view, Saito empathized that Japan has always looked at Iran from a long-term perspective without letting the torrent of temporary affairs and passing developments determine Tokyo's strategic thinking about Iran and its distinctive place in the Middle East, and Asia in general.[52] By the same token, the Japanese orientation toward Tehran has become a rather unique aspect of its foreign policy during the past decades epitomized by the fact that under the Islamic Republic there happened to be several occasions when Tehran's relationship with many US allies plummeted to its lowest ebb, leading to the expulsion of Western ambassadors and senior diplomats from the Persian Gulf country, but such a dreadfully diplomatic development never took place between Iran and Japan.[53]

By and large, Tokyo's formula of success in Tehran derives from a Japanese endeavor to strike a delicate balance between its vested interests in Iran and what the Americans have expected and demanded from Japan with regard to the Iranians. The Japanese simply wanted to formulate their own Iran policy somehow independent of the guidelines which Washington often specified. This approach became more salient during the past two decades when a new generation of ambitious and assertive Japanese leaders strived to boost Japan's global role and presence by means other than pure checkbook diplomacy. Similar to Junichiro Koizumi's bold behavior during the Iraq War of 2003 and the follow-up chaos and insurgency, Shinzo Abe tried to follow a rather proactive policy toward Iran after he returned to the post of Japanese premiership for a second time in late 2012. During his lengthy tenure, which made him the longest-serving prime minister in the history of modern Japan, Abe went out of his way to breathe new life into Tokyo's policy toward Tehran in the face of his hawkish and unyielding position regarding the North Korean nuclear issue in East Asia.[54]

Abe's early fresh steps toward Tehran started to move through the gears since his efforts roughly coincided with the second administration of Barack Obama who sought to settle the Iranian nuclear controversy peacefully; a relatively popular international orientation which eventually led to the issuance of a 159-page agreement known as the JCPOA in June 2015. But Abe's Iran initiatives hit a brick wall on January 20, 2017 when Donald Trump took the helm of US presidency, putting the Japanese leader on his mettle.[55] Abe did not agree with Trump's tough language regarding the JCPOA, urging him repeatedly to stick with diplomacy instead of tossing away the deal. When Trump eventually left the landmark nuclear deal in May 2018, Japan under Abe vowed to commit Tokyo to whatever the JCPOA had stipulated.[56] More important, many top Japanese

2 SANCTIONS REVERBERATE: STOKING UP POLITICAL ALLEGIANCE 35

officials, including Abe himself, frequently asked their Iranian counterparts to stay in the multilateral deal steadfastly and refrain from any measure which may violate what the agreement required Tehran to observe.[57]

The difference of convictions and opinions between Abe and Trump concerning the JCPOA, however, did not deter Tokyo's firm determination to stick to its own Iran policy. On the contrary, Abe's approach toward Tehran had already bought him enough political capital that actually persuaded Trump to unexpectedly dispatch the Japanese prime minister to Iran as a sort of mediator in 2019. This was not the first time that Japan was going to play such a critical task. In 1984 and 1985, for instance, Abe's own father, Foreign Minister Shintaro Abe, somehow made a reputation for his "*Ira-Ira Gaikou*" (Iran–Iraq diplomacy) by attempting to convince both Tehran and Baghdad to come into terms with each other and end their military conflict.[58] A couple of years later, Japan made another attempt to persuade Iran to accept the UN Resolution 598 which virtually ended the eight-year long war with Iraq, though it was not really clear to what extent the Japanese mediating efforts came to fruition then. In the following decades, moreover, the Japanese leaders acted, both formally and informally, as an honest broker offering several proposals to the Americans and Iranians with regard to their thorny sticking points such as sanctions.[59]

When Abe arrived in Tehran in June 2019, therefore, it was the first time that an incumbent prime minster of Japan was visiting Iran since 1978.[60] Conveying Trump message for the Iranian leaders, Abe said he traveled to Iran for the sake of establishing peace and security in the region, and that was a reason which prompted a reformist Iranian newspaper to dub him "the ambassador of peace and security."[61] As *The Japan Times* put it succinctly, nevertheless, Abe's mediating efforts between Washington and Tehran "ended in flames."[62] While the Japanese prime minister was talking to Iran's top leaders in Tehran, a Japan-owned ship was suspiciously attacked near Iran; an isolated incident which many pundits and observers interpreted immediately as the handiwork by some of those sinister forces, inside or outside Iran, which did not wish a rapprochement between Iran and the United States any time soon.[63] The whole uncanny event was subsequently swept under the carpet since neither Japan nor any other party made a formal investigation to find out who was really behind that provocative act.

Of course, Abe's high-stakes diplomacy with Iran had been doomed from the start.[64] The crux of the problem was that the administration of

36   S. AZAD

Donald Trump was not really prepared to either rejoin the JCPOA or remove sanctions before Washington and Tehran could actually engage in formal talks. Trump was determined to score another victory of sorts in foreign policy before the next presidential election scheduled for November 2020, and a potential bargain with Iran over the ongoing nuclear quarrel could significantly boost his popularity among the American voters. But Trump was not willing to pay any corresponding cost; nor did he want to do away with whatever he had already uttered and done with regard to the JCPOA and the relevant Iran sanctions.[65] After hearing Trump's message disclosed through Abe, the Iranian top leadership quickly turned down the proposal for starting dialogue between Iran and the United States, making it pretty much clear to the Japanese leader that such an important move hinged on the Trump administration's willingness to lift all sanctions against Iran first.[66]

Meanwhile, a great number of conservative forces were equally dissatisfied with Abe's Tehran mission, questioning his credibility and power to really make a dent in the whole edifice of the Iranian–American antagonism which had lasted, *mutatis mutandis*, for over four decades. Long before the Japanese premier embarked upon his historic journey, a number of newspapers and social media outlets put provocative titles and urged Abe, and generally Japan, to stay away from the Islamic Republic's top foreign policy matter.[67] They did their utmost to torpedo Abe's short trip to Tehran to such an extent that one conservative Persian newspaper put a discourteous headline, both in Persian and English, challenging the Japanese prime minister's rationale to trust Trump in the first place.[68] By way of contrast, the reformists were generally positive allocating a great deal of their reports and analyses to praise Abe's mediating role and reappraise the history of Iran's relations with Japan in different fields. Additionally, when Abe resigned in August 2020, in a rare move the Iranian foreign ministry issued a statement appreciating his "valuable efforts" toward Tehran.[69]

NOTES

1. Wilson reckoned sanctions to be a superb substitute for war, arguing, "A nation boycotted is a nation that is in sight of surrender. Apply this economic, peaceful, silent, deadly remedy and there will be no need for force. It is a terrible remedy. It does not cost a life outside the nation boycotted, but it brings pressure upon the nation that, in my judgment, no modern

nation could resist." Cited from Barry E. Carter, *International Economic Sanctions: Improving the Haphazard U.S. Legal Regime* (Cambridge: Cambridge University Press, 1988), p. 9.

2. Richard N. Haass, "Sanctioning Madness," *Foreign Affairs*, Vol. 76, No. 6 (November–December 1997), pp. 74–85; and Randall Newnham, *Deutsche Mark Diplomacy: Positive Economic Sanctions in German–Russian Relations* (University Park, PA: The Pennsylvania State University Press, 2002), p. 20.

3. Salim Lamrani, *The Economic War against Cuba: A Historical and Legal Perspective on the U.S. Blockade* (New York: Monthly Review Press, 2013), p. 13.

4. John R. Bolton, *The Room Where It Happened: A White House Memoir* (New York: Simon & Schuster, 2020).

5. Samuel P. Huntington, "Foreign Aid for What and for Whom," *Foreign Policy*, No. 1 (Winter 1970), pp. 161–189.

6. There happened to be some other charges for which Iran could face additional economic penalties. For instance, in 1987 the Reagan administration designated the Middle Eastern power "a major narcotic-trafficking country," putting a ban on almost any type of importing goods into the United States from Iran. O'Sullivan, p. 49.

7. Alan Dowty, "Sanctioning Iraq: The Limits of the New World Order," *The Washington Quarterly*, Vol. 17, No. 3 (summer 1994), pp. 179–198.

8. Kenneth A. Rodman, *Sanctions beyond Borders: Multinational Corporations and U.S. Economic Statecraft* (Lanham, MD: Rowman & Littlefield Publishers, 2001), p. 185.

9. Those four decisive motions against Iran by the UN Security Council came in the form of Resolution 1737 (December 23, 2006), Resolution 1747 (March 24, 2007), Resolution 1803 (March 3, 2008), and Resolution 1929 (June 9, 2010).

10. Jeremy M. Farrall, *United Nations Sanctions and the Rule of Law* (New York: Cambridge University Press, 2007), p. 81.

11. Before participating formally and publicly in those high-profile nuclear talks, the Obama administration had reached out to many top authorities and influential officials of the Islamic Republic from a couple of years earlier in part by opening a secret channel of informal negotiations held in a third country, Oman in particular, between a close coterie of Obama's team and a group of trusted representatives dispatched by Tehran. For more information, see: Hillary Rodham Clinton, *Hard Choices: A Memoir* (New York: Simon & Schuster, 2014); John Kerry, *Every Day Is Extra* (New York: Simon & Schuster, 2018), pp. 408–439; and William J. Burns, *The Back Channel: A Memoir of American Diplomacy and the Case for Its Renewal* (New York: Random House, 2019).

12. Steven Simon, "Iran and President Trump: What Is the Endgame?" *Survival*, Vol. 60, No. 4 (2018), pp. 7–20.
13. Nikki R. Haley, *With All Due Respect: Defending America with Grit and Grace* (New York: St. Martin's Press, 2019).
14. "U.S. Imposes Fresh Sanctions on Iran in Final Days of Trump Presidency," *Reuters*, January 15, 2021; and "Editorial: Biden Must Undo Trump's Original Sin on the Iran Nuclear Deal," *Los Angeles Times*, April 6, 2021.
15. "U.S. Tiptoes through Sanctions Minefield toward Iran Nuclear Deal," *Reuters*, May 17, 2021.
16. Philip H. Gordon, *Losing the Long Game: The False Promise of Regime Change in the Middle East* (New York: St. Martin's Press, 2020).
17. Geoff Simons, *The Scourging of Iraq: Sanctions, Law and Natural Justice*, 2nd Edition (London and New York: Palgrave Macmillan, 1998), p. xvii.
18. "World has had Enough of US Bullying: China Daily Editorial," *China Daily*, August 23, 2020.
19. Moritz Pieper, "Dragon Dance or Panda Trot? China's Position towards the Iranian Nuclear Programme and Its Perception of EU Unilateral Iran Sanctions," *European Journal of East Asian Studies*, Vol. 12, No. 2 (2013), pp. 295–316.
20. Miyagawa, pp. 128–129; and Michael J. Green, *Japan's Reluctant Realism: Foreign Policy Challenges in an Era of Uncertain Power* (New York: Palgrave, 2001), p. 274.
21. Osamu Miyata, "Coping with the 'Iranian Threat': A View from Japan," *Silk Road*, Vol. 1, No. 2 (December 1997), pp. 30–41.
22. Kazuhiko Togo, *Japan's Foreign Policy, 1945–2003: The Quest for a Proactive Policy*, 2nd Edition (Leiden and Boston: Brill, 2005), p. 303.
23. "Korean Firms Face Risk over Iran Sanctions," *Korea Times*, August 19, 2010.
24. Azad, p. 18.
25. "Trump Signs N. Korea, Russia, Iran Sanctions into Law," *Korea Times*, August 3, 2017.
26. "2nd ROK–US Consultation on Snap-back of US Sanctions against Iran Takes Place," *Consulate General of the Republic of Korea in Los Angeles*, July 20, 2018.
27. "'Hangugeun wae miguk malman ddareuna' ilanseo millyeonaneun hanguk kieobdeul" [Korean Companies Pushed out of Iran 'Because Korea Only Follows American Words'] *Hankyoreh*, February 25, 2020.
28. Shirzad Azad, *East Asia's Strategic Advantage in the Middle East* (Lanham, MD: Lexington Books, 2021), pp. 22–23.
29. Joy Gordon, "The Hidden Power of the New Economic Sanctions," *Current History*, Vol. 118, No. 804 (January 2019), pp. 3–10.

30. "Entezar Iran az mottahedan sharghi" [Iran Expectations from Eastern Allies], *Donya-e-Eqtesad*, June 15, 2019, p. 8.
31. Thomas Juneau, "The Enduring Constraints on Iran's Power after the Nuclear Deal," *Political Science Quarterly*, Vol. 134, No. 1 (2019), pp. 39–61.
32. Doxey, p. 18.
33. "Mosalas Tehran, Mosco, pekan batelosehr tamam doshmanihay gharb ast" [The Triangle of Tehran, Moscow and Beijing Checkmates All Western Enmities], *Kayhan*, January 24, 2018, p. 1; and "Iran dar masir etelafsazi ba roosiye va chin" [Iran's Ongoing Coalition-building with Russia and China], *Shahrvand*, July 26, 2020, p. 3.
34. "Iran va roosiye mitavanand America ra mahar konand" [Iran and Russia Can Contain America], *SMT News*, September 9, 2018, p. 2.
35. Bolton, *Surrender is not an Option*, p. 134.
36. "Kick Russia Out of the Iran Nuclear Talks," *Bloomberg*, April 27, 2021.
37. "US Lauds Taiwan for Limiting Iran Ties," *Taipei Times*, December 6, 2012, p. 3.
38. Lenka Caisova, *North Korea's Foreign Policy: The DPRK's Part on the International Scene and Its Audiences* (Abingdon and New York: Routledge, 2019), p. 67.
39. Joseph S. Bermudez, Jr., *North Korean Special Forces* (Annapolis, MD: Naval Institute Press, 1998), pp. 208–209.
40. "'Shuang ezhi' zai bian" ['Dual Containment' Is Changing], *Renmin* (people's Daily), July 17, 1998; and "Xifang jingxiang jiejin yilang" [The West Races to Approach Iran], *Renmin*, August 28, 1998.
41. John Garver, "China–Iran Relations: Cautious Friendship with America's Nemesis," *China Report*, Vol. 49, No. 1 (2013), pp. 69–88.
42. "Iran and China, the Totalitarian Twins," *The Wall Street Journal*, July 20, 2020.
43. Robert R. Bianchi, "China–Middle East Relations in Light of Obama's Pivot to the Pacific," *China Report*, Vol. 49, No. 1 (2013), pp. 103–118.
44. "Yilang yu xifang jixu gaishan guanxi" [Iran and the West Continue to Improve Relations], *Renmin* (people's Daily), May 4, 1999; and "When China Met Iran," *The New York Times*, July 21, 2020.
45. Marc Lanteigne, *Chinese Foreign Policy: An Introduction*, 4th Edition (Abingdon and New York: Routledge, 2020), p. 46.
46. In the wake of all reinstated sanctions by the Trump administration, the two-way trade between Iran and China plummeted to around $20 billion by 2019.
47. "Why China May Have Bought a $400bn Iran Liability," *Arab News*, July 25, 2020; and "China, With $400 Billion Iran Deal, Could Deepen Influence in Mideast," *The New York Times*, March 27, 2021.

48. David K. Schneider, "Iran Sanctions: The View from Beijing," *Diplomatic Courier*, spring 2009, pp. 35–37.
49. Bernt Berger and Phillip Schell, "Toeing the Line, Drawing the Line: China and Iran's Nuclear Ambitions," *China Report*, Vol. 49, No. 1 (2013), pp. 89–101.
50. "Etelaf amniyati jadid dar shargh" [New Security Coalition in the East], *Khorasan News*, July 12, 2018, pp. 1, 16; "Ettehad Iran, roosiye va chin kaboos vahshatnak America" [Alliance of Iran, Russia and China is America's Horrible Nightmare], *Kayhan*, December 29, 2019, p. 1; and "Agar namad ahzab America fil va olagh ast, namad Iranian 'shir' ast" [If Elephant and Donkey are Symbols of American parties, 'Lion' is the Symbol of Iranians], *Asr-e Iranian*, October 13, 2020, pp. 1, 2.
51. "In gorbe shir ast" [This Cat is Lion], *Hamdeli Daily*, December 9, 2018, p. 1; "Shared Vision Binds Iran–China Relations," *Global Times*, August 26, 2019; and "China, Iran Take Path to Shared Future," *China Daily*, April 1, 2021.
52. "Zhapon hargez Iran ra tark nakardeh ast" [Japan Has Never Left Iran], *Hamshahri*, February 19, 2019, pp. 1, 24.
53. "Expert: No Obstacle to Expansion of Japan–Iran Ties," *Iran Daily*, December 26, 2016, p. 1; and "Japan's Iran Dilemma," *The Japan Times*, December 10, 2019.
54. Mari Nukii, "Japan–Iran Relations since the 2015 Iran Nuclear Deal," *Contemporary Review of the Middle East*, Vol. 5, No. 3 (2018), pp. 215–231.
55. "Japan–US Consultation on US Sanctions on Iran," *Ministry of Foreign Affairs of Japan*, June 19, 2018.
56. Pretty similar to the personal relationship between George W. Bush and Junichiro Koizumi, Donald Trump's close ties with Shinzo Abe remained cordial to the very end so that when Abe resigned as Japan's premier in August 2020, Trump's habitual flattery for Abe reached new heights by calling him the "greatest prime minister" in the history of Japan. "Trump Lauds Abe as Japan's 'Greatest Prime Minister' as Bromance Set to End," *The Japan Times*, August 31, 2020.
57. "Japan Urges 'Uninterrupted' Implementation of JCPOA," *Iran Daily*, December 8, 2016, p. 1; and Ministry of Foreign Affairs of Japan, *Diplomatic Bluebook 2020* (Tokyo: Ministry of Foreign Affairs of Japan, 2020), p. 210.
58. Togo, p. 303.
59. "Hatoyama Comes under Fire for Iran Visit, Claims Ambush," *The Japan Times*, April 12, 2012.
60. It was Prime Minister Takeo Fukuda who visited the Shah-ruled Iran in September 1978.

2 SANCTIONS REVERBERATE: STOKING UP POLITICAL ALLEGIANCE   41

61. "Nakhostvazir zhapon dar Tehran: Frestadeh solh" [Japan PM in Tehran: Peace Envoy], *Jahan-e Sanat*, June 12, 2019, p. 1; and "Safir solh va amniyat" [Ambassador of Peace and Security], *Tejarat News*, June 13, 2019, p. 1.
62. "Should Abe Try Again with Iran?" *The Japan Times*, June 28, 2019.
63. Although many observers blamed the internal rivalry between the reformists and conservatives as a possible *casus belli*, the charge against external forces was hard to be discarded immediately then. As a case in point, the Saudi Arabian powerful Crown Prince, Mohammad bin Salman, had already informed Trump's National Security Advisor, John Bolton, that he was pretty unhappy with Abe's planned visit to Iran. For more details, see: Bolton, *The Room Where It Happened*, p. 387.
64. "Iran va zhapon menhay America" [Iran and Japan minus America], *Javan*, June 12, 2019, p. 2; and "The U.S.–Iran Crisis and Tokyo's Response," *The Japan Times*, January 22, 2020.
65. According to a news report by *Kyodo* in September 2020, in June 2019 the Japanese government under Shinzo Abe had proposed a barter deal, worth several billions of dollars, between Iran and the United States with Japan playing an intermediary role to exchange Iranian crude oil with American corn and soybeans. Despite endorsed initially by the Trump administration, the Japanese scheme eventually failed because Washington did not throw its full support behind it. For more details, see: "Japan Secretly Proposed Iranian Oil and U.S. Grain Swap in Failed Mediator Bid," *Kyodo*, September 8, 2020.
66. "'Na' Tehran be vasetegari Abe Shinzo" [Tehran's 'No' to Abe Shinzo's Mediation], *Siasat Rooz*, June 8, 2019, pp. 1, 5; and "Dasthay khali aghay Abe dar Tehran" [Mr. Abe's Empty Hands in Tehran], *Farhikhtegan Daily*, June 10, 2019, pp. 1, 2.
67. "Kolah goshad mozakre ba America inbar ba dallali zhapon!" [The Hoax of Negotiations with America this Time with Japanese Brokerage], *Kayhan*, May 29, 2019, pp. 1, 2; and "Iran va zhapon menhay America" [Iran and Japan minus America], *Javan*, June 12, 2019, p. 2. In similar fashion, many observers and pundits in Japan and other parts of the world believed that Japan was simply unfit to step in the labyrinthine complexities of the American–Iranian problems. "Why Japan Should Stay Out of U.S. –Iran Spat," *The Japan Times*, May 15, 2019.
68. "How Can You Trust A War Criminal, Mr. Abe?" *Farhikhtegan Daily*, June 12, 2019, p. 1.
69. "Iran Hails Japanese PM's 'Valuable Efforts' after Resignation," *Mehr News Agency*, August 29, 2020.

CHAPTER 3

Targeting the Lifeline: Oil and Energy Security in Trouble

Customers Switched: Supplying a Bulk of the Crude to East Asia

In November 1979 when the administration of Jimmy Carter imposed an oil embargo on Iran in the wake of the unresolved hostage crisis, the United States was importing some 400,000 barrels per day (bpd) of oil from Iran directly and bringing in another 200,000–300,000 bpd indirectly. In the same way, several Western European nations were among major importers of Iranian oil with West Germany as the largest European customer, bringing in about 228,000 bpd or 12.6 percent of its total oil imports from the Middle Eastern country. Iran was also supplying some 124,000 bpd to France and 94,000 bpd to Britain, accounting for 5.4 and 7.1 percent of their total oil imports, respectively. The share of Iranian oil from the Netherlands's and Belgium's total oil imports was roughly 8 percent as well.[1] That was not really unusual because since the discovery of oil in Iran in 1908 and particularly after the political crisis over the nationalization of Iranian oil in the early 1950s, the West had positioned itself, by hook or crook, as a top beneficiary of the black gold gushing out of the Persian Gulf country.

Although Japan was importing some 600,000 bpd (or around 13 percent of its total imports) of Iranian oil on November 12, 1979 when Carter issued his executive order to further pressure Tehran through oil embargo, however, the thirsty East Asian power had been destined to

© The Author(s), under exclusive license to Springer Nature Switzerland AG 2022
S. Azad, *East Asia and Iran Sanctions*,
https://doi.org/10.1007/978-3-030-97427-5_3

43

maintain its critical position as a top buyer of crude oil from Iran in the future. And despite persistent arm-twisting by the Carter administration following the oil embargo, it took Japan several months to limit, and definitely not terminate, its imports of Iranian oil. In the period from 1995 to 2008 when the Iranian oil industry came under several bouts of American sanctions, therefore, Iran managed to become the third largest exporter of crude oil to Japan after the United Arab Emirates (UAE) and Saudi Arabia, respectively, supplying on average more than 10 percent of Tokyo's total oil imports.[2] Iran was still the sixth biggest purveyor of Japan's oil imports in 2017 a year before its crude oil supply to the East Asian country dwindled to a trickle because of Trump's withdrawal from the nuclear deal and the heavy-handed sanctions which soon followed.

After Japan, South Korea emerged as the second top customer of Iranian oil from East Asia before the energy position of both of them in Iran was eclipsed by a rising yet oil-dependent China. The ROK proved to be more bullish than Japan for its oil business in Iran when several sets of US sanctions before the Trump presidency aimed to curb the export capacity of the Iranian oil industry.[3] During the presidency of George W. Bush and Barack Obama, for instance, South Korea practically took advantage of oil importation as its ace in the hole in order to capture a rather large share of Iran's bankable markets of automobiles and electronic products. That was a reason why Washington often had a hard time persuading the ROK to scale back its volume of oil imports from Iran. When the Trump administration abandoned the JCPOA in 2018, therefore, Iran was supplying 8.6 percent of South Korea's total oil import, positioning itself as the ROK's fifth largest source of crude oil after Iraq, the United States, Kuwait, and Saudi Arabia, respectively. Surprisingly, in 2009 the share of Iran from South Korea's total importation of crude oil was the same rate of 8.6 percent.[4]

By comparison, 2009 was the year when Iran had also become a key supplier of crude oil to China, providing the rising East Asian giant with almost 14 percent of its total oil imports.[5] From now on, China maintained its critical position as the most important customer among all Eastern and Western countries which could engage, on and off, in oil trade with Iran. Despite all impediments caused by sanctions and regardless of various diversification strategies pursued by Beijing, in 2018 when Trump discarded the nuclear deal, China was still the largest customer of Iran oil, importing 22 million tons of crude oil or about 6.3 percent of its total imports from the Middle Eastern country.[6] Additionally, when China was compelled to bring down its share of Iranian oil exports under certain sanctions diktats, the Chinese were in a good position to replace part of

3 TARGETING THE LIFELINE: OIL AND ENERGY SECURITY IN TROUBLE   45

that missed crude by purchasing it on the spot market. This was another reason why China turned out to be an indispensable partner for the sanctioned-oil which Iran could find a way to sell to the Chinese somehow surreptitiously through third parties.[7]

Meanwhile, China came to play the role of a middleman transferring a small quantity of Iranian oil to other countries such as the land-locked Mongolia and especially North Korea.[8] Although Tehran's first oil deal with Pyongyang dated back to the 1970s during the reign of the Pahlavi monarchy, this business between the two countries became more important under the Islamic Republic which managed to supply the communist DPRK with 500,000 tons of crude oil in 1980 alone.[9] From the early 1990s onward when the communist Soviet Union collapsed and China itself was turned into an oil importer, the role of Iranian crude became critical for North Korea. The Russians were now demanding cash to supply oil to Pyongyang, while the Chinese did not have any sufficient oil for their own increasingly rising consumption. Consequently, it was more affordable and convenient for the cash-strapped Koreans to engage Iran in economic bartering through which Tehran could pay back North Korea's military and defense cooperation by selling to Pyongyang cargoes of crude oil all of which had to sometimes go via China.[10]

Sanctions were, therefore, very instrumental in altering the main patterns of Iranian oil business with the outside world. The corrosive influence of sanctions became clearer over the past decade when the Iranian oil industry was intentionally targeted by the West.[11] In the year before July 1, 2012, when the EU moved to virtually ban all of its oil imports from Iran, for instance, the volume of Iran's oil exports was roughly 2.1 million bpd two-third of which was flowing to Asia with China (550,000 bpd) as the biggest customer followed by India (360,000 bpd), Japan (340,000 bpd), and South Korea (250,000 bpd). At that time, the total volume of Iranian crude supplying to the EU stood at around 550,000 bpd, making Italy (180,000 bpd) and Spain (150,000 bpd) the two largest buyers from Europe. The Mediterranean nation of Greece was also another European customer which had temporarily, yet desperately, become dependent on oil importation from Iran because it was then encountering serious difficulties to acquire credit for purchasing crude oil from other countries.[12]

Later, the materialization of the JCPOA under Obama as well as the post-JCPOA chaos under Trump were to makes new changes to those arrangements in oil trade between Iran and other regions. When the nuclear agreement was reached in Geneva in June 2015, East Asian countries rushed quickly to reclaim their lost markets in Iran by promising to buy larger cargoes of Iranian oil, while the Europeans by and large behaved more cautiously in committing themselves to new oil deals with Tehran as if they knew something terrible was going to happen soon.[13] As a result, when the Trump administration left the JCPOA in May 2018, it was hard for almost all of East Asian customers of Iran oil to come into terms with the grim reality that the Americans were now obliging them to bring to nil their already soared share of crude imports from the Middle Eastern country.[14] On the contrary, as revealed by the Iranian Oil Minister, Bijan Namdar Zanganeh, in early February 2019, even the EU countries of Greece and Italy were no longer taking the call by Iranian officials to talk about bilateral business in oil.[15]

Resource Diplomacy: The Role and Significance of Oil Factor

Despite being an economic commodity, oil has long been used as a political weapon to serve domestic and especially foreign policy objectives.[16] Few goods other than crude oil have really experienced a similar situation in contemporary history, and fewer regions other than the Middle East have undergone turbulent developments and tumultuous times because of possessing oil. For several decades, for instance, the United States has been accused of following an imperial strategy in the Middle East by striving to control the region's oil resources peacefully or violently. Part of the US strategy, as this line of argument goes, has to do with Washington's long-term policy to hold sway over its rising non-Western rivals based on some important lessons gleaned through dealing with the Nazi Germany and the Imperial Japan during the World War II. The paramount significance of this grand strategy could thereby give grounds for the imposition of incessant sanctions against Iran as a potentially menacing threat to the United States and its sedimented interests in the greater Middle East region.[17]

In the same way, oil-producing countries have tried in the past to achieve certain political goals by resorting to their oil weapon. A classic example was the United States which saddled the Imperial Japan with oil embargoes, forcing the Japanese nationalists to go for blitzkrieg to survive by attacking the American military bases in Perl Harbor. Another prominent case was the first oil shock of 1973–1974 during which the Arab states in the Organization of Petroleum Exporting Countries (OPEC) boycotted the United States and its oil-dependent allies and friends for their support for Israel. For all their fleetingly feel-good politics of making use of oil, however, the Arabs in the OPEC largely failed to score any substantial geopolitical gains in the long run. But the whole crisis, which was originally triggered by the Yom Kippur War of 1973, showed that oil could be immensely and imminently susceptible to non-economic developments and political calculations. Accentuated by a second oil shock in the late 1970s in the wake of political turmoil in Iran, the oil plight of 1973–1974 also set in motion many policy circles in industrializing and energy-dependent countries to carve up several measures for minimizing their oil vulnerability under a similar scenario.

Japan was among the countries which took the oil shocks of the 1970s very seriously. In particular, the first oil shock shook Japan to its core reminding the oil-poor country that it had learned almost nothing from its tragic story during the World War II. The entire Japanese society and its modern way of life ground to a standstill, while the quickly advancing Japanese economy required sometime to get the better of various negative consequences of a sudden energy shortage and get back to its pre-oil shock halcyon days.[18] In the following years and decades, the Japanese government came up with a whole host of initiatives to vouchsafe the oil-thirty country's energy security. On top of that, the East Asian power had to reappraise its rather lackadaisical foreign policy toward the Middle East; a pivotal region which was to keep supplying nearly 90 percent of Japan's oil imports regardless of its various diversification plans.[19] Part of the new Japanese orientation was to capitalize on resource diplomacy, and Japan's East Asian rivals were to soon take a leaf out of Tokyo's energy book in Middle Eastern countries, especially Iran.

Unlike Japan and major Western countries, however, China was very late in joining the convoluted and competitive world of energy politics. It took the Chinese one and half decades to become a net importer of oil after they embarked in earnest upon their industrialization and economic growth programs in the late 1970s. But the rising East Asian power soon proved to be far more aggressive than many of its competitors with regard to locating sources of energy in faraway territories. The Chinese energy strategy (*zhongguo nengyuan zhanlue*) pushed Beijing to throw capital, technology, and human resources into some of the most unpredictable and perilous places in the world for the sake of securing a stable and reasonably priced supply of oil in the long-term. Still, the Chinese similar to

48   S. AZAD

their oil-dependent rivals had to ultimately rely more on the Middle East and its treasure-trove of fossil fuels for their energy security. In the region, no country looked more promising than Iran because its untapped reserves of oil and gas had been shunned away due to sanctions and other international restrictions.[20]

The Chinese approach toward Iran ran up against the US-led Western policy to isolate Tehran politically and pressure it economically via an array of punitive technological and financial measures. China was prepared to cooperate with Iran by investing mostly in its up-and-coming energy sector, though there happened to be many other economic fields in the Middle Eastern country which badly needed foreign capital and technology. In the face of Sino–Iranian oil cooperation since the 1970s, however, China's serious involvement in various big-ticket oil and gas projects in Iran started in earnest from the second half of the 1990s onward in lockstep with Beijing's unflinching quest for energy security and its "going-out strategy" (*zouchuqu zhanlue*) in almost every part of the globe. Unless a new set of US-initiated sanctions constrained severely the scope and size of China's oil and gas undertakings in Iran, Beijing's energy diplomacy could win handily one lucrative Iranian project after another without engaging in stiff competition with its more technologically advanced rivals from the West and the East.[21]

At the same time, energy accomplishments of China in Iran could ruffle feathers in Tokyo and Seoul, not to mention some other political capitals in Asia and the West. Many times when a Japanese or South Korean company had to ineluctably forgo a rewarding energy contract in Iran because of sanctions, the Chinese were often more than happy to take on, making their Asian rivals even more disgruntled. True that Japan and the ROK were often promised by their Americans allies to get as much as oil from other places, but they could hardly replace their export markets in Iran where the preference for international trade was to deal with those countries willing to get deeply involved in energy cooperation with Tehran. To cap it all, the Japanese and Koreans, like many other oil-dependent nations, were to jeopardize their energy security in the long run by forsaking their oil leverage in Iran, while the Chinese could take advantage of their expanded energy profile in the Middle Eastern country as a bargaining chip in their tangled relationship with the United States.[22]

Due to its possession of the world's third and second largest reserves of oil and natural gas, respectively, Iran was consequently too important to China's resource diplomacy in the Middle East. Few other oil-producing countries in the OPEC were to be as critical as Iran to China's strategic calculations about its long-term energy security.[23] Besides its gargantuan quantity of oil and gas, Iran happened to be the only country in the greater Middle East region which could supply energy to China overland without any need to pass through the two strategic straits of Hormuz and Malacca. Of course, the strategic nature of the Hormuz Straits through which roughly one-third of global crude passes and Iran's control over this narrow waterway had long been a critical factor in the energy diplomacy of China and its Asian rivals in the Persian Gulf country.[24] South Korean oil tankers, for instance, go through the Straits of Hormuz around 900 times annually, supplying more than 70 percent of the ROK's imports of crude oil. Japan and Taiwan from East Asia are equally dependent on this critical stretch of water for shipping a bulk of their oil imports from the Middle East region.[25]

CHERRY ON THE CAKE: DISCOUNTED OIL

For more than three decades after the ascent of the Islamic Republic to power in 1979, the oil production in Iran was on average 4 million bpd out of which Tehran could export some half of it and allocate the rest for a gradually yet swiftly rising domestic consumption. Prior to 1979, Iran could produce crude oil by more than 6 million bpd a bulk of which for export purposes. Those rather prolific years were the backdrop to the early second decade of the twenty-first century when the US-led West tightened the screws on the Middle Eastern country, bringing down its total oil exports to less than 1 million bpd.[26] Still, Iran's plummeted share of exports from international oil markets had to further go downhill by late 2018 and early 2019 after the Trump administration quit the JCPOA and subsequently targeted Iranian energy exports. Tehran was simply not allowed to sell as much as oil it deemed necessary despite the fact that several top officials of the Islamic Republic threatened unequivocally that they would shut down the Straits of Hormuz and disrupt the flow of oil from the Persian Gulf if Iran could no longer export any crude oil out of the region.[27]

The fact that the Iranian officials now seemed very hapless sharply contradicted their self-assured behavior in the aftermath of the Gulf War of 1991 when Tehran made it possible for its onetime nemesis Saddam Hussein to, as Robert Gates a former defense secretary of the United States put it in his memoirs, "oversee a vast operation smuggling oil across the border into Iran for sale" in addition to the UN-observed "oil-for-food" program under which the Ba'ath Party-dominated regime in Baghdad had been given the permission to sell just enough oil to buy food and medicine.[28] But a big problem was that Iran could not give up its legitimate rights to sell oil because more than two-third of the government budget had to be bankrolled by the incomes coming from the sale of crude oil to other nations. In order to sweeten its dreadfully dwindling deals of oil exports, Iran needed to offer some incentives such as discounted oil to a small number of energy-dependent nations which were prepared to go out of their way to purchase crude oil from the sanctioned-country of the Persian Gulf.

Just as being engulfed with oil sanctions was not really new to Iran, selling concessional crude oil to other nations was not unprecedented to the country either. As a case in point, when Iran nationalized its oil industry in 1953, Britain as a major stakeholder in that critical development led an international oil embargo against the Iranians. Much to the dismay of the British government, the owner of the Japanese oil company Idemitsu dispatched its oil tanker *Nissho Maru* to Iran in March 1953 in order to be loaded with the oil the London-led countries had boycotted. Carrying some 21,793 kiloliters or 137,074 barrels of gasoil and diesel oil, the Japanese ship left the Iranian port city of Abadan in April before completing its months-long contentious journey and returning successfully to the Port of Kawasaki in May.[29] That sanctions-busting move was to be regarded somehow as a heroic act by many Iranians in the decades to come in spite of the fact that the Japanese oil tanker had actually paid for its cargo 30 percent less than market rates in those trying times.[30]

Roughly seven decades after the *Nissho Maru* bravado, international media started to report regularly that Iran was selling its crude at reduced prices but the level of discount was not clearly specified in their news stories. A number of Japanese and Korean newspapers also pointed to the fact that discounted and cheaper oil had motivated their oil companies to "somehow find a way to continue importing" crude oil from Iran even though this sort of violating sanctions could certainly "cause frictions" between their country and the United States.[31] Although the Chinese media remained by and large tight-lipped with regard to any possibility or the precise rate of concessional oil which their state-owned and private companies were supplying from Iran, however, many interested observers and pundits widely believed that China was most probably the biggest beneficiary of a cheaper oil flowing from Iran.[32] The Middle Eastern country had already become badly dependent on China for its oil exports, and the imposition of new restrictions on Iran's energy sector was to only increase the bargaining power of Beijing in Tehran for discounted oil and other lucrative deals in non-energy fields.[33]

Meanwhile, by 2018 Iran's own newspapers were no longer abashed to occasionally report about the bitter reality of the discounted oil which the country had to give primarily to its loyal and devoted Asian customers. More specifically, they were referring to how China was getting "special oil discount" in the wake of Tehran's trouble to secure a sufficient number of committed clients for its superfluous crude oil.[34] But despite such upsetting revelations, the relevant Iranian authorities were often stubbornly refusing to admit the existence of any concessional oil for China or other customers. While acknowledging that no country was actually willing to sign oil contract with Tehran because of Trump's stringent economic sanctions, for instance, in July 2020 the Iranian oil minister tried to brush off the rising concerns with regard to Iran's new energy arrangements with China as part of the ongoing official interactions between the two sides to soon finalize all the details about the controversial 25-year strategic agreement according to which the Chinese were going to invest some $280 billion in various Iranian oil and gas projects alone.[35]

THE PROBLEM WITH INSURANCE AND SHIPPING: THE *SANCHI* DRAMA

For over a century, ship has basically been the prime means of transporting large amounts of crude oil across the globe. Currently, oil tankers in all shapes and sizes are still in charge of carrying more than half of the oil that sails through oceans, high seas, and waterways. Besides the key issues of suitability and safety, ships are essentially the most cost-effective method of transferring crude oil to the far-flung corners of the world. To give an estimate, for instance, if crude oil was carried through pipelines, it would cost around 5 times more than transporting the same amount of crude by oil tanker. In comparison, when the supply of oil is conducted by using train, the cost would staggeringly soar to some 44 times more than crude transportation by tanker.[36] That is no coincidence why most of the East Asian customers of the Middle East oil have for long paid special attention to different types of sea vessels because of their overdependence on these convenient means of transportation to carry sufficient cargoes of fossil fuels from the region all the time.[37]

It was in the aftermath of the first oil shock when the Japanese suddenly worried about their precarious reliance on international oil companies and their vessels to get enough crude oil from the Middle East and some other regions. The relevant ministries in Japan eventually came up with new plans to bring down over time their country's dangerous dependency on foreign tankers by launching a larger number of Japanese-flagged vessels to bring in their required oil. This important measure was actually in line with some other Japanese initiatives concerning oil discovery and extraction abroad in the decades to come. Pretty similar to its late entry into the global politics of energy, however, China moved into the twenty-first century to realize that the Chinese-flagged tankers were responsible for less than 10 percent of all the crude oil Beijing was importing from other countries. In order to partially make up for this limitation, the rising Asian power embarked upon an ambitious project of shipbuilding aiming to import at least 50 percent of its imported crude through the Chinese-flagged tankers by 2020.[38]

The problem of China, and generally other oil-dependent countries of East Asia, in relying too much on foreign oil tankers showed itself annoyingly in 2012 when the EU, in lockstep with a new round of US sanctions levied against Iran, stopped issuing insurance for non-EU tankers of shipping Iranian crude.[39] The European motion which caused temporary rift between Beijing and Brussels, forced the Chinese to ineluctably begin issuing their own insurance for oil tankers after the Japanese thought up such an important plan.[40] Following the EU policy, the Japanese parliament, Diet, enacted a special law to provide guaranteed sovereign insurance up to $7.6 billion for any incident damaging a vessel which transported Iranian crude all the long way to Japan. As a result, Japan bore the brunt of carrying Iranian oil using its own tankers, a scheme which Iran dubbed "unforgettable loyalty."[41] But South Korea's Ministry of Knowledge Economy (MKE) rejected a similar strategy, arguing that an already-struggling Korean economy would consequently face a hard time in coping with the total insurance liability of more than $7 billion.[42]

By 2019, however, a series of mysterious sea incidents involving oil tankers aggravated the dire situation of insured shipment for Iranian crude. The Islamic Republic or its proxies in the region were subsequently blamed for some of those suspicious tankers collisions and tanker attacks, but the whole episode revealed a great deal about Iran's vulnerability and

3 TARGETING THE LIFELINE: OIL AND ENERGY SECURITY IN TROUBLE   53

its endless troubles in shipping oil to especially distant regions such as East Asia.[43] As a corollary, underwriters demanded all of a sudden higher insurance costs for vessels carrying cargos through the Middle East and particularly the Persian Gulf region the entirety of which had now been classified as a high-risk zone.[44] A giant oil tanker could then require up to $500,000, or ten times more than previous rates, to be insured for the vessel itself, its cargo, and its crew members. Additionally, owners of oil tankers started to demand higher fees to cover rising insurance costs and other potential risks before they could dispatch a vessel to transport Iranian crude to a quickly declining number of mostly Asian customers.[45]

Among all shocking sea incidents which befell oil tankers, none of them turned out to be more unfathomable and consequential than the sepulchral sinking of *Sanchi* on January 14, 2018. Built in 2008 by the ROK's Hyundai Samho Heavy Industries for the National Iranian Tanker Company, the unlucky ship had been renamed and reflagged several times before it collided dubiously with the Hong Kong-flagged cargo ship CF *Crystal* some 160 nautical miles (300 km) off of Shanghai in the East China Sea on January 6, 2018.[46] After the collision, *Sanchi* drifted for eight days experiencing several explosions as the Chinese authorities resorted to any sort of dilly-dally tactics to contain the fire, excusing environmental pollution.[47] By the time *Sanchi* sank, there had remained probably little cargo within the ship to cause serious environmental damages, but the moment the vessel submerged completely there was no more hope for the survival of its 32-member crew, including 30 Iranians and 2 Bangladeshis. Only two dead bodies were recovered, and what really happened to other 30 hapless seafarers, similar to whether or not the reported collision with CF *Crystal* was the real culprit behind the whole incident, was to be shrouded in obscurity probably permanently.[48]

At the same time, the sad incident of *Sanchi* flooded Iran with a torrent of griefs, accusations, and rumors. It was reported that the vessel was carrying 136,000 tons (960,000 barrels) of natural-gas condensate for the ROK, but there were other speculations pointing to the possibility of North Korea, and not South Korea, as the main destination of that ill-fated long journey which *Sanchi* had been assigned to undertake surreptitiously. This raised another theory that blamed the United States for the very occurrence given the fact that the ship's radars had been unexpectedly shut down and the attack had also taken place at night. This line of reasoning was insisting that Washington wanted to warn Tehran not to give any further assistance to a sanctioned-DPRK by shipping to Pyongyang

54   S. AZAD

its crude oil or even its armaments (no matter conventional or unconventional arms).[49] Finally, there were other assertions which claimed that China had done the dirty job at the request of top Iranian authorities in order to deflect attention from a recent wave of national unrest and demonstration which had shaken the Islamic Republic to its core.[50]

CRUDE EXPORTS GO VERSATILE: FROM OIL FOR GOODS TO OIL FOR GASOLINE TO OIL FOR GOLD

True that sanctions are by and large more successful when a target state has to rely on its sanctioner or sanctioners and not the other way around, but these economic means of statecraft are pretty much adaptable and can teach a great deal of invaluable lessons to their victim countries and others. The longer and wider a nation is subjected to international punitive measures, the more likely its leaders and policymakers are expected to learn the ropes in coping with different troubles and unanticipated circumstances which sanctions force upon them. The sanctioned-Iraq under the Ba'ath regime of Saddam Hussein proved to be unprofessional and incompetent in dealing with various stringent penalties which were levied against the Middle Eastern country from early 1990s until early 2003. Besides waiting haplessly to lose up to $250 billion in oil incomes, Baghdad's various policies and strategies to dodge sanctions during those trying years turned out to be rather dysfunctional and inadequate mostly because the country had already gained very little experience in adjusting to heavy-handed international restrictions.

Unlike Iraq, however, Iran under the Islamic Republic sharpened its relevant expertise and skills on the whetstone of ample practical experiences after being in the throes of sanctions for more than four decades. In principle, an analogy can be drawn between the Iranian realization and the way many oil-dependent nations learned to revamp their policies of energy security after encountering the oil shocks and more other chaotic fluctuations in crude markets. As countries in advanced and industrializing world strived over time to diversify their sources of energy imports, Iran also came up, albeit rather late, with different plans to bring variety to its export products as well as to its export destinations. Even the mainstay of Iranian exports, crude oil, seemed to experience new patterns of international trade so that the Persian Gulf country could muddle through under changing regimes of sanctions. That is why, over a period of one decade (roughly from 2009 to 2019), Iran's crude exports to East Asia went through more versatility in terms of what Tehran could get in return, and the refined nature of this crucial export item itself.[51]

By late 2010s, sanctions by the UN and the West had compelled the Iranian government to increasingly tap into bartering so that the Middle Eastern country needed to import a larger volume of manufactured goods from East Asian companies, especially South Korean ones, in return for its oil exports to the region. An immediate implication of this strategy was that Iranian markets were soon overwhelmed with Korean brands and goods of any stripe largely at the cost of some well-established Western, Japanese, and domestic products. Furthermore, an unwarranted cultural campaign had been launched all over the country primarily through public media and press in order to increase the popularity and consumption rate of Korean products by the sanctions-stricken Iranian citizens. Since some top Iranian officials had already urged their counterparts in the ROK not to cut substantially the import of Iranian oil for the sake of maintaining their profitable markets in Iran, the Chinese were to soon take a leaf out of South Korea's trade book by demanding a similar barter system for an increasingly expanding commercial relationship between Beijing and Tehran.[52]

Before being extended to cover many other areas of bilateral business involving Iran and China, bartering was applied simultaneously to fix a surprisingly peculiar Iranian problem of gasoline importation from other countries. From September 2009 onward, therefore, a number of state-owned oil companies from China started shipping gasoline to Iran, providing some one-third of what the oil-rich power of the Middle East needed to import to meet its rising domestic demands.[53] Although the Chinese were asserting that their gasoline sales to Iran was quite legal and normal because fuel imports had not been banned by the relevant UN resolutions against Tehran, they still preferred to engage in the business of gasoline exports to Iran primarily through third countries on the spot markets of Asia.[54] This rather complex Chinese method of bartering crude oil and gasoline with Iran was utilized several years before some Western media dubbed the Chinese approach "the maritime sleight of hand" through which China could camouflage its oil imports from Iran by taking advantage of direct means, ship transfers, and third parties such as Malaysia and Russia.[55]

By 2019 when the American withdrawal of the nuclear deal and the follow-up biting sanctions plunged Iran's oil exports to less than 500,000 bpd, moreover, the Iranian government came up with the idea of bartering its crude oil with gold from other countries such as China, Venezuela, Turkey, and so on.[56] In order to disguise the real nature of this business and deflect international attention from its effective function, however, all the parties involved in a crude-for-gold exchange needed to exploit any remaining loopholes of sanctions by applying one or more of those concealing tactics mentioned previously. For instance, Iran could dispatch to Venezuela a flotilla of oil tankers taking Iranian gasoline to the Latin American country, and then fill its ships with Venezuelan crude oil upon unloading their cargo of gasoline and receiving gold from Venezuela for the outstanding. Those Iranian vessels could now sail toward China's territorial waters in order to barter their crude oil with Chinese gold which the cash-strapped Iranian government could easily turn into cold, hard cash in Dubai or elsewhere.[57]

As the case of gasoline sale to Venezuela demonstrated in 2020, therefore, sanctions had already pressed Iran to tackle its chronic problem of gasoline imports by improving the country's refining capacities. More important, sanctions had thought the Iranian government the value and urgency of turning more oil into petrochemicals domestically. Regardless of the fact that selling crude oil as before was just putting national wealth on sale, petrochemicals turned out to be handy and practical in Iran's battle with sanctions. Besides their higher value, petrochemicals could be harder to detect when transported overland instead of using sea vessels, making them an excellent item for exports at a time of expanding rail transportation between Iran and China.[58] That was no coincidence why China emerged as the biggest customer of Iranian petrochemicals by 2016, replacing South Korea which had already made it possible for Iran to process a large volume of its crude oil into petrochemical products by taking advantage of the ROK's technology and advanced facilities.[59]

Dwindling to a Trickle: Waivers and Total Ban

For nearly three decades, Iran had been under sanctions but the country had generally been left to continue selling crude oil to other nations. Exporting crude oil was the main source of generating adequate funds for the annual national budget, making it imperative for the relevant bureaucracy to take care of the business despite all impediments, shortcomings, and fluctuations in the international market of energy.[60] Of course, Sanctions had done a great deal of harm to Iran's oil industry because of various financial and technological restrictions which had virtually prevented successive Iranian governments to invest sufficiently for modernizing and upgrading the vital industry of oil.[61] Obstacles and limitations targeting a particular foreign oil company active in Iran could also have a corrosive impact on the oil industry, one way or the other.[62] As a case in point, in March 1995, the administration of Bill Clinton forced the American company Conoco to stop oil production in Iran, discouraging several other US businesses to engage in various energy and non-energy fields in the Persian Gulf country.[63]

When the Western–Iranian frictions over Tehran's nuclear dossier settled into a grinding stalemate and Ahmadinejad himself called the relevant UN sanctions nothing more than pieces of "torn paper," however, the Obama administration upped the ante by directly getting a bead on Iran's imports and exports of energy products. Obama's Comprehensive Iran Sanctions, Accountability and Divestment Act (CISADA) intended to particularly stop oil companies from other countries to provide Iran with gasoline which the Iranian government had to import increasingly because of rising domestic consumption and limited refining capacity.[64] More important, the National Defense Authorization Act (NDAA) which the United States passed in 2011 basically proposed imposing sanctions on the countries which were importing Iranian crude oil. Hitting the Iranian government where it hurts most, the NDAA was directly and critically challenging several major powers as well as some close US allies and partners which had long been among major consumers of Iran's oil exports. A number of those countries, especially Japan and South Korea, had to put a halt completely yet temporarily their oil imports from Iran in 2012 until a reasonable solution was offered by the Americans.[65]

As a corollary, the Obama admiration eventually came up with the idea of waivers or exempting some countries from doing oil business with Iran in exchange for "significant reduction" in their crude imports from the Middle Eastern country. In reality, the NDAA had given the American president significant authority to interpret the law by taking into account several considerations such as national interests. The biased and double-standard policy of waivers, therefore, let many Asian nations as well as 10 EU members to continue their imports of Iran oil for an initial period of six months.[66] The US administration was going to automatically extend all waivers every 180 days supposedly that those exempted countries had, ceteris paribus, cooperated with Washington in bringing down their level of crude imports from Iran. The exact level of oil reduction was not really very clear, but in 2012, some influential US senators had demanded an 18 percent cut to be qualified for waiver. Although some countries like the ROK went for a 20 percent cut, for other nations, the reduction was more symbolic than substantive.[67]

The Obama administration-initiated system of sanctions waivers continued until Iran and the sextet agreed for the nuclear deal of July 2015.[68] But Trump had to bring back that discriminatory arrangement once his administration withdrew from the JCPOA in May 2018. The reapplication of waivers now seemed to be more urgent and sensible simply because almost all of the countries which were then doing oil business with Iran expressed this displeasure with the US move to quit the nuclear deal.[69] Since the other five signatories vowed categorically and unequivocally to stick to the JCPOA, a widespread international disagreement over the US withdrawal made the new use of waivers a compromise of sorts so that the United States could, for now, steer clear from further diplomatic disputes and potential trade wars with its important commercial partners across the world. As a result, upon leaving the nuclear deal in May, Trump swiftly redialed Iran sanctions in many areas, but sanctions against Iran's oil and banking industries had to be postponed for another six months. It was in November 2018 when the Trump administration announced a ban on importing crude oil from Iran after giving a 180-day waiver to only eight countries, including China, India, Japan, South Korea, Turkey, Italy, Greece, and Taiwan.

Unlike the pre-JCPOA time under Obama, however, the Trump administration-granted waivers turned out to be short-lived. In April 2019, the American officials said that they were not going to reissue waivers after their expiration on May 2, 2019.[70] Some top Replication supporters of Trump and his Iran agenda had already questioned the rationale behind his administration's decision to grant waivers which they practically considered "a direct contradiction" of abandoning the nuclear deal Trump himself had long opposed determinedly and unflinchingly.[71] After discarding the waiver arrangement, the US policy was to "bring Iran's oil exports to zero, denying the regime its principle source of revenue."[72] The Trump administration also made it clear that it will enforce strictly all relevant Iran sanctions and monitor full compliance with them, causing more anxiety among a number of Tehran's major oil partners which were experiencing serious difficulties in adjusting to the new US policy of virtually bringing the export of Iranian crude oil to nil.[73]

When the United States announced that it will not reissue the temporary Significant Reduction Exceptions (SREs) or the waivers, Greece, Italy and particularly Taiwan soon brought down to zero their imports of Iranian oil. In 2017, Taiwan had imported some 4 million barrels or 2.86 percent of its total oil imports from Iran, and that figure dropped by half in 2018. By the time Taipei stopped its crude imports from Iran in early 2019, the Middle Eastern country was supplying only 16,000 bpd to the tiny island state mostly on the spot market. A bulk of Taiwan's oil requirements was traditionally coming from Saudi Arabia and Kuwait, and it was not that difficult for Taipei to quickly make up for its inescapable cutbacks in Iran's crude oil.[74] Additionally, Taiwan like its East Asian rivals started to pay significant attention to Iraq which was increasingly rising as a major crude supplier and a relatively reliable replacement for Iran's lost oil within the OPEC.[75]

Unlike Taiwan, the other three East Asian customers of Iran oil, including Japan, South Korea, and particularly China were not as pliant and manageable as Washington's "toughest sanctions ever" against Tehran entailed. Virtually the only paying customer of Iranian crude at that time, the Chinese initially and publicly said that they would not comply with unilateral US sanctions against Iran.[76] A relevant incident in Hong Kong in 2019 showed that the Chinese were not going to easily give up their oil business in Iran. In late May 2019, the city government of Hong Kong let in the oil tanker *Pacific Bravo*, which was carrying Iranian oil. In spite of serious warning by a senior American official who threatened that "anyone who does business with this ship, the *Pacific Bravo*, would be exposing themselves to US sanctions," local officials in Hong Kong basically ignored the United States by claiming that they were obliged to only observe the UN-imposed sanctions against Iran and not those demanded by Washington.[77] The oil tanker belonged to China's Bank of Kunlun, which as a subsidiary of China National Petroleum Corporation had for years become a main channel of facilitating financial interactions, including oil payments, between Beijing and Tehran. That is why the United States had sanctioned the Chinese bank in 2012 for its violations of Iran sanctions.[78]

But despite scoffing at "American irresponsible behaviors" as demonstrated by the case of *Pacific Bravo* in 2019, China later toed the line, at least tokenistically, and announced that in June 2020, for the first time in at least eight years, it had not imported crude oil from Iran. A month before, the Chinese had decreased their oil imports from Iran to just 60,000 bpd.[79] As a consequence, the total value of China's oil imports from Iran plummeted 83 percent in 2020 as compared to 2019, but some observers and media reports still claimed that the Chinese actually kept importing Iranian crude which was "falsely rebranded" in other countries such as Iraq, Malaysia, Russia, etc.[80] In fact, only bringing down to zero the crucial oil trade between Tehran and Beijing for a rather long period of time could materialize the US determination of imposing "comprehensive embargoes" against the Persian Gulf country. In reality, only time could prove the viability of such unyielding sanctions resolve.

South Korea was equally adamant in keeping up with its crude imports from Iran, but in comparison to China, the ROK had less bargaining power vis-à-vis the United States. For all their stubborn position, the Koreans announced in September 2018 that they had brought to nil their imports of Iranian oil. Before South Korea's oil trade with Iran ground to a halt, it was importing some 180,000 bpd from the Middle Eastern country against a backdrop of purchasing 147 million barrels throughout 2017.[81] But a problem was that Seoul had not committed itself to a permanent halt in September 2018. In May 2019, it was reported surprisingly again that South Korea put an end to its oil imports from Iran before moving in September 2019 to terminate the won-denominated payment account, which for many years had become the main method of sorting out various financial issues between Seoul and Tehran.[82] It seemed that during those several months the ROK took advantage of every useful channel, including the SREs system, to preserve its critical access to Iranian crude.[83]

Although South Korea had been guaranteed for the umpteenth time by the Trump administration to replace easily its lost imports of Iranian crude by more supply of oil from Saudi Arabia, the UAE, and the United States, however, the ROK kept insisting that the Korean petrochemical industry would encounter serious problems by missing the quality condensate flowing from Iran.[84] In the first quarter of 2018, for instance, more than 50 percent of all condensate imports to South Korea had been supplied by Iran through the three Korean companies of SK Incheon Petrochem, Hyundai Oilbank, and Hanwha Total. Before being compelled to end its oil deals with Tehran in May 2019, therefore, all the crude which South Korea imported from the Middle Eastern country during January and February of that year turned out to be 100 percent condensate. For the following months of March and April, the share of condensate from the ROK's Iranian crude was around 70 percent.[85]

Finally, in early September 2018, Japan made it public that the East Asian country will stop buying Iranian oil from the following month, October.[86] But in early second half of February 2019 when a newspaper in Tehran asked Mitsucho Saito, Japan's ambassador to Iran, whether he agreed with some news stating that his country had actually put a halt to its imports of Iranian oil, he immediately rejected such news reports as "quite baseless."[87] After all, Japan like South Korea accounted for some 13 percent of Iran's crude exports during the first quarter of 2019, no matter if both Asian countries had to ineluctably stop their oil deals with Tehran once their SREs allotments expired on May 2, 2019. Thanks to Shinzo Abe's special relationship with Donald Trump, the United States would not probably get up on its soapbox to discredit Japan only because Tokyo had a special yen for Tehran's concessional oil after November 2018 when the Middle Eastern country was bludgeoned into selling its crude at a discount and accepting oil payments in local currencies.[88]

Oil and the Straits: A Leverage to No Avail or a Chastening Experience?

For decades, the visionary regime of the Islamic Republic financed a great deal of its foreign policy adventures by taking advantage of oil revenues which sometimes seemed superfluous because of an unexpected surge in crude oil prices. In fact, some of the most wasteful and unnecessary projects which Tehran under the Islamic Republic committed itself abroad for a long time and made the similar undertakings by the starry-eyed communists of the Maoist China era pale in comparison, had to be underwritten primarily by the incomes flowing from the export of crude oil. Officials of the Islamic Republic, especially ministers and diplomats, moreover, used to often boast about the Middle East country's massive energy resources as a bargaining power in fostering connections to particularly oil-dependent nations.[89] There happened to be other times when those doe-eyed and confident political authorities could overplay their country's power of oil exports to self-assuredly threaten their foreign counterparts not to disrupt a certain pattern of bilateral commercial interactions deemed sufficiently beneficial to the ruling elites in Tehran.[90]

Internally, oil had already become a key instrument in the administrative toolbox in Iran by the time the Islamic Republic was pitchforked into power in early 1979.[91] As the country had to soon bear the brunt of an eight-year long war with the neighboring Iraq, the ensuing economic catastrophes and social disasters only increased the role of oil incomes for governing Iran in the years and decades to come. Various privatization programs and market-friendly initiatives from the late 1980s onward were also neither a panacea nor a placebo in curtailing systematically the national budget's overdependence on oil revenues to make ends meet.[92] By the time when the US-initiated international sanctions drew a bead on Iran's oil exports in the early 2010s, therefore, incomes flowing from selling crude oil to other countries accounted for some 80 percent of the Persian Gulf country's total export earnings and more than half of the government's annual revenues. But could really Tehran still put an invincible faith in its lifeline now that the United States had virtually targeted its international sale?[93]

When many top officials of the Islamic Republic were cheering for the fall of the Ba'ath Party in Baghdad in 2003 they had absolutely no clue that a stable Iraq in the post-Saddam era could boomerang on them by pumping too much oil into the international markets of energy after the supply of Iranian crude was badly interrupted because of sanctions. The oil-rich Iraq under Saddam was itself a glittering crown jewel in the world of fossil fuels and under some propitious circumstances could easily prove its mettle. Besides the newly Islamists-dominated Iraq, the rulers of Saudi Arabia were already waiting in their wings to replace almost all of Iran's lost crude without any delay.[94] Like Saudi Arabia, some other OPEC members were prepared fully to produce above their agreed quota in order to make up for Iranian crude and thereby increase their share of international oil markets at the cost of Iran.[95] The relevant authorities in Tehran could only express their displeasure with a lack of solidarity and sympathy among OPEC countries, but they actually had little power to change the behavior of some OPEC members in exporting more crude oil at Iran's expense.[96]

Meanwhile, the Islamic Republic was to learn an equally bitter lesson with regard to some gratuitous and dangerous statements which were made by a number of its top officials particularly in the run-up to the implementation of the Trump administration-dictated sanctions which targeted the export of Iranian crude oil. On July 13, 2018, for instance, the supreme leader's top advisor for international affairs who was then on an official visit to Russia basically warned that "if Iran was not allowed to export oil, no other country in the region would be able to do that."[97] In less than two weeks later, the Commander of the Islamic Revolutionary

Guard Corps (IRGC) made a similar threat, warning, "any moment we wish, we can cut the world's supply of oil."[98] It all boiled down to Iran's ability to shut down the strategic Straits of Hormuz at one fell swoop. That was why those rhetorical words had been uttered intentionally to leave no doubt that the United States under Trump needed to think twice before daring to impose an international ban on the export of Iranian oil.

True that Iran under those tough times had been left with no recourse but to fight back with forewarnings of the possible closure of Hormuz; nevertheless, such a consequential act involved more than meets the eye. In addition to triggering a spike in oil prices throughout the globe, blocking the world's most critical transit chokepoint could quickly lead to the worst kind of retaliation by the United States and its close allies, if not include other oil-thirsty nations with a background of relatively good connections to Tehran. The Islamic Republic was simply too weak to stand up to an international invasion in the wake of shutting down the narrow waterway of Hormuz. For Iran, this doomsday scenario could result in swift military defeat, further political isolation, economic breakdown, and possibly even the collapse of the whole establishment of the Islamic Republic.[99] As it turned out, Iran decided not to do anything with the Straits of Hormuz, humbling many idealistic and immature officials of the Islamic Republic in the midst of unprecedented international sanctions when the most powerful country in the entire Middle East region was not allowed "to sell one drop of oil."[100]

NOTES

1. Miyagawa, p. 141.
2. Togo, pp. 302–303.
3. "LG, Samsung, Daewoo Worry about Fallout from Iran Sanctions," *Korea Times*, August 12, 2010; and "U.S. Exempts Korea from Iranian Oil Sanctions," *Korea Herald*, June 12, 2012.
4. "Varedat naft kore jonoobi az Iran 8 barabar shod" [South Korea's Oil Imports from Iran Increased Eight-fold], *Rahemardom*, January 16, 2017, p. 5; and "US Exit from Iran Deal May Affect South Korea's Oil Imports," *Korea Times*, May 9, 2018.
5. Bernard D. Cole, *China's Quest for Great Power: Ships, Oil, and Foreign Policy* (Annapolis, MD: Naval Institute Press, 2016), p. 146.
6. "China Unlikely to Follow US Oil Sanctions on Iran," *Global Times*, May 4, 2019.

7. "Bazarhay naft asiai rahi baray dorzadan tahrimhay Iran peidamikonand" [Asia Oil Markets Find Ways to Bypass Iran Sanctions], *Abrar-e Eghtesadi*, May 21, 2018, p. 4; and "Froosh makhfi naft" [Secret Sale of Oil], *Shargh Daily*, May 25, 2019, p. 1.
8. "Chiniha naft Iran ra be mogholistan sader mikonand" [Chinese to Export Iran Oil to Mongolia], *Mehr News Agency*, December 25, 2015.
9. Miyagawa, p. 168.
10. "Vazir naft kore shomali be Tehran amad: Mozakerat nafti Tehran–Pyongyang" [North Korean Oil Minister Arrived in Tehran: Oil Negotiations of Tehran–Pyongyang], *Mehr News Agency*, April 18, 2013.
11. Stephen G. Carter, "Iran, Natural Gas and Asia's Energy Needs: A Spoiler for Sanctions?" *Middle East Policy*, Vol. 21, No. 1 (spring 2014), pp. 41–61.
12. "Iran Threatens Gulf Oil Exports as Sanctions Row Escalates," *Oil and Energy Trends*, February 2012.
13. "Tokyo Gets Tehran's Blessing toward Restoring Oil Imports to Pre-sanctions Levels," *Kyodo*, August 10, 2015; "Iran's Asia Crude Exports Set to Rise," *Iran Daily*, October 29, 2016, p. 1; and "South Korea's Oil Imports from Iran Up Over 100%," *Iran Daily*, November 7, 2016, p. 1.
14. "'Hanguk, ilan chejae yewaeguk yeonjang eoryeobda' taedo bakkun mi…cheongbu, wonyu suib bisang" [Change in U.S. Attitude 'Made it Difficult to Extend to Korea, Iran Sanctions Exception'… The Government, Crude Oil Imports in Hot Situation], *Chosun Ilbo*, March 3, 2019.
15. "General doolat: Europa baray kharid naft javab telephone mara ham nemidahad! [Government General: Europe Does not even Take Our Call for Oil Purchase!], *Javan*, February 6, 2019, p. 1.
16. Hufbauer, et al., p. 21.
17. Simons, p. xvii.
18. Masanari Koike, "Japan Looks for Oil in the Wrong Places," *Far Eastern Economic Review*, Vol. 169, No. 8 (October 2006), pp. 44–47.
19. Yutaka Kawashima, *Japanese Foreign Policy at the Crossroads: Challenges and Options for the Twenty-First Century* (Washington, D.C.: Brookings Institution Press, 2003), pp. 20–21.
20. Zhongqian Yang, "Zhongguo shiyou anquan jiqi zhongdong shiyou zhanlue" [China's Oil Security and its Middle East Oil Strategy], *Shijie jingji yanjiu* [World Economic Studies], No. 1 (2001), pp. 19–22.
21. Manochehr Dorraj and James English, "The Dragon Nests: China's Energy Engagement of the Middle East," *China Report*, Vol. 49, No. 1 (2013), pp. 43–67.

22. "Iran Oil 'Leverage' in China's Trade Talks with US," *Global Times*, May 16, 2019; and "The Iran–China Axis," *The Wall Street Journal*, July 17, 2020.
23. "China Mulls Iran Sanctions," *Global Times*, October 20, 2009.
24. Lanteigne, p. 218.
25. "Asia is Purchasing Nearly All of Iran's Oil," *The Diplomat*, January 5, 2013; and "Ni Iran kaidan Chūtō antei e no ichijo to shitai" [Japan–Iran Talks: Aiming to Stabilize the Middle East], *Yomiuri Shimbun*, December 22, 2019.
26. Juneau.
27. Jeffrey J. Schott, "Economic Sanctions against Iran: Is the Third Decade a Charm?" *Business Economics*, Vol. 47, No. 3 (2012), pp. 190–192.
28. Robert M. Gates, *Duty: Memoirs of A Secretary at War* (New York: Alfred A. Knopf, 2014), p. 27.
29. Mary Ann Heiss, "The International Boycott of Iranian Oil and the Anti-Mosaddeq Coup of 1953," in Malcolm Byrne and Mark J. Gasiorowski, eds., *Mohammad Mosaddeq and the 1953 Coup in Iran* (Syracuse, NY: Syracuse University Press, 2004), pp. 178–200; and "Japan's Iran Moment," *The New York Times*, February 17, 2010.
30. Upon returning back home, however, *Nissho Maru* was reprimanded for its act by the Japanese government, while the British upped the ante by taking legal action in Tokyo against the Japanese owner of the oil tanker and asserting that they owned the cargo *Nissho Maru* had brought in from Iran. But the case was later dropped and the Japanese company emerged triumphant. The saga of *Nissho Maru* was turned into a bestselling novel in 2014 and a film in 2016, both of them in the Japanese language. For more details on the Japanese historical book which could sell astonishingly more than 1,700,000 copies in January 2014 alone, see: Naoki Hyakuta, *Kaizoku to yobareta otoko* [A Man Called Pirate] (Tokyo: Kodansha, 2014).
31. "Sanctions on Iran Create Diplomatic Headache, Rather than Economic Catastrophe, for Oil-dependent Japan," *The Japan Times*, June 27, 2018. Additionally, the condensate which the ROK was importing from Iran happened to be "$2 to $6 cheaper per barrel than crude oil produced in other oil-producing nations." In January 2019, for example, data from Korea National Oil Corporation (KNOC) showed that crude imports from Qatar cost the ROK $61.75 per barrel, but the East Asian country paid only $52.86 per barrel for its crude imports from Iran. "US Embargo on Iranian Oil to Hurt SK Incheon, Hyundai Oilbank," *Korea Times*, April 22, 2019; and "Iran Sanctions Alarm Korean Petrochemical Sector," *Korea Herald*, April 23, 2019.

32. "Chiniha az tahrim Iran sood mibarand" [Chinese Benefit from Iran Sanctions], *Ghanoon Daily*, July 26, 2018, p. 3.
33. "Iran Oil Officials in Beijing to Discuss Oil Supplies, Projects," *Reuters*, April 7, 2015.
34. "Moshtarian asiai naft Iran arzantar be dasteshan miresad" [Asian Customers Get Iran Oil Cheaper], *Eghtesad-e Pooya*, August 11, 2018, p. 4; and "Takhfif vizhe nafti baray chiniha" [Special Oil Discount for Chinese], *Eghtesad-e Pooya*, August 1, 2020, p. 1.
35. "Emtiyaz nafti be chin nemidahim" [We don't Give Oil Concession to China], *Eskenas Newspaper*, July 21, 2020, p. 5.
36. Cole, p. 82.
37. Pieper.
38. Cole, p. 81.
39. "Uncertain Future in HK for Iranian Shipping Line," *South China Morning Post*, March 30, 2011; and "Iran's Hong Kong Shipping Shell Game," *The Wall Street Journal*, August 30, 2011.
40. "China Criticizes New EU Sanctions on Iran, Calls for Talks," *Reuters*, October 16, 2012.
41. "Japan's Inpex in Running for Azadegan Oil Field Deal, Iranian Official Says," *The Japan Times*, January 4, 2017.
42. "SMEs to Take a Hit If Iran Bans South Korean Imports," *The Hankyoreh*, June 28, 2012.
43. "Ship Insurance Costs Soar after Middle East Tanker Attacks," *Reuters*, June 14, 2019.
44. "Nakhostin kashti khareji dar Bandar Abbas pahloo gereft" [First Foreign Ship Berthed in Bandar Abbas], *Mardomsalari*, July 23, 2014, p. 4.
45. "Geroukeshi baray feroosh naft Iran" [Blackmailing for Selling Iran Oil], *Shargh Daily*, August 9, 2018, p. 5; and "Persian Gulf Oil Shipments Cost More than $500,000 to Insure," *Bloomberg*, June 24, 2019.
46. "Burning Iranian Oil Tanker Sinks after January 6 Accident: Chinese State TV," *Reuters*, January 14, 2018.
47. "Rescuers Battle Toxic Oil Blaze off China Coast," *Financial Times*, January 8, 2018.
48. "Hope Fades for Missing Crew Members as Iranian Oil Tanker Sinks," *The New York Times*, January 14, 2018.
49. "Davat kore shomali az Iran baray moghabele ba America" [North Korea Invites Iran to Stand Up to America], *Aftab-e Yazd*, October 17, 2017, p. 15; "Nazdiki Iran va kore shomali; payami be kakhe sefid" [Rapport between Iran and North Korea; A Message to the White House], *Aftab-e Yazd*, April 30, 2019, pp. 1, 15; and "Snapback of U.S. Sanctions on Iran Renews Concerns over Pyongyang–Tehran Ties," *Yonhap News Agency*, September 22, 2020.

50. "Hamle havayi America be naftkesh irani sehhat nadard" [American Air Attack on Iranian Tanker not True], *Tabnak*, January 15, 2018; and "Chera parcham Panama berooy naftkesh irani nasb bood?" [Why did Iranian Tanker Have Panama Flag?], *Tabnak*, January 16, 2018.

51. "Naghsh asiaiha dar kahesh asarbakhshi tahrim nafti" [Role of Asians in Cooling the Effectiveness of Oil Sanctions], *Tejarat News*, June 3, 2018, p. 1.

52. "Iran to 'Reconsider' Ties If S. Korea Cuts Oil Imports," *Korea Herald*, June 29, 2012.

53. Iran's gasoline problem was compounded in 2010 when the Obama administration passed the Comprehensive Iran Sanctions, Accountability and Divestment Act (CISADA) which aimed, among other things, to deter foreign oil companies from supplying gasoline to the Middle Eastern country.

54. "China Supplying Gasoline to Iran: Report," *Global Times*, September 24, 2009; and "China Sweats Iran Trade Ties," *Global Times*, September 30, 2009.

55. "Chin 8 million boshke naft Iran ra bedoon sabt dar gomrok kharid" [China Purchased 8 Million Barrels of Iran Oil without Customs Registration], *Servat News*, August 5, 2020, p. 5; and "China is Still Brimming with Iranian Oil," *Atlantic Council*, February 10, 2021.

56. "Chungguk, hwanjeog, che3gukkyeongyu tonghae 'ilan wonyu uhoesuib' uihog" [China Suspected of 'Importing Bypassed Iran Crude Oil' through Transshipment and Third Country], *Hanguk Kyeongje*, July 3, 2019.

57. "China is Still Brimming with Iranian Oil," *Atlantic Council*, February 10, 2021.

58. "China Firms Dominate Iran Oil Expo," *Global Times*, April 18, 2011.

59. "Chin bozorgtarin moshtari petroshimi Iran shod" [China Becomes Biggest Customer of Iran Petrochemicals], *Asrar Daily*, June 25, 2016, p. 1; and "Ba hazf kore az list moshtarian; Chin bozorgtarin moshtari petrochimi Iran shod" [After Eliminating Korea from the List of Customers; China Becomes Largest Customer of Iran Petrochemicals], *Kaenat*, June 25, 2016, p. 10.

60. Jones, p. 5.

61. David Wood, "Iran's Strong Case for Nuclear Power is Obscured by UN Sanctions and Geopolitics," *Atoms for Peace: An International Journal*, Vol. 1, No. 4 (2007), pp. 287–300.

62. "European Oil Majors March Back to Iran," *The Wall Street Journal*, March 10, 1999.

63. Suzanne Maloney, "Sanctioning Iran: If Only It Were So Simple," *The Washington Quarterly*, Vol. 33, No. 1 (2010), pp. 131–147.

64. Greg Ryan, *US Foreign Policy towards China, Cuba and Iran: The Politics of Recognition* (Abingdon and New York: Routledge, 2018), p. 111.
65. "Korea to Reduce Oil Imports from Iran in Steps," *Korea Herald*, January 17, 2012; and "Japan Slashes Iran Oil Imports Amid Sanctions," *Japan Today*, May 31, 2012.
66. "Sanctions Exemption Shows China's Power," *Global Times*, June 30, 2012.
67. "Korea Faces 18% Iranian Oil Cut Guideline: Sources," *Korea Times*, February 3, 2012.
68. "U.S. oil Sanctions Waiver Extended," *Kyodo*, September 7, 2013.
69. "Cheshm omid be shargh" [Pinning Hope on the East], *Vatan Emrooz*, June 12, 2018, p. 2; and "Seoul Granted Waiver to Buy Iranian Oil," *Korea Herald*, November 5, 2018.
70. "Seoul Seeks Exemptions from Trump's Iran Sanctions," *Korea Herald*, August 16, 2018.
71. "U.S. to Eliminate Iran Oil Waivers for Countries Including Japan after May 2 Expiration," *The Japan Times*, April 22, 2019.
72. "United States Unexpectedly Cancels Iran Sanctions Waivers; Puts Pressure on Market, Mideast Tensions." *Oil and Energy Trends*, No. 44 (2019), pp. 18–19.
73. "'Hanguk, ilan chejae yewaeguk yeonjang eoryeobda' taedo bakkun mi…cheongbu, wonyu suib bisang" [Change in U.S. Attitude 'Made it Difficult to Extend to Korea, Iran Sanctions Exception'…The Government, Crude Oil Imports in Hot Situation] *Chosun Ilbo*, March 3, 2019.
74. "Taiwan Hopes for Iran Oil Sanction Waiver," *Taiwan News*, November 3, 2018.
75. "Taiwan va Sri Lanka moshtarian jadid nafti Iran: Vorood be bazaar shargh Asia" [Taiwan and Sri Lanka New Customers of Iran Oil: Entry into East Asia's Market], *Jahan-e Sanat*, May 12, 2016, p. 13.
76. "Khyanat be Iran, inbar tavasot chin!" [Betraying Iran, this Time by China!], *Kelid Newspaper*, May 20, 2018, p. 4.
77. "HK Ignores US Sanctions on Iran as Tanker Heads East," *Asia Times*, May 30, 2019.
78. "Hong Kong Rejects U.S. Warning on Ship Breaching Iran Sanctions," *Bloomberg*, May 29, 2019.
79. Before the Trump administration quit the nuclear deal and reinstated all Iran sanctions, China was importing some 600,000 bpd of crude oil from the Persian Gulf country.
80. "United States Should Derail Prospects for an Iran–China Alliance," *The Heritage Foundation*, October 6, 2020.

81. "Hanguo tingzhi jinkou yilang shiyou" [South Korea Stops Importing Iranian Oil], *Xinhua*, September 24, 2018; and "Kore jonoobi varedat naft az Iran ra betoor kamel motavaghef kard" [South Korea Stopped Importing Iran Oil Completely], *Abrar-e Eghtesadi*, September 24, 2018, p. 1.

82. "Iranian Vendors of S. Korean Products Shutting Down Due to Lack of Supplies," *The Hankyoreh*, February 29, 2020.

83. The South Korean government was probably not also happy when it had to reimburse its oil companies for "excess transportation costs" caused by the replacement of Iranian crude supplied by non-Middle Eastern countries located in Africa, Europe, and the Americas. "Ilanchejae daeeung...wonyudo ibseon dabyeonhwa butamgeum hwangeub 3nyeon yeonjang" [Response to Iran Sanctions...Diversification of Crude Oil Imports and Extension of Charges Refund by 3 Years], *Hanguk Kyeongje*, May 3, 2019.

84. In sharp contrast to 2016, South Korea's oil imports from the United States increased by 520 percent in 2017 and 3400 percent in 2018. For more details, see: "S. Korea's Imports of US Crude Oil Have Risen Drastically during Trump Era," *The Hankyoreh*, March 17, 2019.

85. With regard to the quality of Iranian crude, a Korean newspaper once revealed that "Iranian condensate's naphtha content surpasses approximately 70 percent, while that of other countries' condensate remains around 50 percent. This means domestic petrochemical firms need more oil to produce the same amount of naphtha if they use ultra-light oil from other countries." "US Embargo on Iranian Oil to Hurt SK Incheon, Hyundai Oilbank," *Korea Times*, April 22, 2019.

86. "Japan Reportedly to Halt Iran Oil Imports Under U.S. Pressure," *Japan Today*, September 4, 2018.

87. "Zhapon hargez Iran ra tark nakardeh ast" [Japan Has Never Left Iran], *Hamshahri*, February 19, 2019, pp. 1, 24.

88. "Tai Iran Nihon, yureru dokuji gaikō" [Japan against Iran, Shaking Independent Diplomacy], *Nihon Keizai Shimbun*, July 12, 2018.

89. "Ba dastoor dolat: Faghat az keshvarhai ken aft Iran ra bekharand kala vared mikonim" [Government Instructed: We Import Goods only from Countries Which Buy Iran Oil], *Abrar-e Eghtesadi*, July 5, 2018, p. 4.

90. "Namaknashnasi koreiha" [Ungratefulness of Koreans], *Khorasan News*, September 16, 2018, p. 4.

91. Iran's oil incomes had soared from around $1.1 billion in 1970 to more than $20 billion by 1976 or a few years before the Islamic Republic replaced the Pahlavi monarchy.

92. Jahangir Amuzegar, "Iran's Oil as a Blessing and a Curse," *Brown Journal of World Affairs*, Vol. 15, No. 1 (fall/winter 2008), pp. 47–61.

93. "Saderat gaz Iran tahrimshodani nist" [Exports of Iran Gas not Sanctionable], *Eghtesad-e Meli*, May 28, 2018, p. 5.
94. "Oil Prices Fall as U.S. May Grant Some Waivers on Iran Crude Sanctions," *Reuters*, October 8, 2018.
95. "US Sanctions on Iran, Trade War with China and Trade Peace with Mexico," *Oil and Energy Trends*, No. 43 (2018), p. 7.
96. Additionally, the mysterious global crisis of coronavirus, also known as COVID-19, from the early 2020 onward had a role to play in lowering demands for crude oil in many energy-dependent countries some of which used to be regular consumers of Iranian oil for decades.
97. "Velayati dar Moscow: Agar Iran natavanad naft sader konad hichkas dar mantaghe nemitavanad" [Velayati in Moscow: If Iran not Allowed to Export Oil No Other Country in the Region Will], *Kayhan*, July 14, 2018, pp. 1, 10.
98. "Farmandeh sepah: Har lahze erade konim, sodoor naft donya rag hate mikonim" [Commander of IRGC: Any Moment We Wish, We Can Cut the World's Supply of Oil,], *Abrar News*, July 26, 2018, p. 2.
99. J. Peter Pham, "Iran's Threat to the Strait of Hormuz: A Realist Assessment," *American Foreign Policy Interests: The Journal of the National Committee on American Foreign Policy*, Vol. 32, No. 2 (2010), pp. 64–74.
100. "Ejaze feroosh yek ghatre naft ra be ma nemidahand" [They Do not Let Us to Sell One Drop of Oil], *Akhbar-e Sanat*, September 5, 2020, p. 2.

CHAPTER 4

In Other Party's Terms: Frozen Oil Funds

Asset Freeze and Blocked Funds: The Prehistory

Out of the broader category of economic sanctions, assets freeze has continued to become a major practice of American foreign policy in exercising its domineering financial power over other nations during the past several decades. Historically, freezing assets and properties of other countries took place when there was a major war or internecine hostility which could be exploited to put additional pressure on the other party, or normally the weaker side. But in recent decades, successive American administrations have made recourse to financial blockade and assets freeze inimical to foreign countries and their citizens more in time of peace than during outright military conflict.[1] From blocking some or all of financial resources belonging to most sought-after terrorists and drug traffickers to freezing funds and properties of sovereign nation-states as well as their top leaders and close associates, Washington's use or abuse of this often potent tool of penalty and international punishment has undoubtedly been an undertaking of different order of magnitude than anything seen in history.[2]

Concerning the US behavior in modern times, however, the first biggest act of seizing assets and funds of other countries by the United States happened in late 1979 when Washington froze Iranian assets amounting to some $12 billion in the wake of occupying the American embassy in Tehran and taking its personnel hostage. After Washington failed to quickly release its citizens in Tehran, on November 14, 1979, the administration

© The Author(s), under exclusive license to Springer Nature
Switzerland AG 2022
S. Azad, *East Asia and Iran Sanctions*,
https://doi.org/10.1007/978-3-030-97427-5_4

71

of Jimmy Carter issued Executive Order 12170, confirming unequivocally that "The President has today acted to block all official Iranian assets in the United States, including deposits in United States banks and their foreign branches and subsidiaries. This Order is in response to reports that the Government of Iran is about to withdraw funds."[3] Incorporating a bulk of Iran's accessible foreign exchange reserves, the blocked Iranian assets included various deposits and securities held by US banks in the United States and their branches in Western Europe. Golds belonging to the Central Bank of Iran (CBI) were also part of the blocked assets.[4]

At that time, $12 billion was simply a king's ransom. Prior to the US financial move against the newly established Islamic Republic in 1979, for instance, the United States had frozen assets of the Cuban and North Vietnamese governments, but the total value of those resources was insignificant compared to what Washington blocked for Iran. A decade later, when the Iranian government applied to get a loan from the World Bank to partially finance its ongoing reconstruction programs carved out after the conclusion of the Iran–Iraq War, all Tehran could receive from that international institution was a sum of $250 million which was really insubstantial in comparison to the remarkable amount of $12 billion frozen with a stroke of a pen at the White House in November 1979. After all, Iran had very little chance to have the World Bank agreed to its financial request without practically getting along with the US-led coalition's extensive blockade against Baghdad following Saddam Hussein's reckless and ill-advised invasion of the neighboring Kuwait in 1990.[5]

Despite being out of the ordinary, nevertheless, the biggest freezing of foreign funds in the United States was to be later regarded as a rather successful experience of financial sanctions. A number of scholarly works even gave credits to the Carter administration for the financial move against Iran because in their view it was the very act of freezing Iranian assets which provided the ground to free the American hostages in Tehran after some 444 days. The United States had created a bargaining chip of sorts, as such writings argue; its outstanding leverage through both official and unofficial negotiations with Iran had virtually left few options for top authorities of the Islamic Republic but to release the US citizens based on the Algiers Accords.[6] Whether or not freezing Iranian assets was effectively the main factor behind the ultimate release of American hostages, however, the move was a gross violation of international law and contrary to all relevant conventions and treaties which the United States and Iran had already signed. It also set a precedent which continues until the present day to essentially poison many aspects of relationship between Washington, Tehran, and a whole host of other nations.[7]

At a national level, for decades, numerous court rulings across the United States held the regime of the Islamic Republic accountable for various charges such as hostage taking and terrorism, condemning Iran to pay a hefty sum of indemnity to American victims or other beneficiaries with dual nationality through its frozen assets and properties in the United States or other countries.[8] Internationally, the US Congress and the executive branch of the American political system kept ordering other countries to freeze Iranian financial assets generated primarily and largely by selling crude oil to international energy markets. Despite the fact that US requests for blocking Iranian assets and properties by other governments started in 1979 in the wake of the hostage crisis, Americans stepped up their extraterritorial demands at a blistering pace during the past decade and half when stalemates over Iran's nuclear dossier and all related international sanctions and penalties provided the ground for many countries, East Asians in particular, to freeze unprecedentedly a bulk of Iranian oil incomes.

THE BANKING BARRIER AND UNRETURNED OIL REVENUES

Until 2008, international banking was possible for Iran as many foreign financial institutions were able to take advantage of their American subsidiaries to transfer money to Iranian banks. This method of financial interactions with Iran hit a brick wall in 2008 when anxiety and disputation over the Middle Eastern country's WMDs intentions reached fever pitch and Tehran was basically suspected of making use of international financial transactions in order to pour funds into its ongoing nuclear and missile programs.[9] The Islamic Republic was, moreover, subject to four UN Security Council resolutions, beginning with Resolution 1737 on December 23, 2006 and culminating in Resolution 1929 on June 9, 2010. Under these uncompromising resolutions which curtailed substantially Iran's previous access to international banks and other financial institutions, all UN members had been required to block funds and assets belonging to the Iranian entities and individuals who were supposedly playing a critical role in the country's nuclear and missile programs.[10]

To cap it all, the United States as the biggest proponent of pressuring Iran at the UN system, carved out its own sanctions and punitive measures targeting Tehran. Several US bills such as the Iran Threat Reduction and

Syrian Human Rights Act of 2012 plus all the four crippling sanction resolutions which had already been adopted by the Security Council from December 2006 to June 2010 were meant to strikingly strangulate Iran's access to the international financial system. As a result, Iran became subject to an international monetary blockade which was enforced more vigorously by the United States roughly from 2010 until almost January 2016 when the nuclear deal between Tehran and the sextet was implemented.[11] Financial sanctions led to a detrimental devaluation of Iranian currency, rial. More important, they locked up tens of billions of dollars which Iran owned for its exports to other countries. American banks and financial institutions had simply threatened their foreign clients, including major international banks, not to transfer any funds to Iran or otherwise they would risk losing their access to US banking system.[12]

Barred from international banking, therefore, Iran increasingly tapped into bartering and using local currencies to handle part of its external commercial interactions. By 2015, for instance, more than $5 billion of Iranian oil incomes had been frozen in India alone. Taking fully advantage of the situation, Indian officials had made it clear to their Iranian counterparts that Tehran could not invest its frozen funds in India's stock markets, nor was it possible for Iran to get any interest for its blocked assets. The only option left to Iran was to import more goods from the South Asian nation, turning India into one of the biggest exporters to the Persian Gulf country before the JCPOA was agreed in 2015.[13] In the same way, bartering suddenly became a useful method to return back a large sum of Tehran's frozen funds in Ankara. Thus, Iran's gold imports from Turkey reached new heights to the extent that gold trade between the two neighboring countries ratcheted up astonishingly from 1 ton in 2011 to some 126 tons in 2012, valued around $6.5 billion. In 2012, Turkey also exported gold to Dubai, worth $4.6 billion, a great deal of which had reportedly ended up in Iran. But the United States later discovered and put a stop to this tactic of circumventing sanctions involving Iran and Turkey.[14]

As major customers of Iranian oil, moreover, the East Asian countries of Japan, China, and South Korea had to freeze lots of funds which Iran owned for its crude exports. While the prolonged nuclear negotiations were going on between Iran and the 5+1 group, those East Asian nations released some of Iran's assets in line with the payment schedule promised in the interim agreement, but a bulk of the blocked funds had to remain frozen until the implementation of the JCPOA.[15] By the time the nuclear deal was sorted out, however, no one really knew the exact figures for Iran's frozen funds in other countries, including those located in East Asia. In the run-up to the JCPOA, the US President, Barack Obama, announced that Iran had some $150 billion frozen abroad, his Secretary of the Treasury, Jack Lew, put the figure at around $100 billion, and the relevant data for the Iranian government turned out to be an extremely fluctuated number of $22–60 billion. Some Iranian sources asserted then that China alone had to pay back roughly $40 billion to the Persian Gulf country for the crude oil and other exports which Iran had already shipped to the East Asian power.[16]

As much as Iran's frozen funds abroad were concerned, however, the JCPOA was not really what it was cracked up to be. The correct figure for Iran's blocked assets before the JCPOA had been a matter of debate, while the total amount of cash which was given to the Middle Eastern country after the implementation of the nuclear deal turned out to be equally disputable as well. All the money which Iran could get back from its frozen funds in other countries was probably less than $30 billion or just one-fifth of the $150 billion figure which Barack Obama had already divulged.[17] A major problem was that some countries in which Iran had a large sum of frozen assets took a wait-and-see approach with regard to clearing Iran's oil dues as if something unpleasant was going to happen soon. That troublesome development happened to be the political rise of Donald Trump who eventually withdrew the United States from the JCPOA in 2018, unwinding what the Obama administration had helped create, and forcing Iran to once again rely on bartering, at least temporarily, to muddle through.[18]

What at first made the bartering system work was that most of Iran's major trading partners did not support Trump's policy to quit the JCPOA. From November 2018 onward, Iran and India increasingly returned to their dollar-free bartering mechanism, while China and Russia expanded their commercial interactions with Iran using their own national currencies, yuan and ruble. Even the European countries of Germany, France and Britain launched INSTEX which was basically a bartering system designed not to be subject to US dollar-based trading interactions.[19] Many more countries were going to employ bartering and local currency, making a de-dollarized international trading system with Iran in the offing before the Trump administration moved to largely shut it down. The top leader of the Islamic Republic had already raised the rhetoric another notch by calling the US Department of the Treasury under Trump "the economic war room" for its overbearing role in enforcing and monitoring various financial sanctions related to Iran's trade with the outside world.[20]

By the time the administration of Joe Biden was commenced on January 20, 2021, therefore, more than $100 billion of Iran's revenues from crude oil and other exports had been locked up abroad. From Italy and Luxembourg in Western Europe to Japan and South Korea in East Asia, Iran's trading partners across the world had been bludgeoned into freezing tens of billions of dollars belonging to the Persian Gulf country's public and private sectors during the final years of the Trump presidency alone.[21] Even the war-torn neighboring country of Iraq was now refusing to release Iran's frozen assets by excusing US sanctions and other international impediments.[22] Although part of those frozen assets had actually been piled up because of a rather complex bartering system which Iran had employed to sort out its commercial connections to other larger economies by exploiting Baghdad as a conduit, nonetheless, various impediments concerning international financial transactions such as the double-edged sword of SWIFT had hindered Iraq to transfer funds to Iran for its debts accumulated for electricity and other goods supplied by Tehran.[23]

China: The Contentious Currency Deal

Considering all foreign destinations where Iranian assets were frozen, the status of Iran's funds in China was both less known and more controversial. Part of the problem could be attributed to the fact that rhetorical flourishes by Chinese officials and state media had hardly matched the way the East Asian power used to treat Iran in practice. In early December 2011, when the US Senate passed some harsh sanctions against Iran, promising to prevent major Asian countries from more oil business with Iran and punish their financial institutions if they dared to engage the Iranian central bank, an editorial by China's *Global Times* criticized the move by stating that "Under such an arrogant bill, it is hard to imagine how the US would borrow money from the central banks of its creditors to make up its bleak budget in the future. China needs not to pay attention to it."[24] As it turned out, China's oil deals as well as its financial interactions with Iran were to be influenced negatively by all UN, US, and EU sanctions in the years to come. China also went out of its way to occasionally freeze banking accounts of many Iranian students and businessmen active in the mainland by excusing sanctions and other international financial restrictions.[25]

China's foreign and economic policy was, therefore, pragmatic enough to carefully balance its global commitments and vested interests in Iran. On one side, those parts of China which happened to be more internationalized and well-connected to major centers of power and wealth in the West, tried to as much as possible stay away from potential troubles coming from economic interactions and financial transactions involving the Iranian entities and individuals sanctioned by Western countries or top international institutions. After a hiatus of some eight years, for instance, it was in June 2016 when Hong Kong Monetary Authority removed its financial restrictions on Iran's Bank Melli which had come under some EU sanctions since 2008.[26] The timing of the action was actually more than five months after the implementation of the JCPOA on January 16, 2016, when all nuclear program-related sanctions and financial limitations on the Persian Gulf country had to be lifted in lockstep with the nuclear deal which Iran and its 5+1 party had agreed in Geneva in June 2015.

On the other side, the rising Asian power had designed its special methods and institutions to cater to Beijing's peculiar relationship with Iran and some other nations. A prominent case in point was Bank of Kunlun which at times was responsible for more than two-third of all financial transactions between Beijing and Tehran. Sanctioned by Washington despite having no meaningful connections to the United States, this Chinese bank could handle the whole financial issues involving the supply of crude oil from Iran to China, though the bank had also been given the mandate to sort out some other monetary matters coming from wider commercial interactions between China and Iran.[27] The United States could accuse other major Chinese companies, such as the giant Huawei, of certain bank frauds to advance their growing commercial interests in Iran, but Bank of Kunlun had been protected from similar allegations because its Iran-related transactions did not have to go through the US-dominated global banking system.[28] Despite Beijing's rather unique approach to handle its financial issues with Tehran in the heydays of sanctions, there was always widespread speculation that Iran had some assets frozen by Chinese banks, including Bank of Kunlun, but Iranian officials often rejected such opinions.

Shortly before the nuclear deal was agreed in 2015, for instance, Iran's oil minister claimed that China was not holding any Iranian frozen assets piled up by importing crude oil from the Middle Eastern country. Still, he was not quite sure about the issue and referred to the Central Bank of Iran to comment on the real status of Iranian frozen assets in other countries.[29] Some five and half years later, the spokesman for the Iranian Foreign Ministry took similar position by asserting than "Iran has resources in China, which it uses to supply its needs and this is different from the money blocked in Japan, Iraq or South Korea."[30] While such official statements talked of Iran's "resources" or "revenues" in China which Tehran could have easy access to whenever it wished, however, by the time Trump left the White House in January 2021, some Iranian media and observers insisted that Iran had approximately $18–20 billion of frozen assets in China. More important, they kept arguing that the $18–20 billion figure was still separate from the frozen 22 billion euros (about $25 billion) which the government of Ahmadinejad had transferred from Europe to Chinese banks in the run-up to the implementation of the nuclear program-related sanctions.[31] There were some reports that China had agreed to unfreeze the 22 billion frozen euros after the JCPOA went into effect in early 2016, but the issue was to remain highly controversial from the very moment a number of Iranian media and press heard of it.[32]

Ahmadinejad himself or his successors never provided any details with regard to the widely debated currency deal which Iran had signed with China before moving its Europe-based assets to Chinese banks. In July 2015, however, Tahmasb Mazaheri, the governor of the Central Bank of Iran from September 2007 to September 2008, revealed more details about the case during his interview with an Iranian newspaper. In his view, the real status of Iranian frozen euros in China was actually worse than the situation of Iran's frozen assets in other countries because the Chinese were going to give them back to Iran not in their original form but through the supply of low-quality Chinese products contrary to the promise made by many other nations to unfreeze Iran's blocked funds upon the implementation of the nuclear deal.[33] Following that contentious interview, many other people inside and outside Iran kept believing that China had exploited sanctions by throwing Iranian frozen assets into its own bankable projects, and compelling the government in Tehran to either accept Chinese goods or Chinese finance for Iranian projects for the Middle East country's blocked funds in China.[34]

Japan: Stuck Between a Domineering Ally and an Unfeigned Friend

From the early months of the hostage crisis in 1979, Japan was pretty reluctant to get along with some American retaliatory measures against Tehran. After significant US arm-twisting, the Japanese government decided to go along with their Western allies and impose limited financial sanctions on the newly established theocratic regime of the Islamic Republic. In coming years and decades, however, Japanese banks and financial institutions kept their cautious connections to Tehran going, helping Iran benefit from international transactions involving the American greenback.[35] Japan's next move in saddling Iran with financial restrictions came about in the aftermath of the UN Security Council resolutions of 2006–2010 when the East Asian country, like many other major powers, had little option but to impose, albeit more seriously this time, certain financial sanctions against Tehran, culminating in a decision by the Japanese government of Prime Minister Naoto Kan in early September 2010 to freeze Iranian assets of 88 entities, 15 banks, and 24 individuals in addition to other 75 entities and 41 individuals whose assets had already been blocked by Tokyo in line with what the relevant UN resolutions had clearly stipulated.[36]

By around this time, Japan was importing at least 10 percent of its crude oil from Iran, providing the ground for the Iranian government to store part of its oil revenues in Tokyo. The situation prompted a New York-based court in May 2012 to ask Bank of Tokyo-Mitsubishi UFJ to give $2.6 billion of Iranian assets to the families and survivors of 241 American marines who had died of a bomb attack in Beirut, Lebanon, in 1983. Despite persistent denial by Iran, the United States had since then accused Tehran of its involvement, either directly or indirectly, in the bloody incident. The Japanese bank simply turned down the request made by the American court, excusing its lack of any jurisdiction over the Iranian assets held in Japan.[37] Still, Bank of Tokyo-Mitsubishi UFJ which was already responsible for some 80 percent of all financial settlements between Iran and Japan, had to do exactly what several UN and US sanctions required by keeping Iranian assets frozen until 2016 when the giant Japanese bank recommenced its financial transactions with Iranian banks.[38]

But Japan had to again cut down its financial relationship with Iran following Trump's withdrawal from the JCPOA. Iran's crude supply to the thirsty East Asian nation subsequently dwindled to a trickle, while the

Middle Eastern country's non-oil exports of petrochemicals, sea foods, and fruits to Japan plummeted to less than $1 billion in total. In Early 2021, the Iranian Foreign Minister, Mohammad Javad Zarif, revealed that Iran had some $3 billion of frozen assets in Japan after calling the East Asian country "an old friend" and asking the Japanese government to expedite the process of clearing Iran's blocked funds.[39] The timing of request was interesting because the Iranian government had already been engaged in a diplomatic kerfuffle with South Korea over Iran's frozen assets by the ROK. Contrary to the way many Iranian top officials and media outlets treated Koreans, Iran decided to go pretty soft on Japan with regard to its frozen assets in Tokyo and this had a lot to do with Tehran's overall impression of Tokyo and its timely assistance to the Islamic Republic during more than four decades of Western sanctions.

South Korea: "Alliance Spirit" Goes Through Its Paces

In July 2010 when the United States passed the Comprehensive Iran Sanctions, Accountability, and Divestment Act, three South Korea-based Iranian entities had been included in the US list: Iran Petrochemical Commercial Company, the CISCO Shipping Company, and the Seoul branch of Bank Mellat. At that time, Iran's Bank Mellat had foreign branches in only three countries, including Turkey, Armenia, and South Korea. Since South Korea's financial institutions which were going to continue their cooperation with the Seoul branch of Bank Mellat could not engage in business with American banks and financial bodies, the Iranian bank soon became a target of US demands from the ROK.[40] In early August 2010, Washington dispatched to Seoul the US State Department's coordinator for North Korean and Iran sanctions, Robert Einhorn, asking the South Korean government to freeze Bank Mellat's assets and shut down its activity in the ROK.[41] By early next month, the South Korean government carried out the US request after its officials from the Financial Supervisory Service (FSS) accused the Seoul branch of Bank Mellat of having "engaged in obscure foreign currency transactions aiding Iran's nuclear activities during a regular inquiry on the bank."[42]

Within a year after the move against Iran's Bank Mellat, the South Korean conservative government of Lee Myung-bak was persuaded by the Democrat administration of Barack Obama to initiate its own tougher initiatives against Tehran in addition to the implementation of relevant

UN and US sanctions for which the ROK was already under tense pressure by Washington.[43] Basically, South Koreans were encouraged to more than ever appreciate their alliance and friendly relationship with the United States as a powerful bulwark to counterbalance North Korea's saber-rattling jingoism and China's frighteningly growing clout in the region. On top of that, US officials asked their Korean counterparts not to contradict themselves by actively backing all types of financial sanctions against Pyongyang, while at the same time taking a rather reluctant position with regard to carrying through punitive financial measures against Tehran. As a result, by December 2011 or roughly one year after the Seoul branch of Bank Mellat was blacklisted by the ROK, the South Korean government financially sanctioned some 201 entities and 30 individuals from Iran for their alleged role in the Iranian nuclear program.[44]

Meanwhile, another equally vexing trouble was the economic fallouts of Iran sanctions for the ROK's conglomerates (*chaebol*) and a large number of Korean smaller firms which were doing business with the Persian Gulf country. One early solution was to use banks and financial institutions of a third party, such as the UAE, to sort out various monetary matters between Korean companies and their business partners in Iran. Since dollar-based economic interactions between Iran and other nations had been banned, Seoul and Tehran still wanted to circumvent sanctions by using the Korean national currency, won. Thus, with a tacit approval of the US government, in 2010 the ROK's state-run Woori Bank and Industrial Bank of Korea (IBK) were given the mandate to open a won-based "escrow account" for the Central Bank of Iran through which the two countries could settle their financial transactions.[45] To clear up payments, the same account could be used by Iranian importers of Korean products and South Korea's importers of Iranian crude oil and condensate.[46]

For South Korea, however, the rewards from operating the won-based settlement system with Iran was more than met the eye. In essence, the US government had shot itself in the foot by ruling out the use of dollar in Iran's international trade since 2010, providing a conducive ground for some major trading partners of Tehran such as the ROK to reap the benefits. That was no coincidence why the Korean government had intentionally selected two state-run financial institutions to manage the won-based settlement system with Iran, though "security reasons" was its main justification. In practice, the two Korean banks made a lot of profits because both of them could handle, on average, some 10 trillion won (more than

$9 billion) of Iran-related funds annually. Each bank almost always enjoyed a few trillion won in deposits which it could invest in some profitable business. In 2011 or one year after presiding over the system, for example, Woori Bank witnessed a remarkable inflow of 3.4 trillion won (roughly $2.9 billion) into its pool of deposits from the ROK's energy business with Iran. At that time, the entire deposits of South Korea's fourth largest bank, Hana Bank, was less than the 3.4 trillion won figure which Woori Bank had incorporated into its financial stock.[47] Since the won-based settlement system between the ROK and Iran was to keep going for at least a decade, the rosy prospect of bringing in huge earnings for the two Korean banks became stark in its clarity.

Despite its enormous advantage for the ROK, the won-based settlement mechanism could hardly satisfy the Iranian government which demanded some adjustments to the system once Tehran started to fulfill its commitments under the nuclear deal in early 2016. Woori Bank soon declared its willingness to set up a representative office in Tehran to essentially become the first Korean financial institution to commence its banking business in Iran.[48] In August 2016, moreover, South Korea's finance minister announced that his country was going to start a euro-based payment system for doing business with Iran.[49] None of these initiatives turned out to be really functional, and the ongoing won-based settlement system between the two countries needed to continue its assigned task. But a big problem was that the Iranian government was still not permitted to have complete access to its Woori Bank's and IBK's accounts despite its full commitment to the JCPOA. The South Korean government had unblocked only a small fraction of Iran's frozen assets, and the two Korean banks were going to keep the rest of the Iranian funds frozen for an unforeseeable future.[50]

On May 2, 2019, however, the entire won-based settlement system came to a standstill after the Trump administration's temporary oil waivers for South Korea and seven other nations expired. The liberal Korean government of Moon Jae-in made an appeal to Washington to let the won-based settlement system between the ROK and Iran run as usual by arguing that this financial mechanism was actually different from the oil waiver system. The United States simply ignored what the Moon-led Korean government asked, and it thereby created a whole host of troubles for South Korea–Iran relations as well as for those 2111 Korean companies which had some commercial interactions with the Middle Eastern country.[51] Unlike his conservative predecessors, South Korea's Moon

Jae-in had already demonstrated more willingness to cooperate with the Trump administration regarding Iran sanctions partly because he desperately needed Washington's favor to go ahead with some of his Pyongyang-friendly policies. In the following months after the won-based settlement system stopped its services, Moon's sustained close cooperation with Washington was to only frustrate many Iranian officials and aggregate the already tense situation between the East Asian country and Iran.[52]

By mid-2020, therefor, a confluence of crippling economic pressures and the deterioration of the COVID-19 pandemic brought the ROK–Iran tensions out into the open as the Iranian government increasingly publicized its quest for unblocking the frozen assets in South Korea. To partially assuage Iran's anger over its frozen assets, the Korean government had already dispatched Song Wong-yup, a board member of Korea International Cooperation Agency (KOICA), to Tehran, to deal with the worsening diplomatic crisis between Tehran and Seoul.[53] As another sign of its good intentions, the ROK also shipped to Iran some $500,000 worth of medicine to help the Iranian government better cope with its coronavirus plight.[54] But none of those initiatives prevented the spokesman for the Iranian foreign ministry to go out of his way and lay the blame on South Korea for "having a master-servant relationship with the United States" during one of his regular official briefings in July 2020. The South Korean government immediately summoned Iran's ambassador to Seoul to file a complaint with regard to the "inappropriate comments" uttered by the Iranian official. In response, all the Iranian top envoy to the ROK had to say was that those comments were not the official position of the Iranian government; a typical diplomatic nicety (no pun intended).[55]

But in Tehran, the Iranian government upped the ante by raising the possibility of taking legal action against South Korea with regard to its frozen assets in Seoul. Iranian media reported that the country could take South Korea to the International Court of Justice (ICJ) over the frozen assets. The main argument was that ROK's policy behavior was in obvious violation of international law as Seoul could unblock Iranian assets without infringing sanctions rules and regulations. Later, the CBI's Governor, Abdolnaser Hemmati, said in an interview that South Korea should also pay appropriate compensation for its illegal freezing of Iran's funds. In his view, there was not really any legal impediment to unfreeze the assets, and the only problem was the lack of political will on the side of the South Korean government.[56] The Iranian foreign minister echoed a similar attitude, stressing that the ROK seized Iranian assets "upon US orders" at a trying time when his country critically needed those funds to spend on its required foods and medicines.[57] Additionally, he tried to overplay the factor of Iran's consumption markets by warning that South Korea and its companies will be "the final losers in this game."[58]

Since the threat of banning or limiting South Korean access to Iran's rather bankable markets had long been exploited by many Iranian officials to caution the ROK against taking hostile steps toward Tehran, therefore, it was a good time to widely capitalize on such an ace in the hole.[59] A number of Iranian lawmakers announced that they were planning to pass a motion in the parliament in order to prohibit completely the import of Korean goods.[60] Some of them even suggested that the Islamic Republic should take advantage of its influence in the Islamic world and promote the idea of boycotting Korean products by other fellow Muslims.[61] Many Iranian observers and pundits, however, rejected such "naïve proposals," pointing out that such measures would only serve China and its products of subpar quality in the wake of limited or no access to quality Korean goods. The Trump administration-imposed sanctions had already curtailed substantially the availability of some Koreans brands and goods for the average Iranian shopper, and any move by the government to outlaw the restricted supply and sale of South Korean products could only add more pressures on the country's struggling consumption markets.[62]

Still, there were many other powerful forces, mostly conservative opinion-makers and analysts in the media and press, who thought that South Korea's rather easy access to Iranian profitable markets was actually the root cause of the problem.[63] In their views, the Iranian government was to be blamed partly for the setback over the frozen assets in the ROK because it had provided unwarrantedly a lot of great opportunities for a whole slew of Korean companies over years, making Koreans "stubborn and insolent" to the extent that they could now dare to ignore Iran's legitimately repeated requests to have access to its blocked funds in the East Asian country.[64] They were also questioning the government how Woori Bank could "shamelessly" ask from Tehran to pay maintenance fee after making the most of Iranian frozen funds, though the South Korean bank had previously issued a statement, emphasizing, "Woori has continued to pay interest on Iran's deposits without demanding any maintenance fee."[65] It was, therefore, this group of largely partisan and zealot individuals or their stalwart peers and friends in the establishment of the Islamic Republic who advocated a harsher, and probably even violent, response by Iran with regard to its frozen assets in South Korea.[66]

Resorting to Gunboat Diplomacy: Seizing Korean Oil Tanker

On January 4, 2021, the Islamic Republic's IRGC seized the South Korean oil tanker, MT Hankuk Chemi, near the Straits of Hormuz in the Persian Gulf. The Korean ship carrying 7200 tons of ethanol was then taken to Bandar Abbas along with its 20 crew members, including 5 Koreans, 11 Myanmares, 2 Indonesians, and 2 Vietnamese. The charge put forward against the vessel was that it had "repeatedly violated maritime environmental rules of Iran," though Iranian officials never presented any evidence with regard to the leaking of toxic chemicals into the Persian Gulf by the Korean tanker.[67] Iran and South Korea had already been at loggerheads over the frozen funds for some two years, and almost any interested observer could instantaneously link the incident to Tehran's failure in forcing South Korea to unblock its assets. Some two weeks had left before the inauguration of Joe Biden's presidency in the United States, and the only thing the lame duck administration of Donald Trump could do was to urge Iran to "immediately release" the Korean tanker and its crew.[68]

For South Korea, IRGC's move was at first tantamount to hostage taking, but the spokesman for the Iranian government, Ali Rabiei, discarded such allegations by stressing that "if there is any hostage taking, it is the Korean government that is holding $7 billion of Iran's assets on baseless grounds." The ROK government even considered taking legal action against the ship seizure by Iran—a highly problematic action which could deal a serious blow to the entire foundation of South Korea–Iran relations in various areas.[69] Given the prospect of a potentially major shift in Washington's policy behavior toward Tehran under Biden, however, South Korea's government as well as its media and press soon embraced a more conciliatory tone and favored diplomacy to settle the crisis. The ROK's Vice Foreign Minister, Choi Jong-kun, led a delegation to Tehran, but after two days he left Iran empty-handed and went to Doha to ask for Qatar's mediation given the small Arab sheikhdom's rather friendly ties with Tehran.[70] The Iranian government basically declined to accept another nation to act as an intermediary, saying, "we don't accept political mediation on technical issues."[71]

Meanwhile, during and after Choi's visit to Tehran, several proposals were discussed by the two countries to iron out both the seizure of tanker and frozen assets issues.[72] When some of those proposed solutions were leaked to media and press, one party often accused the other side for raising the idea in the first place, though none of those suggestions could quickly break the deadlock over their differences. One proposal was to barter almost all of Iran's frozen funds to import ambulance vehicles and coronavirus test kits from South Korea which had the responsibility to win over Washington's potential displeasure with such deals. Another more controversial idea was that the South Korean government could use Iranian frozen assets to pay some $16 million for Iran's UN membership fees and debts, but the main impediment was that the ROK had to first convert the money from Korean won to US dollar and this was not possible under Iran sanctions. It was also reported that the US government had basically rejected any payment for Iran to the UN system through South Korea.[73]

Whether or not the two governments had already bargained over a satisfactory deal, in early February 2021, Iran freed 19 members of the crew, but the tanker and its captain remained in custody. It took another two months until the Iranian government decided to release the Korean ship and its captain in April.[74] This time the prospect for a lasting settlement looked bright because a few days after the release of tanker, South Korea's Prime Minister, Chung Sye-kyun, paid an official visit to Iran. It was the first time a South Korean premier was traveling to Iran after some 44 years amid lingering tensions between Seoul and Tehran over the frozen funds. Despite high expectations, Chung was both chastised and cold-shouldered by Iranian officials. He even failed to secure a short meeting with the Iranian president who used to host many other foreign dignitaries of lower rank, including deputy prime ministers and foreign ministers. Besides acknowledging Iran's legitimate right to have access to its frozen funds, all that the Korean premier could offer in Tehran was to express his country's willingness to give "sideline support" for Iran's ongoing negotiations with representatives from the Biden administration and other 5+1 governments over the fate of the JCPOA.[75] As the new US Secretary of State, Antony Blinken, had already made clear, any potentially grand bargain between South Korean and Iranian leaders concerning the frozen assets required Iran's "full compliance with the nuclear deal."[76] The hands of South Korean leaders had simply been tied by such clear-cut American guidelines.

It turned out, therefore, that by late April 2021, Iran had received only $30 million out of some $7 billion of its frozen assets in South Korea.[77] This was in sharp contrast to some reports that the ROK government had pledged in February to help release at least $1 billion from Iranian blocked funds most of which kept by Woori Bank and the IBK.[78] Such a negligible achievement also greatly contradicted the sentiments and views of some Iranian conservative media and press over the ostensible submission of South Korea to Iran's will power. They were basking in joy while they were reporting about the arrival in Tehran by South Korea's vice foreign minister and prime minister in January and April, respectively, attributing it largely to Iran's tough language expressed through the IRGC's gunboat diplomacy.[79] But only time will judge whether the seizure of South Korea's cargo ship was really a worthy accomplishment or it will go down in history as a badge of shame akin to some other terrible blunders in the past such as ransacking embassy and shooting down commercial plane.

NOTES

1. Joy Gordon, "The Not So Targeted Instrument of Asset Freezes," *Ethics & International Affairs*, Vol. 33, No. 3 (2019), pp. 303–314.
2. Kern Alexander, "United States Financial Sanctions and International Terrorism," *Butterworths Journal of International Banking and Financial Law*, Vol. 17, No. 5 (2002), pp. 212–223.
3. Exec. Order No. 12,170, 44 Fed. Reg. 66,279 (November 14, 1979).
4. Palgrave, p. 46.
5. Simons, p. 198; and "In Iraq, Hunger Wins," *The New York Times*, July 21, 1993, p. A 7.
6. Drury, p. 11; and Robert Carswell, "Economic Sanctions and the Iran Experience," *Foreign Affairs*, Vol. 60, No. 2 (winter, 1981), pp. 247–265.
7. Ray Takeyh and Suzanne Maloney, "The Self-limiting Success of Iran Sanctions," *International Affairs*, Vol. 87, No. 6 (2011), pp. 1297–1312; and Peksen.
8. "Rahzani 3.5 milyard dolari America az Iran" [America's $3.5 Billion Banditry from Iran], *Farhikhtegan Daily*, April 30, 2017, p. 1; "Dozd gereftim" [We Caught Thief], *Vatan Emrooz*, January 5, 2021, p. 1; and "U.S. Collects $7 mln in Iranian Assets for Victims of Terrorism Fund—Justice Dept," *Reuters*, January 5, 2021. Among other Iranian assets which were later seized by the United States, there happened to be a Manhattan-based skyscraper valued more than one billion US dollars.
9. "Prosecutors Link Money from China to Iran," *The New York Times*, August 29, 2012.
10. Jonathan Brewer, "UN Financial Sanctions on Iran," *The RUSI Journal*, Vol. 161, No. 4 (2016), pp. 22–26.
11. "Sanctions: War by Other Means," *Financial Times*, March 31, 2014.

12. If foreign beneficiaries still dared to disregard what American banks demanded, they would just subject themselves to any potential US retaliation such as being cut off from the powerful Society for Worldwide Interbank Financial Telecommunication (SWIFT) which is controlled by the United States. Access to the SWIFT system is a must for any business involving international financial transactions. "Iran's Banks Face Increasing Pressure from the West," *The Wall Street Journal*, February 18, 2012.
13. "Block 5 milyard dollar pool Iran dar hend" [$5 Billion of Iran Money Frozen in India], *Tabnak*, August 14, 2013.
14. "Gold and the Monetary Blockade on Iran," *BullionStar*, June 3, 2018. For more information on this issue, also see: "Iran's Turkish Gold Rush," *Foreign Policy*, December 26, 2013.
15. "Iran Gets $1 Billion in Japan Oil Revenue under Extended Nuclear Deal: IRNA," *The Japan Times*, September 5, 2014.
16. "40 milyard dollar az chin talabkarim" [China Owes Iran $40 Billion], *Arman Daily*, October 12, 2015, p. 1.
17. "What Iran Will Really Do with Its Sanctions Relief Windfall," *The Washington Post*, November 4, 2015.
18. Juneau.
19. "Yureob, indo kieob, ilangwa 'mudalleo keorae'" [European and Indian Companies Engage in 'Trade without Dollar' with Iran], *Hanguk Kyeongje*, May 31, 2019.
20. "Vezarat khazanedari America otagh jang aleih Iran ast" [US Treasure Department is the War Room against Iran], *Kayhan*, May 1, 2018, p. 1.
21. "4 ta 5 miliard dollar pool blockeshode Iran dar italia" [$4–5 Billion Iranian Blocked Money in Italy], *Aftab-e Eghtesadi*, November 10, 2020, p. 1; "Vezarat khareje and bank markazi movazzaf shodand: Mamooriat azadsazi arzhay blockeshode" [Foreign Ministry and Central Bank Obliged: Mission for Unfreezing Blocked Moneys], *Iran*, November 11, 2020, pp. 1, 8; and "Hajm darayihay blockeshode Iran 100 milliard dollar" [$100 Billion of Iran Assets Frozen], *Abrar-e Eghtesadi*, January 6, 2021, p. 1.
22. "Faghat 2 darsad az pool saderat naft be hesab Iran variz shodeast" [Only 2 Percent of Exported Oil Deposited to Iran Account], *Javan*, August 16, 2016, p. 1; "Hajm darayihay blockeshode Iran 100 milliard dollar" [$100 Billion of Iran Assets Frozen], *Abrar-e Eghtesadi*, January 6, 2021, p. 1; and "Blockekardan pool Iran rahzani beinolmelali ast" [Blocking Iran Money is International Piracy], *Eqtesad Ayandeh*, March 9, 2021, p. 3.
23. "Varedat vasetei kala az aragh" [Importing Intermediary Goods from Iraq], *Aftab-e Yazd*, September 16, 2020, p. 5; "40 milliard dollar pool blockeshode darim" [We Have $40 Frozen Money], *Abrar-e Eghtesadi*, October 27, 2020, p. 1; and "Poolhay blockeshode Iran dar aragh

azadshod" [Iran's Frozen Assets in Iraq Released], *Abrar-e Eghtesadi*, March 7, 2021, p. 1.

24. "China Not Obliged to Besiege Iran," *Global Times*, December 3, 2011.
25. "Moshkel hesanbay Iranian dar chin halshod" [Problem of Iranian Accounts in China Settled], *Tabnak*, January 30, 2018; and "Tahrim chini shahrvandan irani" [China Sanctions Iranian Citizens], *Shahrvand*, November 1, 2017, p. 2.
26. "Sanctions on Bank Melli in Hong Kong Lifted," *Iran Front Page*, June 28, 2016.
27. "Chinese Bank to Back Iran–China Transactions as of Dec. 2," *Tehran Times*, November 29, 2018.
28. "Huawei's 'Wolf Culture' Helped It Grow, and Got It into Trouble," *The New York Times*, December 18, 2018.
29. "'China Holding No Frozen Iran Cash'," *Press TV*, April 14, 2015.
30. "Iran Has No Frozen Assets in China," *Financial Tribune*, October 19, 2020; and "Sokhangooy vezarat khareje: Pool blockeshode dar chin nadarim" [Foreign Ministry Spokesman: We do not Have Frozen Money in China], *Abrar News*, October 20, 2020, p. 2.
31. "The Payoff for Iran," *The Washington Post*, June 28, 2015; and "Sarnevesht ajib poolhay blocke Iran dar chin" [Strange Fate of Iran Frozen Assets in China], *Azarbaijan Newspaper*, February 23, 2021, p. 6.
32. "22 milyard euro blockeshode dar chin azadshod" [22 Billion Frozen Euros in China Released], *Tabnak*, January 24, 2016.
33. "Goftogoo ba Tahmasb Mazaherin dar mored arzhay bloukeshode" [Dialogue with Tahmasb Mazaheri on Blocked Funds], *Shargh Daily*, July 25, 2015, p. 1.
34. "Factbox: Countries Where Iranian Oil and Gas Revenues are Blocked," *Reuters*, January 5, 2021.
35. Alexander, p. 125.
36. "Japan Approves Economic Sanctions against Iran," *The Jerusalem Post*, September 3, 2010.
37. "Japanese Bank Freezes Iranian Assets," *Financial Times*, May 17, 2012.
38. "Iran torihiki teishi e" [Toward Suspending Iran Trade], *Nihon Keizai Shimbun*, July 13, 2018.
39. "Zarif Asks Japan to Free Iran's Frozen Assets," *Tasnim News Agency*, February 16, 2021; and "Zarif: Majmooe daraihay masdood shode Iran dar zhapon va kore jonoobi hodood 10 milyard dollar ast" [Zarif: Iran's Total Frozen Assets in Japan and South Korea is around $10 Billion], *Abrar News*, February 17, 2021, p. 2.
40. "Korea Considers Alternate Payment Methods Over Fresh Iran Sanctions," *Korea Times*, August 8, 2010.
41. "Migug-ui ilan chejae dongcham yogu" [American Request to Join Iran Sanctions], *Chosun Ilbo*, August 4, 2010.

42. "Builders, Traders Face Damage from Iran Sanctions," *Korea Herald*, September 8, 2010.
43. "U.S. Ambassador Pushes for Sanctions on Iran," *Korea Times*, August 25, 2010; and "S. Korea Welcomes IAEA Resolution on Iran's Nuke Program," *Korea Herald*, November 19, 2011.
44. "105 Firms, Individuals Face New Iran Sanctions," *Korea Times*, December 16, 2011.
45. "Seoul Gets Exemption from Re-imposed Iran Sanctions," *Korea Times*, November 5, 2018.
46. "Woori Bank, IBK to Stop Iran Payments Due to U.S., Sanctions," *Korea Herald*, November 2, 2018.
47. "Woori, IBK Score with Sanctions on Iran," *Korea Times*, June 3, 2012.
48. "Tehran, Seoul Promoting Banking Relation," *Tehran Times*, May 3, 2016.
49. "S. Korea to Open Euro-based Payment System for Trade with Iran: Finance Minister," *Yonhap News Agency*, August 25, 2016.
50. "Ilan suchul misugeum 2300eog…janggigan mot padeul sudo" [Iran Exports Due 230 Billion…May not be Receivable for Quite Long], *Hanguk Kyeongje*, October 7, 2018.
51. "Korean Exporters Hit by US Sanctions on Iran," *Korea Times*, May 7, 2019.
52. "Seoul Should Adopt 'Independent' Attitude towards Tehran," *Mehr News Agency*, January 11, 2021.
53. "Seoul in Tight Spot Over Late Payments for Iranian Oil," *Korea Times*, December 16, 2019.
54. "Ministry Calls in Iranian Envoy to Protest Reported Threat to Sue South Korea Over Frozen Assets," *Korea Times*, July 21, 2020.
55. "South Korea Summons Iranian Ambassador after 'Inappropriate' Comments," *Al Arabiya*, July 21, 2020.
56. During the interview when the reporter asked Hemmati about the feasibility of transferring Iranian frozen assets in South Korea to INSTEX, which happened to be a Swiss-proposed monetary channel to facilitate financial transactions between Europe and Iran, he replied that the Korean government basically lacked the political will to consider such suggestions, after highlighting the fact that INSTEX had been to no avail because of certain sanctions and restrictions pushed by the United States. "South Korean Banks Should Pay Damages on Iran's Frozen Funds: CBI Governor," *Press TV*, January 19, 2021.
57. Mark Fitzpatrick, "Sanctioning Pandemic-plagued Iran," *Survival*, Vol. 62, No. 3 (May 2020), pp. 93–102.
58. "South Korea Seizing Iranian People's Food, Drug Money: Zarif," *Iran Front Page*, January 20, 2021.
59. "Seoul May Lose Iranian Market Forever," *Tehran Times*, August 3, 2020.

60. "Tarh tahrim kajahay korei rooy miz majlis" [Proposal for Boycotting Korean Goods on the Parliament Desk], *Asr-e Iranian*, July 23, 2020, pp. 1, 2; and "Mamnooiyat varedat kala az kore jonoobi" [Banning Goods Imports from South Korea], *Emrooz* (Today Online), December 27, 2020, p. 1.

61. "MP Urges S Korea to Immediately Unblock Iran FOREX Resources," *Mehr News Agency*, January 13, 2021.

62. "Mahigiri koreiha az ab gelalood" [Koreans Fishing from Muddied Waters], *Tejarat News*, June 11, 2020, p. 1; and "Mozakerat ba kore jonoobi be tahdid ham keshid" [Negotiations with South Korea Led to Threat Too], *Aftab-e Yazd*, September 24, 2020, p. 5.

63. "Joziyat rahzani korei" [Details of Korean Banditry], *Khorasan News*, June 13, 2020, pp. 1, 10.

64. "Che kesani koreiha ra gostakh kardand?" [Who Made Koreans Insolent?], *Kayhan*, July 28, 2020, p. 2; and "Seoul May Lose Iranian Market Forever," *Tehran Times*, August 3, 2020.

65. "Are Tehran's Demands Unreasonable?" *Korea Times*, July 14, 2020.

66. There were also some suggestions urging Iranian policymakers to downgrade the level of politico-diplomatic relationship between Iran and South Korea in order to put additional pressures on the ROK government to unfreeze the blocked funds. "Lezoom kahesh sathe ravabet ba kore jonoobi" [Downgrading Relations with South Korea a Must], *Resalat*, July 26, 2020, p. 1.

67. "Iran Seizes South Korean Tanker for Polluting Persian Gulf Waters," *Tehran Times*, January 4, 2021; "Iran Says S. Korean Vice Foreign Minister's Visit Unrelated to Tanker Seizure," *KBS World Radio*, January 6, 2021; and "Iran's Islamic Revolutionary Guard Corps above the Government," *The Dong-A Ilbo*, January 6, 2021.

68. "US Urges 'Immediate Release' of Korean Tanker from Iran," *Korea Times*, January 5, 2021; "Iran Sends Warning to US Friends with South Korea Tanker Seizure," *Nikkei Asia*, January 7, 2021; and "Iran Challenges Biden with South Korea Tanker Seizure," *Nikkei Asia*, January 24, 2021.

69. "S. Korea to Hold NSC Meeting on Iran Issue," *Korea Herald*, January 6, 2020; "Joziyat rahzani korei" [Details of Korean Banditry], *Khorasan News*, June 13, 2020, pp. 1, 10; and "Seoul Considers Legal Action against Iran after Tanker Seized," *Korea Herald*, January 6, 2021.

70. "South Korea Asks Qatar to Help Get Back Ship from Iran," *Anadolu Agency*, January 14, 2021; and "S. Korea Urges Qatar to Mediate for Release of Vessel in Iran," *Mehr News Agency*, January 14, 2021.

71. "Iran Rules out Mediation on South Korean-flagged Tanker," *Tehran Times*, January 24, 2021.

72. Of course, before the ROK's vice foreign minister arrived in Tehran to meet Iranian officials over the seizure of oil tanker, the two countries had explored a whole host of proposals, including an unwise allocation of all Iranian frozen funds to purchase coronavirus vaccines from South Korea. "7 miliard dollar pool blockeshode Iran dar kore jonoobi sarf kharid vaccine mishavad?" [$7 Billion Frozen Assets in South Korea Spend on Purchasing Vaccine?] *Aftab-e Yazd*, August 22, 2020, p. 1.

73. "Iran, South Korea Close to Unlocking Frozen Assets," *Tehran Times*, February 23, 2021.

74. "Iran Agrees to Free South Korean Ship's Crew," *The New York Times*, February 2, 2021; and "Iran Releases South Korean Oil Tanker," *The New York Times*, April 9, 2021.

75. "South Korea's PM: Iran's Frozen Funds Should be Quickly Returned," *Yonhap News Agency*, April 12, 2021; and "Korea Willing to Help Iran Advance Dialogue for Restoring Nuclear Deal: PM," *Korea Times*, April 12, 2021.

76. "Blinken Says Seoul Isn't Sending Iran Sanctions-Linked Cash," *Bloomberg*, March 11, 2021.

77. "S. Korea Unfreezes $30m Iranian Funds for Medical Purchases," *CGTN*, April 22, 2021.

78. "Iran Sees Light at End of Tunnel for Assets Frozen in Korea," *Korea JoongAng Daily*, February 23, 2021.

79. "Ghodrat sakht sepah kore jonoobi ra saraghl avard" [Hard Power of IRGC Made South Korea Wise], *Kayhan*, January 13, 2021, p. 2; and "Kart be kart: Vaghti diplomacy az eghtedar charge mishavad" [Card to Card: When Authority Charges Diplomacy], *Vatan Emrooz*, April 12, 2021, p. 1.

CHAPTER 5

Clogged Up: The World of Non-oil Banking and Credit Matters

Tightening Financial Noose: The Trauma of Banking Transactions

Like trade penalties, financial sanctions are a form of economic sanctions which seek to interfere with the circulation of capital and financial resources from and to a target country unlike curbing the movement of goods as trade sanctions do. In that sense, financial sanctions aim to disrupt a target country's financial relationship with the outside world by limiting or banning in total its financial transactions with other nations.[1] Thanks to an increasingly swift process of globalization and interdependence, technologically and financially, over the past three decades, moreover, financial sanctions have become much easier to impose compared to other types of punitive economic measures. In the same way, it has become very difficult for sanctioned countries to chip away at their international financial impediments especially when their national economy is largely dependent on maintaining sustainable relationship with other economies.[2] This is exactly what happened to Iran's non-oil economy in the decades that followed the establishment of the Islamic Republic in the early 1979.

Iranians have had financial interactions with other nations from time immemorial, and their country's dependency on exporting crude oil and bringing in its pecuniary earnings is only a contemporary phenomenon. Until the export of Iranian crude oil came under more constraints from the early 2010s onward, therefore, the Persian Gulf country's non-oil

---

© The Author(s), under exclusive license to Springer Nature Switzerland AG 2022

S. Azad, *East Asia and Iran Sanctions*, https://doi.org/10.1007/978-3-030-97427-5_5

93

commercial relations with other nations involved a great deal of financial transactions, though this area had also been affected previously and negatively by sanctions and other international restrictions. Almost from the moment the crude oil-related financial transactions between Iran and other countries encountered stringent controls and obstacles, various monetary issues arising from non-oil commercial dealings between Iranians and their foreign counterparts equally ran into troubles. The crux of the problem was that both oil trade and non-oil commerce involving Iran and other nations could no longer arrange their regular activities without going through the international banking system. And when Iranian banks lost their previous access to foreign financial institutions, they became powerless in terms of providing a ground for average Iranian citizens to sort out their international financial transactions.[3]

Imposing limitations on Iranian banks' connections to the outside world began as part of the fourth UN sanctions resolution in 2010 when that international body tried to keep to minimum monetary transactions between Iran and foreign financial institutions. Later, the United States and EU countries carved out their own relevant banking restrictions against Iranian banks, culminating in sanctioning the Central Bank of Iran (CBI) by Washington in 2012. When the CBI was not able to engage in financial transactions with banks from outside Iran, other Iranian banks were ineluctably in no position to provide any substantial international financial service for their clients.[4] It took almost 1400 days, or roughly 46 months, before the international ban against the CBI and other Iranian banks was lifted in 2016 when Iran implemented the nuclear deal. Still, a whole host of non-nuclear financial sanctions against Iran remained in place after 2016, limiting the scope and size of international monetary services which the CBI and other Iranian banks could have access to.[5]

The situation was compounded in September 2019 when the United States under the Trump administration once again blacklisted the CBI after bringing back a slew of other financial penalties targeting Iran and its state-owned and private banks. In 2012, the CBI had been sanctioned for smoothing the way for financing the Iranian nuclear program, but this time the CBI was accused of facilitating financial transactions for terrorist groups no matter if some of those groups which Washington now called terrorist were part of the establishment of the Islamic Republic. In fact, it was in April 2019 when the United States moved to unprecedentedly designate the IRGC as well as its elite Quds Force as a Foreign Terrorist Organization (FTO), marking the first time the US government was formally drawing a bid on another country's military force as a terrorist entity.[6] As a Result, there had been much water under the bridge by

September 2019 when Washington tightened the screws on the CBI which had never seen so much international animosity and restrictions in its entire history.

Now, Iranian banks were again denied access to the system of Society for Worldwide Interbank Financial Telecommunication (SWIFT) in order to conduct any financial transaction with banks and financial institutions from other parts of the world. Aside from putting a brake on monetary processing between the Middle Eastern country and other nations through the channel of Iran's banks, SWIFT's unavailability was to confront Iranians with a myriad of other problems. Just as the Iranian government could not bring back the revenues made through exporting crude oil, many businesses from the private sector failed to either engage in commercial interactions with other countries or run into serious hurdles while trying to sort out their relevant financial matters. Additionally, direct and indirect costs of international transactions increased substantially for those who could bypass banks and settle their monetary issues involving a foreign currency. More important, the curtailed supply of foreign currencies, especially the US dollar, had a very corrosive impact on the value of Iran's own national currency, rial, forcing the government to deliberately hike the price of dollar to muddle through under a worsening climate of financial sanctions.[7]

Swindling State and Paranoid Population: Hoarding Gold and Foreign Currency

In February 2021, the Iranian president's chief of staff, Mahmoud Vaezi, made it known that the price of the US dollar was not real in Iran. Confessing to a bitter reality that some economic experts had already dubbed "currency coup," Vaezi revealed that the government had to hike arbitrarily the price of dollar in order to manage the country's economy in the wake of Trump's "maximum pressure" policy against the Islamic Republic.[8] What had forced the Iranian government to intentionally raise the value of the US dollar, as Vaezi argued, was that Iran could previously export crude oil as much as 2.8 million bpd, but under tougher circumstances forced upon Tehran by the Trump administration, the sale of crude oil by the Persian Gulf country plummeted to less than 100,000 bpd. Iran was also not able to bring in the revenues from its oil exports, leaving the government with little option but to gradually increase the price of the US dollar by around 1000 percent in order to tackle critically the country's growing demands for dollar and other foreign currencies, including the Chinese yuan.[9]

The so-called currency coup d'état orchestrated by the CBI, however, turned out to be terrorizing far more than met the eye. It simply wreaked havoc on the whole Iranian society as the price of almost every single commodity and service increased exorbitantly.[10] In particular, the price of many foreign products such as automobiles surged equally by 1000 percent, while the citizenry's salaries and incomes remained relatively stagnant.[11] This gloomy situation galvanized a throng of people into action, firing up their growing thirst for hoarding foreign currencies, especially dollar and euro, and gold as a safe bet to guard against a sharply nosediving value of their savings.[12] Although the relevant data and statistics were often hard to come by, some experts and observers estimated that Iranian citizens hoarded about $20–50 billion worth of foreign currencies as well as around 215 tons of gold, including some 15 tons of gold coins.[13] For the country that was already in the throes of economic stagflation and social despondency, an unproductive stockpiling of so much foreign currencies, gold jewelries, and gold coins was to only supply grist to the mills of Trump's psychological warfare of "maximum pressure" against Iran.

More recently, there has been a burgeoning desire among many Iranians to go for purchase of digital foreign currency—a new phenomenon which would exacerbate the somber situation of capital flight from the Middle Eastern country. Of course, the exodus of capital, like brain drain, is not a recent development in Iran, but the government's decision to depreciate dreadfully the value of rial added fuel to the fire, convincing a larger number of Iranians to simply opt for emigration and take along all their wealth after converting its equivalent value to a foreign currency. Based on some estimates, in recent years at least $30 billion left Iran, though this figure did not include the real value of all those talented and skillful people who departed the country in search of building a new life somewhere else.[14] Amidst such massive fleeing of capital and other precious economic and social resources, blundering officials of the Iranian government had to plead for financial support by other nations, including East Asian states, to manage the state of affairs in an atmosphere of despair and agony caused by international sanctions.

Loans and Credits: Hostage to Political Will

Given a potentially positive role of loans and financial credits in economic growth and development, they have long been used as an instrument of financial sanctions.[15] More specifically, the United States has been predisposed to exploit loans and credits as an effective tool of sanctions against any nation it wishes, though Washington has also frequently tapped into such financial instruments in bilateral relations with its allies and friends. As a case in point, Iran under the Pahlavi monarchy used to be a recipient of American military aids for a few decades, but after the regime of the Islamic Republic came to power in 1979, the United States cut all types of its aids and loans to Iran as part of the successive sets of sanctions it levied against the Middle Eastern country. More importantly, the United States often used its power and influence to convince other countries not to give substantial amount of loans and financial credits to the Islamic Republic. In the same way, major international banks and financial institutions came under constant US pressure to decline any financial request submitted by Iran.[16]

It took the Islamic Republic more than a decade, therefore, to get its first loan of $250 million from the World Bank in the early 1990s, but even such a meager achievement was hardly cost-free diplomatically. It was a sensitive time in international politics when the United States needed Iran to join its multinational economic and financial blockade of Baghdad following Saddam Hussein's invasion of the neighboring Kuwait. As soon as Iran agreed to cooperate with Washington regarding the US-led coalition's siege of Saddam, the World Bank under US recommendation gave the nod and provided Tehran with the loan as a reward of sorts.[17] Likewise, for some two and half decades before the Iranian nuclear program became a hot-button international issue, many Western countries and Japan were persistently under American arm-twisting not to extend their loans and financial credits to Iran since Washington usually argued that such pecuniary international cooperation with Tehran would only embolden Iranian leaders and encourage them to keep up with their "bad behaviors" in the Middle East region and beyond.

After 2005 when Iran's nuclear and missile programs turned out to become a vexing dilemma in international politics, it became more much difficult for Tehran to have its loan and credit requests approved by major banks and financial institutions in the world. It was now easy to reject Iran's loan applications by excusing that any international financial assistance could only help Tehran advance its controversial nuclear ambitions. That is why when Iran and its international partners in the 5+1 group managed to strike a bargain in the form of the JCPOA in June 2015, some rich and resourceful countries expressed their willingness to offer some types of loans and financial credits to the Persian Gulf country. In May 2016 and less than a year after the nuclear deal was reached, for example, Japan announced that it was going to give a yen-based loan to Iran so that Tehran could allocate part of that financial aid to renovate some of its dilapidated oil refineries.[18] The move, which was to be repeated later, gave Japan a good chance to raise its post-JCPOA profile in Tehran after a hiatus of some 15 years during which Tokyo had always encountered Washington's objection to lend any significant financial package to Iran.[19]

From Iran's Own Pocket: The Chinese Way of Financing

From the time the JCPOA was agreed to in June 2015, and until Trump quit the nuclear deal some three years later in May 2018, Iran managed to sign financing agreements worth tens of billions of dollars mostly with East Asian and European countries. The largest deal which was agreed with South Korea was a $10 billion loan dubbed as the "golden loan" by some observers.[20] But not all of those colossal credit lines and fancy financing pacts were going to be materialized in the wake of changing political atmosphere in Washington once Trump acceded to power. European foot-dragging on their loan commitments to Iran was soon followed by second thoughts among some resourceful East Asian countries to fulfill their financing promises for Iranian projects. At the end of the day, China remained virtually as the biggest foreign actor which was still willing to finance a significant number of Iranian projects throughout the Persian Gulf country. Even before the JCPOA was clinched, China was in effect the only active investor in many projects across Iran.[21]

For all its promise of supplying large financing packages to Iran, however, the Chinese approach almost always became clouded with suspicion and controversy. Many Iranian experts and analysts were of the opinion that what China was offering Iran in the name of finance and credit line was actually Iran's own money which the East Asian power had already frozen by taking advantage of international sanctions against Tehran.

Since 2014, there happened to be a lot of reports by Iranian media and press, announcing that China was going to finance various projects in Iran valued twice as much as the Iranian frozen assets kept by Beijing.[22] There was hardly a credible report regarding the exact amount of financing promised and accomplished by China, and most of the figures released by the press varied astonishingly between $35 billion and $70 billion.[23] Part of the problem could be attributed to the fact that few people really knew the total value of Iran's frozen assets in China against a backdrop of the Iranian government's official position that often denied Iran had any funds blocked by the Chinese in the first place.

Aside from offering Iran's own oil incomes masquerading as finance and credit lines, the Chinese had apparently put forward some unfair and unreasonable demands for their loan and lending cooperation with Tehran. For example, China was asking for risk guarantees which many Iranian interlocutors found ridiculous since at least half of what the Chinese were promising to finance happened to be Iran's own frozen assets. Capitalizing on Iran's peculiar circumstances, moreover, the Chinese had become choosy, preferring to fixate upon underwriting oil and gas projects which were supposedly more promising and could be of use to China's own energy requirements in the long run. Thus, some of the projects which the Chinese wanted to sponsor financially were not productive and efficient economically, forcing the relevant Iranian officials and administrators to sometimes change the rules and process in midstream.[24] In the face of all those contentious matters, China was still Iran's best bet of credit lines as its financing role was to only expand in size and scope for the foreseeable future.

To be Delivered: Joint Banks, Stock Exchange Ties, and East Asian MasterCard

During the months that followed the conclusion and implementation of the nuclear deal, many economic and financial officials in Iran were in a state of euphoria concerning the prospect of larger banking and monetary cooperation between Tehran and its major trading partners in East Asia. In particular, authorities from the Central Bank of Iran promised that Iran will let East Asian banks to set up their branches in the country, and in some cases, several joint banking branches will be established in Tehran and some other major cities. Besides their pledge about a widespread use of SWIFT between Iran and East Asian countries in the future, moreover, officials of the CBI predicted that Iranians will receive their first international banking cards of Asian types by late 2016, enabling them to enjoy from lots of benefits which some well-known international banking cards from the West such as Visa and MasterCard could offer.[25] Since better economic ties and higher volumes of trade require closer banking and monetary relationship, as CBI and many other economic officials argued then, East Asian countries were now willing to help Iran bring up to date its banking technologies and capabilities.

Based on previous experiences, Iran prioritized Japan for closer interbanking and financial connections with East Asia. Prior to the signing of the JCPOA, Japanese banks had apparently provided better services to their Iranian clients, encouraging the CBI to call on Japanese financial institutions to set up their branches in Iran.[26] As Japanese banks similar to many financial institutions in the West demonstrated a wait-and-see attitude toward improved banking ties with Iran in the aftermath of implementing the nuclear deal, Iranian officials approached South Korea for close banking ties between the two countries. In 2015, Iran and the ROK had signed an agreement on stock exchange cooperation in addition to convening a joint workshop in Tehran about stocks and capital markets.[27] Later, Woori Bank was prepared to set up a branch in Tehran, and the future of better banking ties between Iran and South Korea looked more promising after the prohibition of using euro in their bilateral commercial relationship was removed in August 2016.[28] In view of larger economic interactions between Iran and South Korea at that time, it was more urgent for the ROK than Japan to smooth the way for its banking connections to the Persian Gulf country, though Koreans soon proved to be as reluctant and cautious as their Japanese counterparts to rush into building sizeable banking connections to Tehran after Trump was catapulted to power in the United States.

Compared to South Korea, however, a lack of close banking relationship involving Iran and its largest trading partner, China, was far more consequential. For a couple of years before the JCPOA was clinched in June 2015, Iran had urged China to set up joint banks, but the Chinese had often refused to take any concrete action with regard to developing better banking ties with Tehran. Part of the reason had to do with the fact that the channel of Kunlun Bank, as almost the only financial mechanism to sort out myriad monetary matters between Iran and China, was more beneficial to the East Asian power. When Iran encountered more stringent international financial restrictions as part of some relevant UN and US sanctions, for instance, Kunlun Bank gradually embraced a new policy by increasing its service rates from 5 percent of a deal to much higher rates of 10–15 percent of a whole transaction. Under normal circumstances, the standard rate for Kunlun's financial transactions had to be under 0.01 percent of a whole deal, but the Chinese bank demanded exorbitant service rates by taking advantage of sanctions and Iran's financial susceptibility.[29]

Despite Iran's unhappiness with the overpriced rating service which Kunlun Bank had already forced upon the Middle Eastern country, in June 2019 Iranian press reported that Kunlun had commenced its banking activities in Iran without providing enough details about the nature and scope of its financial operation there.[30] As it turned out, however, the Chinese quickly took a leaf out of their Japanese and Korean competitors' banking book, refusing to engage in close and unrestricted financial interactions with Iran.[31] In a move similar to Russia, China also demanded Iran to join the Financial Action Task Force (FATF) before Beijing could increase substantially its level of banking cooperation with Tehran.[32] Many Western and some Eastern nations had already asked Iran to become a member of the FATF for the sake of international campaign against money-laundering and other illegal financial crimes, but Iranian officials did not expect that their Chinese counterparts now stubbornly insist on Tehran's compliance with the FATF regulations prior to any enhanced banking liaison between the two countries.[33]

NOTES

1. Farrall, p. 107.
2. Eyler, p. 79.
3. Emre Hatipoglu and Dursun Peksen, "Economic Sanctions and Banking Crises in Target Economies," *Defence and Peace Economics*, Vol. 29, No. 2 (October 2016), pp. 171–189.
4. "Iran's Banks Face Increasing Pressure from the West," *The Wall Street Journal*, February 18, 2012.
5. "Vasl SWIFT pas az 1400 rooz" [SWIFT Reconnected after 1400 Days], *Donya-e-Eqtesad*, January 19, 2016.
6. "U.S. Tiptoes Through Sanctions Minefield toward Iran Nuclear Deal," *Reuters*, May 17, 2021.

7. "Eteraf dolat be dastkari nerkh arz" [Government Confession to Interference with the Price of Foreign Currency], *Asr-e Eghtesad*, February 27, 2021, p. 1.

8. "Dolat dar geran shodan dollar zinafe bood" [Government Benefited from Dollar Hike], *Kelid Newspaper*, October 7, 2018, p. 1; and "Bank markazi amel mohem afzayesh nerkh arz ast" [Central Bank Main Cause of Dollar Hike], *Emrooz* (Today Online), May 18, 2021, p. 2.

9. "Rais daftar raisjomhoor: nerkh dollar 25 hezar tooman nist" [President Chief of Staff: Price of Dollar is not 25,000 Tooman], *Emrooz* (Today Online), February 27, 2021, p. 1.

10. "Taid 'koodetay arzi' az sooy khobregan eghtesadi" ['Currency Coup' Admitted by Economic Experts], *Arman Daily*, July 30, 2018, p. 1.

11. "Afzayesh ghimat dollar jamae ra be naboodi keshand" [Hike in Dollar Price Destroyed Society], *Eghtesad-e Pooya*, January 19, 2021, p. 1.

12. To dissuade people, there happened to be rumors circulating in the press and social media warning the public not to hoard dollars because the US government was probably going to declare the serial numbers of those hoarded dollars invalid and thereby making them worthless.

13. "Anbasht 215 ton tala dar khaneha" [215 Tons of Gold Hoarded at Homes], *Tabnak*, July 26, 2018; and "20 milliard dollar arz dar khaneha" [$20 Billion Foreign Currency Horded at Homes], *Emrooz* (Today Online), June 24, 2020, pp. 1, 3.

14. "Khorooj 30 milyard dollar 'sarmaye arzi' az keshvar" [Exidus of $30 Billion 'Foreign Currency' from the Country], *Eghtesad-e Meli*, September 2, 2018, p. 2; and "Tsunami khorooj sarmaye az keshvar" [Tsunami of Capital Flight from Iran], *Eskenas Newspaper*, February 24, 2021, p. 3.

15. Richard S. Olson, "Economic Coercion in World Politics: With a Focus on North–South Relations," *World Politics*, Vol. 31, No. 4 (July 1979), pp. 471–494.

16. Eyler, p. 185.

17. Simons, p. 198.

18. In 1993 when Japan offered a yen-based loan to Iran, it came under tremendous US pressures, forcing Tokyo to release only the first instalment of $394 million and suspend the second instalment (to the tune of $450 million) two years later (1995). Still, some Western observers accused Japan that it had little altruistic reasons in offering loans to Iran, and offering economic aid was mostly a calculated policy by Tokyo to vouchsafe its commercial interests in the Middle Eastern country. For more details, see: Reinhard Drifte, *Japan's Foreign Policy in the 1990s: From Economic Superpower to What Power?* (London: Macmillan Press LTD, 1996), p. 125.

19. "Zhapon be 'yen' be Iran vam midahad" [Japan Gives Loan to Iran in 'Yen'], *Tabnak*, May 23, 2016; and "Tamin etebar 120 million euroi

zhapon dar petroshimi Apadana" [Japan Finances 120 Million Euro for Apadana Petrochemicals], *Servat*, December 10, 2019, p. 2.

20. "Vam talai Seoul be Tehran" [Seoul's Golden Loan to Tehran], *Shahrvand*, August 26, 2017, p. 1.

21. "China Provides $10 Billion Credit Line to Iran," *AFP*, September 16, 2017.

22. "Ghofl finance chini bazshode ast?" [Is the Lock of Chinese Finance Unfastened?], *Eghtesad News*, December 26, 2014.

23. "Tazetarin tavafoghat finance Iran ba chiniha, saghf bazgoshaei finance ta 70 miliard dollar afzayesh yaft" [Most Recent Financing Agreements between Iran and Chinese, Maximum Financing Increased to $70 Billion], *Mehr News Agency*, September 13, 2014.

24. "Chiniha pool naft khodeman ra be esm finance be ma midadand" [Chinese Gave Us Our Own Oil Money in the Name of Finance], *Eghtesad Online*, April 24, 2017.

25. "Vorood avvalin kart banki beinolmelali" [Arrival of First International Banking Card] *Tafahom News*, July 11, 2016, pp. 1, 4; and "Tehran, Beijing to Expand Banking Relations," *Financial Tribune*, August 5, 2017.

26. "Pishnahad tasis bank zhaponi dar Iran" [Establishing Japanese Bank in Iran Proposed], *Tabnak*, August 8, 2015.

27. While visiting Tehran in October 2015 and signing a memorandum of understanding (MOU) with Iran regarding bilateral cooperation on stock exchange, South Korea's CEO of Stock Exchange, Choi Kyung-soo, announced that his country "is eager to share its 60-year experience in stock exchange with Iran." "Tehran, Seoul Stock Exchanges Ink MoU," *Mehr News Agency*, October 25, 2015.

28. "Bardashteshodan mamnooiyat estefade az Euro dar mobadelat tejari Iran va kore jonoobi" [Prohibition of Using Euro in Iran–South Korea Trade Exchanges Removed], *Tejarat News*, August 27, 2016, p. 10.

29. "Ghate moravedat banki bankhay irani ba Kunlun bank china" [Banking Interactions between Iranian Banks and Chinese Kunlun Bank Cut], *Bultan News*, December 11, 2014.

30. "Aghaz bekar Kunlun bank chin dar Iran" [Chinese Kunlun Bank Begins Its Activity in Iran], *Abrar-e Eghtesadi*, June 8, 2019, p. 1.

31. "Prosecutors Link Money from China to Iran," *The New York Times*, August 29, 2012; "Chinese Bank Denies Reports on Blocking Iranian Accounts," *Trend News Agency*, August 15, 2017; and "Hal bohran bozorg hesab iranian dar chin" [Settling the Big Crisis of Accounts of Iranians in China], *Tejarat News*, September 16, 2017, p. 6.

32. "Peigham chin va roosiye: Iran 'FATF' ra bepazirad" [Chinese and Russian Message: Iran Accept 'FATF'], *Iran*, December 26, 2019, pp. 2, 8; and "Bankhay roosi va chini az eraeye khadamat be iraniha khoddari mikonand"

[Russian and Chinese Banks Refuse to Give Services to Iranians], *Aftab-e Yazd*, August 2, 2020, p. 8.

33. "Iran dar list siyah FATF gharargereft? Ma va kore shomali!" [Iran on the Black List of FATF? We and North Korea!], *Ebtekar News*, December 16, 2019, p. 1.

CHAPTER 6

The Minefield for Moneymakers: Investments in a Fluctuating Land

FEARING THE SWORD OF DAMOCLES: THE "SECONDARY SANCTIONS"

Early American sanctions against Iran had actually little to do with dissuading foreign investors to throw their financial resources into the Persian Gulf country. Although the newly established theocracy's strong aversion to capitalists as well as the catastrophic Iran–Iraq War of 1980–1988 all played a significant role in disheartening many resourceful entrepreneurs and international companies to venture into Iran, nevertheless, the United States did not come up with certain measures to stave off systematically the flow of foreign capital to the country.[1] In fact, a great deal of all sanctions which the Carter and Reagan administrations levied against Tehran had to do with preventing the export of American arms and advanced technologies to the Middle Eastern country, though Japan and other Western countries had also been barred by Washington to supply similar high-cost products to Iran. After all, a fair number of American energy companies were still allowed to work on Iranian oil projects primarily to export their produced crude oil to the United States.[2]

By and large, it started with the Clinton administration and its "dual containment" policy as the main plank of Washington's approach toward Iran under Clinton. After encouraging European and Japanese companies to minimize their economic presence in Iran, the Clinton administration moved to virtually prohibit American oil companies from further

© The Author(s), under exclusive license to Springer Nature Switzerland AG 2022
S. Azad, *East Asia and Iran Sanctions*,
https://doi.org/10.1007/978-3-030-97427-5_6

105

cooperation with Iranians. In 1995, the American company Conoco was bludgeoned into abandoning its written commitment to develop Iran's Sirri oil fields, putting an end to any substantial energy investments by US companies in Iran for many years, if not decades, to come. One year later, the United States formulated its first major sanctions motion targeting investments in Iran through the Iran Sanctions Act (ISA) according to which any foreign company that invested upwards of $40 million in Iran over a period of one year was to be subject to US sanctions. In 1997, an updated version of the draconian fiat of ISA moved the goalposts, threatened any non-American company which dared to invest more than $20 million in Iran per annum.[3]

The investment boycott by the United States exacted a heavy toll on Iran's ability to attract sufficiently foreign financing for its oil and gas projects. The National Iranian Oil Corporation (NIOC) simply lost its previous leverage as few and fewer resourceful foreign corporations were now bidding for a specific energy project offered by NIOC. That was a reason why NIOC had to inevitably come up with more tempting packages from the late 1990s onward in order to win over those few foreign investors who were willing to put their company on the line by taking on a potentially lucrative energy deal in Iran. More important, the Islamic Republic had to find, by-hook-or-by-crook, the minimum amount of capital and technology to develop some of its critical oil projects because the export of crude oil used to be the mainstay of the government's revenues without which the total bankruptcy of the whole governing system was all but a foregone conclusion. No matter how much the core political ideology of the Islamic Republic was unsympathetic to the idea of foreign investment, smoothing the way for the presence of foreign companies in Iran's oil and gas projects had to be taken for granted.

Meanwhile, the Clinton administration's policy of fending off foreign investments in Iran continued, *mutatis mutandis*, under the presidency of George H. Bush who advocated a much tougher language in dealing with the regime of the Islamic Republic which he cast aspersions on as a part of the "axis of evil." Any plucky and ambitious foreign investor who now wanted to go Iran had to live under a climate of perpetual fear and possible military conflict between the United States and the Middle Eastern country. Under Obama, the international controversy over the Iranian nuclear program and the relevant US and UN sanctions only made things worse, though the nuclear deal of June 2015 which his administration helped bring into being temporarily left some wiggle room for foreign companies to think about pouring their resources into Iran's up-and-coming projects. Compared to his predecessors, Trump showed very little patience for foreign companies which were interested in cooperating with Tehran. After tossing away the JCPOA in May 2018, he just scared the hell out of international investors and many other business partners of Tehran by sending out an intimidating Tweet on August 7, 2018, warning that "Anyone doing business with Iran will not be doing business with the United States."[4]

The bottom line was about the extra-territorial extension of American laws and regulations so that the United States could easily sanction those foreign businesses which had the temerity to ignore Washington's demands by investing in an Iranian project. A number of US-initiated sanctions simply had an unnerving provision obliging both federal and state entities in the Unites States to divest unconditionally from any foreign company which engaged in any type of economic and technological cooperation with Iranians. For obvious reasons, many international entrepreneurs and corporations had a lot of business to do in the United States, preferring to often forfeit potentially short-term profits from Iranian projects in favor of vouchsafing their vital connections to American markets in the long run. Even those foreign companies which did not have much interests in the United States needed to still worry from any imminent retaliation by Washington such as being excluded from using the American-controlled SWIFT without which all the comfort and convenience of international financial transactions go into a tailspin in the twinkling of an eye.

Fallout: Scrapped Deals

Sanctions were not going to have a corrosive impact only on future investments in Iran; they more often backpedaled much of the progress made by a major project involving a foreign company and the Middle Eastern country. When an international investor made a pitch for an Iranian megaproject, the whole process usually required several years of tough negotiations and adequate preparations before they began to seriously implement their finalized agreement. Troubles arose when an ongoing project hit a brick wall out of the blue by a sanctions bill drafted in the US Congress or by an executive order announced at the White House, compelling that foreign company to either postpone its progressing contract in Iran or just cancel it in total. Under such dismal circumstances, project delay or continuous work on the project at slow pace often happened to be preferable to Iran than contract cancelation and project abandonment by an international contractor. Aside from some other nagging issues such as loss and indemnity, an abandoned agreement still required a replacement as quick as possible because the project had to move forward, one way or the other.[5]

Examples abound about the number of international, especially East Asian, companies which left Iran in the lurch halfway through an unfinished project. The history of abandoned contracts predates the Clinton administration's "dual containment" policy, harkening back to the dawn of governing Iran by the Islamic Republic. An early case was the Iran–Japan Petrochemical Complex (IJPC) in which the Japanese Mitsui was a major stakeholder. The project which had been agreed to between Iran and the Japanese company was in essence 73 percent finished before the Iran–Iraq War broke out in September 1980, providing the skeptical and hesitating Mitsui with a better justification to quit the contract permanently by excusing that its risky undertaking was no longer viable economically. True that the Japanese government had advised its major companies in April 1979 not to sign any new deal with Iran in various areas from oil to steel, but the IJPC project had been contracted under the Pahlavi monarchy, and Mitsui's abandonment seemed to have a lot to do with the treacherous world of politics than economic reasons.[6]

Another prominent example was the futile Japanese involvement in Iran's oil-exploration project of Azadegan. After several years of negotiations, in February 2004 Japan's Inpex Corporation managed to became a major partner in developing the Azadegan oil field at a total cost of around $2 billion. As one of the largest oil fields in the entire Middle East region, the Azadegan project was gauged at that time to have an estimated deposit of 26 billion barrels, persuading top politicians in Tokyo to throw their support behind Inpex in which more than 35 percent of controlling stake actually belonged to the Japanese government.[7] Japan under the leadership of Junichiro Koizumi had already done its heavy lifting in terms of backing the US wars in Afghanistan and Iraq under the banner of "war on terror," and it was time for Washington to partially reward Tokyo by turning a blind eye to Inpex's major oil deal with Iran. In sharp contrast to such expectations, however, both Inpex and the Japanese government soon came under heavy US pressures to do away with the Azadegan oil project in Iran. In October 2006, the Japanese eventually gave up as Inpex brought down its stake in the Azadegan oil field from 75 percent to only 10 percent with the hope that under some favorable circumstance in the future the company would be able to claw back its lost development rights in the Iranian megaproject.[8] Japan pulled out of the Azadegan project completely in 2010 as a result of unabated American pressures.

Similar to Japan, South Korea had to force its companies to pull out many projects in Iran particularly when the Iranian nuclear program led to several sets of crippling sanctions against Tehran. Prior to that, South Korean contractors in Iran used to take on smaller contracts or their non-energy Iranian projects often escaped Washington's suspicion and denunciation. Koreans were even given a good chance to deal with various Iranian projects which had previously been abandoned by some Western and Japanese companies. By 2010 when Iran had already become the fifth-biggest construction market for Korean contractors in the world, mounting international pressures over Tehran's nuclear dossier forced Koreans to relinquish a great number of their agreements in the Persian Gulf country. From Daelim and Doosan to Hyundai Heavy Industries and GS, almost all top construction and engineering corporations from South Korea were bludgeoned into leaving their relatively lucrative Iranian projects.[9] When the JCPOA was agreed in 2015, most of those Korean companies returned back and won over some more ambitious and expensive contracts. But Trump's withdrawal from the nuclear deal in 2018 signified that Koreans had to soon walk away from several major construction deals worth more than $5.2 billion. As a case in point, Daelim Industrial Corporation abandoned a refining Iranian project valued around $2 billion.[10]

Meanwhile, whenever a major Iranian project was abandoned by a sophisticated and resourceful Western or Eastern company, an immediate issue was about its replacement in order to get the job done. During the 1980s and 1990s when some critical criteria such as sufficient investment and advanced technology barred Chinese companies to compete with their Western or East Asian rivals, Japanese and South Koreans were in a better position to take over from an Iranian project relinquished by a Western investor. From the early twenty-first century onward when Chinese companies could somehow catch up financially and technologically, it became rather axiomatic that the Chinese were waiting in the wings to fill the void as soon as an Iranian project was abandoned by a Western, Japanese, or Korean company.[11] Such international one-upmanship in Iran intensified when a number of Chinese state-owned or private conglomerates emerged to challenge their Western and particularly their Eastern rivals, offering to take over swiftly and complete the abandoned project with all the characteristics which the Iranian partner of the contract had originally wished for.[12]

In the Face of Sanctions: A Fertile Ground for Investment

A slew of international sanctions and restrictions certainly made Iran a tough place to invest significantly and survive in the long haul victoriously. A simple international financial transaction was often difficult to sort out, making monetary matters an unremitting bugbear of foreign investors who were ultimately after making more money and taking it with them. The country was by and large isolated diplomatically, and its perpetually antagonistic relationship with the West set war drums to pound harder one decade after another. After all, few peace-loving entrepreneurs and pragmatist business people were really excited about taking their capital and expertise into a potentially conflict zone. Domestically, Iran's politico-economic environment seemed equally dispiriting to many hard-boiled international investors. The country's official political ideology was hardly foreign business-friendly, and its much vaunted bureaucratic and economic reforms were for the most part cosmetic and window-dressing because those measures could hardly make a serious dent in the interfering and menacing role of the government or semi-governmental entities in Iran's micro and macroeconomic policies.[13]

In spite of all those problems and impediments, however, Iran sanctions could be a great chance to flourish in an atmosphere suffused with less cut-throat international competition and collusion. It was all about turning those sanctions and limitations into possibility and opportunity.[14] As proved by South Korean contractors in Saudi Arabia during the second half of the 1970s and the first half of the 1980s, nascent companies and startups had actually a better chance to succeed and thrive by bidding for small and particularly unwanted business undertakings. Since Western and to some extent Japanese companies and entrepreneurs largely remained wary of retaliations and penalties from the United States for venturing into Iranian projects, newly established Korean firms or later fledgling Chinese businesses could often find ample opportunities to make a name for themselves by taking risk and making a humble bid for a normally profitable project in Iran. Amid a climate of pessimism and potential setbacks, thus, ambitious and determined foreign companies and investors could still find a silver lining in the dark clouds of Iran sanctions and restrictions.[15]

Basically, the Iranian government itself was the biggest sponsor and guarantor of projects, offering small to largescale contracts in almost every economic area. There was always a new state-financed infrastructure to be built in Iran, from refineries and railways to ports and power plants, and from highways and high-rise apartment buildings to schools and sanitation systems.[16] Since the conclusion of the Iran–Iraq War in 1988 until the present day, successive Iranian governments have regularly carved out a throng of small and large projects most of which required foreign capital and technology to carry out. In practice, sanctions could not prevent some gigantic Iranian projects from ever happening. The Tehran subway system was, for example, a monumental infrastructure project which was executed by China, giving the Chinese builders a unique opportunity to tuck under their belt significant credibility and experiences for completing the crucial Iranian mega plan under international sanctions. Some European as well as other East Asian contractors had already been offered to engineer the big-ticket subway project, but only China displayed more passion and perseverance to take on a huge scheme fraught with danger and uncertainty.[17]

At the same time, Iran's consumption market was equally encouraging and full of promises for foreign investments. As the second most populous country in the entire Middle East region, the country always offered huge markets with insatiable demands for almost every industry. Addicted to foreign goods and products for more than half a century, the so-called great appetite of Iranian citizens for foreign brands and high-quality stuff had only been whetted in the wake of continuous international sanctions over more than four decades. From automobiles and domestic appliances to clothing and cosmetics products, Iran's unquenchable consumption markets could hardly disappoint resourceful and committed foreign investors who were prepared to benefit from unexpectedly great business opportunities coupled with immensely high stakes.[18] In sum, various unsound social and economic policies of the Islamic Republic had just turned the country's markets into a gravy train of sorts, triggering an intense yet invisible rivalry especially among East Asian countries which had already experienced firsthand Iran's high potentials for remunerative foreign investments in both public and private sectors.[19]

Economic Rivalry: Rushing to "the World's Largest Emerging Market"

From June 2015 until the very early moments when some diplomatic insiders in Washington realized that the Trump administration had finally decided to quit the JCPOA, the approach of many countries toward Tehran was a snapshot of what may follow in a sanctions-free Iran. As almost all interested observers and pundits expected that Iran was coming in from the cold, a large number of European and Asian companies along with high-profile political delegations were visiting the Middle Eastern country with the hope of establishing their commercial foothold in the post-sanctions era.[20] Expectations were quite high simply because some $100 billion of Iranian frozen assets were going to be unlocked in different foreign locations, providing the government in Iran with a strong financial muscle to reboot the country's economy by modernizing and upgrading its industries and infrastructures after decades of suffering from sanctions and the lack of proper investment and technology. A watershed moment was in the offing, and any hesitation in reaching out to "the world's largest emerging market" could be economically detrimental, one way or the other.[21]

On top of that, Iran happened to be the home to the world's second-largest deposits of natural gas and the fourth-biggest reserves of crude oil, buoying up some experts and pundits to argue that only sizeable development of the country's massive offshore gas fields could help Iran emerge virtually as "a regional economic superpower."[22] In lockstep with its return to international community and opening a new chapter in relationship with the outside world, moreover, the energy-rich Middle Eastern country was going to regain its rightful share from international oil markets upon building up its production capacity and exporting larger cargoes of crude oil. In order to make many sanctions-era restrictions increasingly irrelevant, even Iran's own oil products had to be taken care of properly this time. That was a reason why the Iranian oil ministry engaged in serious negotiations with Japan, South Korea, and China to improve both quantity and quality of its refined products at a number of major oil refineries located in Abadan, Isfahan, Bandar Abbas, and Lavan. Drop in oil prices and sanctions had previously damaged those vital refineries; it was now time to refurbish them, primarily by injecting sufficient capital and technology supplied by those East Asian nations.[23] Still, Iran's fresh ties with each of those three resourceful Asian countries involved more than met the eye.

As soon as Iran started to implement the nuclear deal on January 16, 2016, the Japanese government lifted its sanctions on Iran and came up with a series of proactive policies to give a boost to Tokyo–Tehran relations. In the following month, for instance, Japan signed a crucial bilateral investment pact with Iran in order to smooth the way for Japanese companies to claw back their lost share from Iranian markets. To expedite the process, the state-backed Japan Bank for International Cooperation (JBIC) and Nippon Export and Investment Insurance provided Iran with a credit line to the tune of $10 billion. In addition to thinking in earnest about paying an official visit to Tehran, the Japanese leader, Shinzo Abe, believed that his country "must not be left behind" as many other countries were in a rush to beef up their connections to Iran.[24] Although most of Japanese businesses, especially its major corporations, took a wait-and-see approach because many financial impediments in doing business with Iran had still remained in place, the Japanese government had a second thought with regard to its serious push for fostering closer connections to the Persian Gulf country.[25]

First and foremost, Japan was worried about the Chinese growing clout in Iran under sanctions, and Tokyo did not wish China's influence in Tehran become more powerful after the regime of Iran sanctions was abolished. More specifically, Japan wanted to regain its fair share from Iran's energy projects. About one and half decades earlier, the Japanese government had done its utmost to help Inpex Corporation secure a 75 percent stake in Iran's Azadegan oil field, and it now wanted Inpex to claw back its one-time domineering role in the big-ticket Iranian oil project. Not only Inpex was the first international company which had signed a memorandum with Iran in 2016 concerning the Azadegan oil field, some officials from Iran's oil ministry had also made it public that with Tehran's blessing Japan could practically return to the Azadegan oil project.[26] After all, Japanese brands and products were still highly popular in Iran, and the Iranian government expected that Japanese companies play an active role in its newly myriad infrastructure schemes, ranging from oil projects to manufacturing undertakings.[27]

In comparison to Japan, however, South Korea displayed more interest to rekindle its rather multifaceted relations with Iran. Various UN and US sanctions had greatly harmed the ROK's commercial interactions with Iran to the extent that the two-way trade between South Korea and Iran had sharply nosedived from around $17.4 billion in 2011 to only $6.2 billion in 2015.[28] To help South Korea take back its market share in Iran, President Park Geun-hye made a three-day state visit to Tehran in early May 2016. Accompanied by "the largest-ever economic delegation" composed of representatives from 236 businesses and institutions, Park could sign provisional agreements in construction and energy worth more than $45 billion which was an incredible feat brought about "at a single summit."[29] In August 2017, moreover, South Korea through its Exim Bank provided Iran with a credit line of 8 billion euros ($9.54 billion) in the form of loans to finance various Iranian projects, ranging from construction to energy development, which were going to be carried out by Korean companies.[30]

South Koreans were also more optimistic than their East Asian competitors were, as Park was predicting the possibility of "a second Middle East boom" in Iran. Koreans had benefited tremendously from "the first Middle East boom" in the wake of the oil shocks during the 1970s and 1980s, and they now anticipated that a new boom in the region would work as a great stimulus to the flatlining Korean economy.[31] At the same time, South Korea was at a rather defensive mood for its policy behavior toward Iran under sanctions. Apart from Seoul's close cooperation with Washington regarding sanctions, many Iranian officials believed that the ROK was essentially a major beneficiary of bankable imports markets in Iran during those tough times, and it was now a propitious moment for Koreans to partially pay back their huge benefits by throwing more capital and technology into Iranian projects.[32] To better appease Iranians, in November 2017, South Korean Ambassador to Tehran, Kim Seung-ho, made it known that his country had reappraised its commercial priority in Iran "from trade to investment."[33]

Meanwhile, China turned out to be a horse of a different color. The increasingly expanding interests of this Eastern enchilada in Iran had already rendered pangs of jealousy and resentment among its rivals both in the West and in the East. Since almost all Western and Eastern nations were flooding in Iran to virtually eat China's lunch in the Middle Eastern country after implementing the nuclear deal in the early 2016, the Chinese had to do something about their threatened sedimented interests in Iran.[34] As a member of the 5+1 party which had given birth to the JCPOA in Geneva in June 2015, China had previously conducted its share of formal and informal talks as well as preliminary negotiations with Iranians on the possible direction of Iranian political and economic relationship with the outside world in the post-sanctions era. It was now time for Beijing to prove that it had a less difficult job than many other countries with regard to securing its present and future interests in the Persian Gulf country. It was no coincidence that the Chinese President, Xi Jinping, became the first foreign head of state to pay an official visit to Iran in January 2016. What happened during and after his trip to Tehran was to supply grist to the mills of countless debates, analyses, rumors, and contentious issues involving Sino–Iranian relations.[35]

UPPED THE STAKES: AT THE CENTER OF THE CHINESE BRI

After Xi Jinping became the president of China in March 2013, the Chinese communist system under his leadership launched an unprecedented campaign at home and abroad to promote the Belt and Road Initiative (BRI). By 2017 when the BRI was enshrined into the constitution of the Chinese Communist Party (CCP), this highly ambitious scheme had already received the support of more than one hundred countries and tens of major international organizations, buttressing Beijing's new aspiration to restore, through its multitrillion dollars project, the glorious function of the ancient Silk Road by connecting all the three continents of Asia, Europe, and Africa, if not beyond.[36] Regardless of all grand strategic and economic interests which had inspired the Chinese to think up the BRI and its different versions, China's mega plan had to ineluctably pass through the Middle East as the intersection of all those major regions which the BRI aimed to link. On top of that, the BRI needed to travel across the sanctioned-Iran as the geographic heartland of the Chinese big-ticket project.[37]

From a Chinese perspective, Iran was "a natural partner" as well as "an important fulcrum" of various BRI projects. Aside from its irreplaceable location in straddling Central Asia and the Persian Gulf region, Iran was at the focal point of the China-Central Asia-West Asia corridor of the BRI in order to connect Chinese and European markets.[38] Iran could also be very critical to a Chinese security strategy to one day get rid of its so-called Malacca Dilemma by setting up overland routes for supplying Middle Eastern, and even African, energy resources and other raw materials to China.[39] Additionally, a great deal of Iran's ongoing energy projects and its infrastructure plans, including rail links, dovetailed neatly with various BRI designs in the Middle East and Central Asia.[40] Chinese leaders, therefore, needed to persuade their Iranian counterparts to cooperate with

Beijing concerning some long-term objectives of certain BRI undertakings in Iran and its neighboring countries.[41] It was part of Xi Jinping's mission to Tehran in January 2016, though in the previous years the Chinese had taken advantage of different occasions here and there to give enough publicity to their BRI plans among Iranians.

From the outset, the Iranian government emerged among major international proponents of the Chinese BRI. In fact, when China started to promote its BRI thought, Iran was under many crippling US and UN sanctions, and Tehran had to rely on Beijing as a lifeline for its international commerce. The rising East Asian power was also a major stakeholder in a whole array of energy and infrastructure projects under way throughout Iran. The BRI idea was, therefore, a unique opportunity for the Iranian government in almost all political, economic, technological, and cultural areas. By jumping on the Chinese BRI bandwagon, Iran could make use of China's massive financial and technological resources to carry out its own economic projects. For that important reason, Iran did not abandon its staunch support for the BRI after clinching the JCPOA and the follow-up visits to Tehran by a flurry of rich and resourceful Western and Eastern companies.[42] On the contrary, Iran and China moved to accentuate the place of the BRI in their ensuing "25-year agreement" which Xi had broached during his trip to Tehran in January 2016.

The Contentious 25-Year Iran–China Agreement

In January 2016, Xi Jinping became the first Chinese president to visit Iran after 14 years. During his trip to Tehran, Iran and China talked about the prospect of a $600 billion trade within a period of just one decade. At its pinnacle, the two-way commercial interactions between the two countries had reached $51.85 billion in 2014, making the $600 billion figure a rather ambitious forecast unless the Chinese were prepared to invest significantly in Iran.[43] More important than that sanguine trade prediction, however, both Chinese and Iranian leaders discussed about a 25-year agreement which was to be known as "comprehensive strategic partnership" while Xi was in Tehran. It took several years for the two countries to iron out various details regarding the 25-year agreement, providing ample opportunities for policy circles and the media as well as experts and the lay public to often speculate, and sometimes rumor, about the pending Sino–Iranian pact. On March 27, 2021, the foreign ministers of Iran and China eventually signed the long-awaited bilateral agreement in Tehran.[44]

Iran and China did not publish all the details of their 25-year document, but most of its content had already been leaked into the press around the world.[45] As it turned out, the agreement was indeed comprehensive, covering a whole array of issues, ranging from stocks and banking to communications and military affairs. Based on the agreement, for instance, Iran and China aimed to set up a joint bank to cater exclusively to their commercial interactions, bypassing various US-based rules and regulations regarding international financial transactions, including accession to the Financial Action Task Force (FATF) which many conservative forces within the establishment of the Islamic Republic loathed.[46] More important, the critical document signified an estimated $400 billion of Chinese investments in Iran over the course of two and half decades. Out of $400 billion, some $280 billion or 70 percent will be invested in Iran's oil and gas as well as petrochemical projects, and the rest of $120 billion or 30 percent will be capitalized on various Iranian infrastructures, including transportation and manufacturing undertakings.[47]

Based on the previous Chinese record of investment in the Persian Gulf country, the $400 billion figure sounded very ambitious, and it became a subject of many discussions and analyses concerning the Sino–Iranian pact. From 2005 to 2019, for instance, China's total investment in Iran was $26.92 billion. Prior to 2005, Iran's share of foreign direct investment (FDI) by the East Asian country was marginal at best.[48] Thanks to the JCPOA, the Chinese invested some $3.72 billion in Iran in 2016, but then their investments in the Middle Eastern country plummeted to around $2 billion in 2018 and only $1.5 billion in 2019 in the midst of uncertainty over the Iranian nuclear deal following the US withdrawal in May 2018. Additionally, it was not really clear what percentage of the agreed Chinese investments in Iran had strong connection to China's own BRI projects for the greater Middle East region. Many observers strongly believed that at least some Iranian infrastructure projects, particularly railways, had been designed to be of service to China's BRI undertakings in Iran and beyond.[49]

Meanwhile, what happened to be far more disputable were the rewards and advantages which the Chinese were going to be offered in the wake of their prospective investments in Iran according to the 25-year agreement. Major gains and benefits for China rumored to be heavily discounted Iranian crude oil, potential deployment of Chinese security forces around the projects they were going to carry out in Iran, and renting out some Iranian islands in the Persian Gulf, Kish in particular.[50] Many Iranians across the world came forward to question such illegitimate advantages promised to China by the regime of the Islamic Republic, denouncing the 25-year agreement as a "colonial pact" resembling the Treaty of Turkmenchay which Persia (now Iran) had signed with the Tsarist Russia at the end of the Russo–Persian War (1826–1828) in February 1828.[51] A few years ago, the Turkmenchay analogy had also been used by many Iranians with regard to the currency deal which the Ahmadinejad government had signed with the Chinese before transferring 22 billion euros of Iranian assets from Europe to China in the run-up to stringent UN and US financial sanctions against Iran.[52]

In spite of all those contentious matters and criticisms, however, the Iranian government as well as a throng of conservative forces in the parliament and other key institutions of the Islamic Republic strongly defended the 25-year agreement with China and denied that Iran had offered to the Chinese any of those rumored benefits for their anticipated investments in the Middle Eastern country. Although Iran had signed the agreement with China when it was in a cash crunch and its economy had been shattered by crushing international sanctions, the proponents of the deal argued that the general public was by and large unaware about a lot of important gains flowing from close Sino–Iranian cooperation in line with what the strategic agreement stipulated.[53] A number of staunch advocates, moreover, upped the ante by calling the 25-year agreement with China "the third strategic, diplomatic decision" of the Islamic Republic after accepting UN Resolution 598, which ended the internecine Iran–Iraq War of 1980–1988, and negotiating the JCPOA, respectively.[54]

NOTES

1. Jonathan Eaton and Maxim Engers, "Sanctions," *Journal of Political Economy*, Vol. 100, No. 5 (October 1992), pp. 899–928.
2. O'Sullivan, p. 71.
3. Still, the ISA had given substantial authority to the US president to give waivers if it served American interests. In 1998, for instance, under the Clinton administration the French Total, Russian Gazprom, and Malaysian Petronas were given a waiver to invest $2 billion in Iran's energy sector.
4. "Trump Says Firms Doing Business in Iran to be Barred from U.S. as Sanctions Hit," *Reuters*, August 7, 2018.

5. "France 12 hezar milyard tooman be khodrosazi keshvar khesarat zad" [12,000 Billion Tooman French Damage to the Country's Auto-making Industry], *Kayhan*, March 13, 2018.
6. Miyagawa, p. 149.
7. "Japan, Iran Sign Huge Oilfield Deal Despite US Opposition," *Mainichi Daily News*, February 19, 2004; and "Japan Mulls Options for Iran Oil Project," *Kyodo*, November 24, 2006.
8. Michael Penn, *Japan and the War on Terror: Military Force and Political Pressure in the US–Japanese Alliance* (London and New York: I.B. Tauris Publishers, 2014), pp. 197–198.
9. "Builders, Traders Face Damage from Iran Sanctions," *Korea Herald*, September 8, 2010.
10. "Daelim Revokes W2tln Deal with Iranian Oil Company in Wake," *Korea Herald*, June 1, 2018; and "Builders Hit by US Sanctions against Iran," *Korea Times*, June 3, 2018.
11. Since 2004, China actively involved in developing Iran's energy projects, and the Chinese participation contributed significantly to its growing commercial connections to the Persian Gulf country to an extent that bilateral trade interactions between the two countries ratcheted up almost 12 times over a decade from 2001 to 2011.
12. "Iran Says China to Help Develop Azadegan Fields," *Global Times*, March 14, 2011; "Sherkat chini jaigozin Total shod" [Chinese Company Replaced Total], *Tejarat News*, November 26, 2018, p. 5; and "Ekhraj hend esteghrar chin" [Expelling India Establishing China], *Eghtesad-e Pooya*, July 21, 2020, p. 1.
13. "Syasathay sandoogh beinalmelali pool darhal ejrast" [Implementation of IMF Policies Underway], *Jam-e Jam Daily*, December 3, 2019, pp. 1, 3.
14. "Turning Sanctions into Opportunity," *Global Times*, December 13, 2012; and "Yi he wenti zaiqi bolan" [Iranian Nuclear Issue Is Resurging], *Xinhua*, June 23, 2020.
15. "Ilan kyeongje chejae, chunggukman shinnadda" [Only China is Excited for Iran Economic Sanctions], *Chosun Ilbo*, March 2, 2011; and "Iran torihiki teishi e" [Toward Suspending Iran Trade], *Nihon Keizai Shimbun*, July 13, 2018.
16. "'Maskan korei' dar rah ast" ['Korean Housing' is Coming], *Tabnak*, October 29, 2015.
17. "China Signs $4 Billion Metro Contract with Iran: Report," *Global Times*, July 21, 2011; and "Tafahom ba chin baray khat 3 ghatar shahri" [Agreement with China for Subway Line 3], *Khorasan News*, October 28, 2017, p. 1.

18. "'Ilan chejae'… hangugeun 'pihae,' chunggugeun 'suhye'" ['Iran Sanctions'…Korea 'Suffers,' China 'Benefits'] *OhmyNews*, September 14, 2010.

19. Tetsuya Watanabe, *Sekai to nihon keizaidai yosoku 2020* [The World and Japanese Economic Forecast 2020] (Tokyo: PHP kenkyūjo [PHP Institute], 2019), pp. 81–84.

20. "Ilan, gugchesahoe boggwireul shijaghaessda" [Iran Starts Returning to International Community], *Chosun Ilbo*, January 20, 2016.

21. "Vazir eghtesad elam kard: Tabdil Iran be bozorgtarin bazaar nowzohoor jahan" [Minister of Economics Declared: Turning Iran into the World's Largest Emerging Market], *Jahan-e Eghtesad*, December 7, 2016, p. 5.

22. Carter.

23. "Palayeshgahay Iran dar astane varshekastegi" [Iran Refineries on the Verge of Going Bankrupt], *Tabnak*, January 10, 2016.

24. "Building Stronger Ties with Iran," *The Japan Times*, August 18, 2016.

25. "Sanctions Eased but Japan Inc. Treads Warily in Return to Iran," *The Japan Times*, March 16, 2016.

26. "Tokyo Gets Tehran's Blessing toward Restoring Oil Imports to Pre-sanctions Levels," *Kyodo*, August 10, 2015; and "Japan's Inpex in Running for Azadegan Oil Field Deal, Iranian Official Says," *The Japan Times*, January 4, 2017.

27. "Sanctions-free Iran Looks to Japan's Carmakers for Eco-friendly Vehicles," *Kyodo*, August 14, 2015; and "Kyodo: Japan to Boost Iran Investment," *Iran Daily*, September 5, 2016, pp. 1, 2.

28. "S. Korea Trading Firms Turn Eyes to Post-sanctions Iran," *Korea Times*, January 20, 2016.

29. "Korea-Iran Summit Paves Way for $45.6b Business Deals," *Korea Herald*, May 2, 2016; and "Is 'Sales Diplomacy' Really Just an Empty Slogan?" *The Hankyoreh*, May 19, 2016.

30. "Ekhtesas khat etebari 7 milyard euroei kore jonoobi be Iran" [Allocating Credit Line of 8 Billion Euro to Iran by South Korea], *Ettelaat*, August 26, 2017, p. 1.

31. "Tycoons in Search of Growth in Iran," *Korea Herald*, May 2, 2016; "Korea to Benefit from Lifting of Iran Sanctions," *Korea Times*, January 17, 2016; and "Iran Opportunities," *Korea Times*, January 18, 2016.

32. "Sarmayegozari shart varedat khodro" [Investment Precondition for Car Imports], *Hamshahri*, December 3, 2016, p. 1; and "'Finance' abzar tosye eghtesadi" ['Finance' Means of Economic Development], *Tejarat News*, October 2, 2017, p. 5.

33. "Iran, South Korea Sign Agreement on Technology Transfer," *Xinhua*, December 12, 2017.

34. "Chinese Firms Face Competition in Developing Iranian Oilfields," *Tehran Times*, December 26, 2016, p. 5; and "China's Investments in Iran Surge as Those Coming from Western Nations Flounder," *The Japan Times*, December 1, 2017.

35. "Zarif: Chin dar syasat khareji Iran naghsh balai darad" [Zarif: China Got a Big Role in Iranian Foreign Policy], *Abrar News*, February 20, 2019, p. 1; and "United States Should Derail Prospects for an Iran–China Alliance," *The Heritage Foundation*, October 6, 2020.

36. "'Debt Trap' Diplomacy is a Card China Seldom Plays in Belt and Road Initiative," *The Japan Times*, September 1, 2020.

37. Lanteigne, pp. 79, 216.

38. "Mosharekat Iran dar rahandazi corridor chin-eurupa" [Iran Partnership in Launching China–Europe Corridor], *Afkar*, October 26, 2019, p. 4.

39. Marc Lanteigne, "China's Maritime Security and the 'Malacca Dilemma'," *Asian Security*, Vol. 4, No. 2 (2008), pp. 143–161.

40. Around mid-February 2016, the first freight train from China arrived in Tehran, making a maiden journey of 10,399 kilometers from Yiwu city in east China's Zhejiang province south of Shanghai. The train's long-distance travel took only 14 days, while it usually takes cargo ships some 45 days to sail from Shanghai to the port of Bandar Abbas in Iran. Referred to as the Silk Road train and carrying 32 containers, the Chinese freight train had also passed through Kazakhstan and Turkmenistan before crossing Iran's border. "First Train from China to Iran Stimulates Silk Road Revival," *China Daily*, February 16, 2016; and "First Freight Trains from China Arrive in Tehran," *Financial Times*, May 10, 2016.

41. "Hich keshvari bedoon Iran nemitavanad jadde abrisham besazad" [No Country Can Build Silk Road without Iran], *Servat*, September 4, 2019, p. 6; and "Rahahan jadid Iran ra be shargh chin vasl mikonad" [New Railway Connects Iran to East China], *Aftab-e Eghtesadi*, November 11, 2020, p. 2.

42. "Iran's Leader Says Never Trusted the West, Seeks Closer Ties with China', *Reuters*, January 23, 2016; "Iran Welcomes Reviving Silk Road," *Tehran Times*, September 2016, pp. 1, 2; and "Iran Looks toward Cultural Cooperation with China," *Global Times*, November 29, 2019.

43. "6 vazir 600 hamrah 600 milyard dollar tabadol: Iran va chin sanad hamkari 25 sale emza kardand" [6 Ministers, 600-Member Entourage, and $600 Billion Interaction, Iran and China Signed 25-Year Cooperation Document], *Ghanoon Daily*, January 24, 2016, p. 1.

44. "China's 25-year Deal with Iran Marks 'Momentous' Change as Ties with US Sour, Says Former Ambassador, *South China Morning Post*, March 29, 2021; and "China, Iran Ink Blueprint, Oppose Unilateral Sanctions," *China Daily*, March 29, 2021.

45. "Secretive China–Iran Deal Likely to Fuel Further Suspicions," *The Straits Times*, March 31, 2021.
46. "Iran va chin bank moshtarek tasis mikonand" [Iran and China Set Up Joint Bank], *Servat*, April 7, 2021, p. 5; and "Chiniha vared bourse Iran mishavand" [Chinese Enter Iran's Stocks], *Servat News*, May 11, 2021, p. 5.
47. "The China–Iran Deal and the Lack of Transparency," *Modern Diplomacy*, April 4, 2021.
48. "Sahm Iran az sarmayehay chini taghriban hich" [Iran's Share of Chinese Investments Almost Nothing], *Taadol Newspaper*, June 1, 2016, p. 9.
49. "What China's New Deal with Iran Says about Its Ambitions in the Region," *Time*, July 29, 2020; and "Azadrah Ghadir bakhshi az jadde abrisham ast" [Ghadir Highway is Part of Silk Road], *Bahar Daily*, February 27, 2021, p. 2.
50. "Safir Iran dar Chin: Edeay vagozari jazire Kish be chin, tohin be mellat Iran ast" [Iran Ambassador to China: Claim about Giving Kish Island to China, Insult to Iranian People], *Afkar*, July 12, 2020, p. 2; and "Vezarat khareje eddeai ejareh jazayer irani be chin ra takzib kard" [Foreign Ministry Denied China Rented Iranian Islands], *Ettelaat*, July 19, 2020, p. 1.
51. "Iran's Mullahs Clutching at Straws in Deal with China," *United Press International*, July 27, 2020; and "Is China Iran's Last Resort for Survival?" *Asia Times*, November 3, 2020.
52. "Aya gharadad arzi Iran va chin Turkmenchay bood?" [Was Currency Deal between Iran and China Turkmenchay?], *Jahan News*, July 20, 2015.
53. "Sokhangooy vezarat khareje khatab be mardom: Az tamam ertebatat Iran va chin khabar nadarid" [Foreign Ministry Spokesman to People: You are not Informed of All Iran–China Communications], *Aftab-e Yazd*, March 2, 2021, p. 5.
54. "Sanad hamkari 25 sale Iran va chin eftekharamiz ast" [25-Year Cooperation Document of Iran and China Honorable], *Eskenas Newspaper*, June 30, 2020, p. 1.

CHAPTER 7

Tipped to Profit: The Non-stop Gravy Train of Trade

DECISIVE REORIENTATION IN COMMERCIAL PARTNERS: TIME FAVORS EAST ASIANS

In the early 1980s and despite the existence and effectiveness of some US sanctions, the West was generally Iran's most favorite region in the world to engage economically. The share of US goods and services in Iranian import markets was markedly and swiftly shrinking, but many Western European countries still maintained significant commercial interactions with the Persian Gulf country despite avowedly direct and downright American displeasure with Europe's unbroken trade ties with Tehran. Not only Western European countries were importing more than a quarter of Iranian oil exports, thousands of their nationals kept working on various oil and non-energy projects in Iran. Likewise, a number of Western European nations, including Britain and France, were among major exporters to Iran regardless of the fact that the West's one-time quasi-monopoly over Iran's import markets was evaporating briskly like a wisp of morning mist. The main reason was that Europe had to increasingly, yet arbitrarily, sacrifice its sedimented economic interests in Iran in favor of its political allegiance to the United States. This was what had already happened to American businesses in the face of a rich and long-established philosophy and practice of free trade, private enterprise, and capitalism in general.[1]

© The Author(s), under exclusive license to Springer Nature Switzerland AG 2022
S. Azad, *East Asia and Iran Sanctions*,
https://doi.org/10.1007/978-3-030-97427-5_7

123

124   S. AZAD

Meanwhile, a fundamental shift was simultaneously under way in Iran's commercial connections to the outside world *pari passu* with the West's diminishing role in the Middle Eastern country, diplomatically and especially economically. In terms of meeting Tehran's economic and technological requirements, the Soviet Union and some of its satellite states in Eastern Europe had a lot of things to offer. India and many of its fellow countries in the Non-Aligned Movement (NAM) were other options which Iran could engage commercially, though those nations were close to the Islamic Republic politically and ideologically as well. But the crux of the problem was that almost all of those non-Western countries were then rather backward technologically no matter if some of them had for a while embarked upon their own quest for modernization and economic development. More important, they were not really in a position to purchase a great deal of Iranian crude oil without which Iran could hardly enter into some sort of economically symbiotic relationship over a long period of time.[2]

As it turned out, the actual and enduring swing of pendulum in Iran's trade ties with the world was too far from Western Europe to Eastern Asia. Of course, Japan was at the time among top economic partners of Iran, and the oil-thirsty and technologically advanced nation of East Asia was quite determined to keep up with its commercial interactions with Tehran in spite of some ups and downs in diplomatic relationship between the two countries in the wake of unabating US economic sanctions and political pressures against Iranians. Apart from Japan, the Chinese were then quite irrelevant technologically, and even their communist comrades in North Korea were doing fairly better in terms of supplying some industrial equipment to Iran in the early 1980s, though both communist countries of East Asia had been destined to emerge as major exporters of armaments to the Persian Gulf country during the 1980s. The last but not least important politico-economic player in the region was South Korea which required at least another two decades before the quality of its industrialized products could seriously compete with similar goods supplied to Iranian markets by Japan and a few European countries. But before international sanctions give South Koreans a golden opportunity to come out as the dark horse of Iranian import markets in the early twenty-first century, all they could afford for now was to bid their time, keep buying crude oil from the Mideast country, and prepare to contract some Iranian infrastructure projects especially from the early 1990s onward.

The Pinnacle of Commercial Ties

By almost every economic and financial estimate, Japan was Iran's top trading partner from the region of East Asia during the twentieth century. By 1990, for instance, the two-way trade between Japan and Iran had climbed to more than $5 billion, positioning the East Asian economic giant as a very crucial commercial partner of Iran. Throughout the 1990s, however, economic interactions involving the two countries did not improve significantly as the total volume of their trade was still less than $6 billion in 2000. Statistically, the first decade of the twenty-first century signified the acme of Japanese–Iranian economic relations as Japan was increasingly losing the ground in Iran to its East Asian rivals (i.e., South Korea and China). In 2004, Japan was still the second top trade partner of Iran after the EU, capturing some 11.4 percent of the Persian Gulf country's foreign trade and ahead of China (8.7 percent) and South Korea (5.9 percent). Although the Japanese–Iranian bilateral trade recorded a turnover of around $14 billion in 2007, the ensuing international dilemma over the Iranian nuclear program was to further sabotage Japan's commercial performance in Iran, probably permanently.[3] As a corollary, 2019 marked the 90th anniversary of the commencement of diplomatic relationship between Japan and Iran by remarkably little fanfare except that Tehran and Tokyo were stuck in gridlock over the issue of some $3 billion Iranian frozen assets in the East Asian country.[4]

Unlike Japan, South Korea began to experience its momentous years of economic accomplishment in Iran when Tehran's nuclear dossier was turned into a hot-button issue in international relations. In 2008, the two-way trade between the ROK and Iran astonishingly rose to $12.6 billion as Korean brands and products were unexpectedly capturing a big share of Iranian consumption markets. Despite all crippling UN and US sanctions over Iran's nuclear controversy, the total bilateral economic interactions involving South Korea and the Middle Eastern country jumped to more than $14.5 billion which turned out to be the highest level of their commercial ties until now.[5] By this time, some 25 *chaebol* (conglomerates) and upwards of 2000 small and medium-sized enterprises (SMEs) from South Korea were exporting goods and services to Iran, which was the fourth largest supplier of crude oil to the ROK, accounting for some 10 percent of its total oil imports.[6] In fact, in the critical sanctions period of 2008–2015, South Korea managed to export to Iran, on average, some $4.75 billion worth of goods and services on a yearly basis, buoying up some Korean leaders to dream about acquiring a record of $80 billion exports to the Mideast country by 2025.[7] Although Trump later ruined their dreams by quitting the JCPOA, in 2016 the ROK was still among the top five countries (China, the UAE, South Korea, Turkey, and Germany, respectively) which were the sources of some 60 percent of Iran's total imports.[8]

Similar to South Korea, China reached the zenith of its commercial interactions with Iran during the second decade of the twenty-first century and under heavy international sanctions. Iran and China scaled the heights of their bilateral trade in 2014 when their two-way trade ratcheted up to around $52 billion against a backdrop of only $314 million in 1990 and $700 million in 1993. In 2015, their total trade nosedived some 35 percent because of a drop in oil prices and the follow-up plunge in the value of petrochemicals and refined products. In the following years, the value of bilateral trade between the two countries was, on average, $20 billion annually in the wake of sanctions and continuous fall in crude prices.[9] A major stumbling block was that the United States kept in place non-nuclear related sanctions against Iran, putting a stop to international financial transactions in US dollar involving Iranian banks and businesses. In spite of those hurdles, by 2020 China still remained Iran's top commercial partner, accounting for roughly a quarter ($18.6 billion) of the Persian Gulf country's total trade ($73 billion).[10]

The foregoing statistics, however, did not represent the true value of Iran's economic relations with its major partners from East Asia. A main reason was that because of sanctions Iran often brought in a lot of East Asian products through its neighboring countries, especially the UAE. In 2009, for example, the official figure for the two-way trade between Iran and China was $21.2 billion, but the two countries also traded indirectly some $7 billion through the UAE. In the previous and next years, the same problem existed with regard to Iran's commercial interactions with South Korea and to some extent with Japan. The more Iran strived to sidestep sanctions, the more the role of informal trade grew in Iran's commercial interactions with East Asia and some other regions. Additionally, Iran's informal trade was conducted in myriad forms, making it rather difficult, if not impossible to keep accurate reports of all foreign goods and products that entered the relatively large and populous Mideast country. Consequently, those factors all contributed substantially to the omnipresence of East Asian brands and goods in Iranian markets decade after another.

Unwarranted Imports: "Worse than the Mongol Invasion"

As late as the post-oil shock of 1973–1974, an uncalculated policy of importing large quantity of foreign goods and products established a poisonous procedure which afflicted Iran's national economy until the present day. Under the Islamic Republic, dependency on foreign products was to only get worse one decade after another because the visionary theocratic system had no serious intention or well-thought plans to boost domestic production structurally and bring into being internationally competitive non-energy industries and brands.[11] Emigration became the zeitgeist of a growingly large crowd of entrepreneurs and talented graduates, leaving a great deal of economic and financial activities in Iran in the hands of incompetent and unproductive forces who often turned out to be more predisposed to relying on foreign goods and services than many inept policymakers and blundering bureaucrats across the political spectrum.[12] Decades of political isolation and economic sanctions did not also make a true dent in the whole edifice of this largely barren and futile system of governing the country other than turning Iran virtually into an Eldorado for certain foreign products and brands, especially those supplied by East Asian companies.[13]

The flow of foreign products to Iran became far more conspicuous and consequential, however, when the Middle Eastern country became subject to a comprehensive regime of international penalties and restrictions, including strict financial sanctions, over the Iranian nuclear program. Iran was no longer able to bring back its oil revenues, compelling its government to engage in certain bartering arrangements with a number of countries, including East Asian states, which could import Iranian crude oil and freeze its money.[14] The government had to now think up a "Barter Committee" in "the oil for goods era" in order to redirect the country's foreign trade toward doing more commercial interactions with a few countries with which the barter mechanism appeared to be more agreeable.[15] The more those few fortunate countries purchased Iranian oil, the more Iran imported their manufactured goods and products of almost any type no matter if some of those imported stuff could be procured domestically with higher quality and at a lower cost.[16]

On one side, imports covered the alpha and omega; from big-ticket requirements such as Airbus planes and Korean bulk carriers to inessential and unwanted goods like Chinese blood and Indian stationery.[17] On the other side, certain foreign products and brands were let to ultimately establish a near-monopoly control over Iranian markets. For instance, three Korean car companies of Hyundai, Kia, and Ssangyang could once capture some 40–50 percent of the entire market of imported vehicles in Iran.[18] Likewise, the total share of the Korean Samsung and LG brands from Iran's markets of mobile and home appliances could sometimes go beyond 50 percent with an annual turnover of roughly $4–5 billion, whetting the appetite of South Koreans to steadfastly take care of their largest market in the greater Middle East region by fair means or foul.[19] In similar fashion, markets for less-expensive goods, including shoes and textiles, were equally invaded by a tsunami of foreign products in the face of long-established Iranian expertise and mastery in manufacturing such products.

Imports became such a bankable business that literally "everyone wanted to be an importer" simply because profits from importing foreign goods and products far outweighed any profit and reward made by building and manufacturing. Based on some estimates, earnings from imports could be as high as five-fold more than what manufacturing and production could yield.[20] Importing some fashionable and sought-after foreign goods and products could actually bear much higher rewards under varied circumstances rendered by international sanctions.[21] Additionally, importers could have access to some state benefits, including subsidized foreign currency, making it possible to potentially make more money by bringing in certain required goods and products licensed by the government. Besides the government, banks and financial institutions were also among major supporters and guardians of importers. It was once reported, for instance, that more than two-third of Iranian banking resources were practically in the service of imports rather than giving assistance to domestic production and manufacturing.

As a result, uncalculated imports wreaked havoc on domestic industries and employment as some major casualties of bringing in large quantities of unrequired foreign goods and products one decade after another. Over time, many national brands and established businesses just went bankrupt as subsequent conservative and reformist governments under the Islamic Republic opened widely the country's gateways to the flood of foreign products. Corrosive repercussions were not constrained only to business bankruptcy; from high rates of youth unemployment to incessant brain drain and from social depression to rampant drug addiction, all had something to do with unreasonable and immoderate volumes of imported products.[22] These national malaises prompted some pundits and observers to consider the contemporary phenomenon of excessive imports to be "worse than the Mongol invasion" of Iran several centuries ago. Such a sense of national susceptibility was to be accentuated after Chinese goods as well as Chinese laborers and predators started to flock in.

RENTING OUT: FROM CHINESE WORKERS TO CHINESE FISHERS

After the conclusion and implementation of the nuclear deal, China continued to secure tightly its place as Iran's top trading partner because other major commercial players from the East and the West either refused to come back in full force or they could no longer compete with Chinese domineering position in Iranian markets. Statistically, Sino–Iranian commercial interactions plummeted to less than $32 billion in 2016 and even much lower in the following years, but such data was not rally revealing the whole truth about China's encroachment upon Iran's import markets.[23] More important, Chinese products started to ride on the crest of a wave in Iran as soon as the Trump administration quit the JCPOA in May 2018.[24] From now on, Chinese brands and goods began to gradually displace their main rivals in Iranian consumption markets: Korean brands and products. The Chinese mobile brands of Xiaomi and Huawei engaged in a tight race with the Korean Samsung, while a gang of Chinese automobile brands such as Chery and Changan went head to head with South Korea's popular Hyundai and Kia cars.[25]

At the same time, the emerging "empire of Chinese commodity in Iran" had a lot to do with an increasingly large share of imports from China. In 2015, Chinese goods accounted for roughly 25 percent of Iran's total imports, but by 2020, China and the UAE were the source countries for half of the products imported into Iranian markets.[26] Since a significant part of what the UAE was shipping to Iran was originally coming from China, the overall share of Chinese goods was definitely more than a quarter of all foreign goods and products which Iran was importing.[27] On top of that, in 2015 when machinery made up some 50 percent of Iran's imports from China, brand-new Chinese cars were really a tough-sell in Iranian markets; but by 2019, even second-hand Chinese vehicles were in high demand partly because of high inflation and substantial depreciation of the Iranian currency, rial. Under such circumstances, any China-related issue could swiftly become very controversial and gain public attention

130   S. AZAD

particularly when the Chinese mounted a new assault on some sacrosanct Iranian businesses, including the fishing industry.[28]

Basically, as late as 2018 a relatively large presence of Chinese fishing boats in southern waters of Iran in the Persian Gulf became a national *cause célèbre*. A number of Iranian media and press were reporting that the Chinese fishers were like vacuum cleaners hallowing out fishes and other types of sea foods, disrupting the traditional livelihood of many Iranian fishermen in the region. In the same way that the conservative government of Mahmoud Ahmadinejad had previously denied vehemently the presence of Chinese workers in Iran, the so-called moderate government of Hasan Rouhani first contradicted such news stories by asserting that there were no Chinese fishing boats in Iranian waters at all.[29] Subsequently, different branches of the governing institutions in Iran issued some contradictory statements, but it was no longer possible to trample the contentious matter under the carpet completely.[30] Finally, the government insisted that the Chinese fishing boats in the Persian Gulf were under constant supervision because they were actually working for Iran, but it still refused to provide any important details regarding the nature of any potential Iran–China agreement under which a herd of Chinese fishermen had been permitted to enter Iranian territorial waters.[31]

LEAVING IN THE LURCH: FROM DISPENSING TO DENIAL, AND FROM DUMPING TO DOMINATION

At some point in 2019, international sanctions against Iran were tightened again, bringing the roaring juggernaut of official imports to a screeching halt. The popular markets for domestic appliances and automobiles were, subsequently yet swiftly, affected.[32] Samsung and LG which had already captured some 60 percent of the market for home appliances were left with little option but to suspend their production lines and depart. Prior to their departure, the two Korean brands were basically assembling their products inside the Persian Gulf country, but now sanctions made it impractical for both companies to bring in their required components.[33] After leaving Iran, moreover, the Korean giants also stopped providing a great deal of their promised customer services by citing sanctions and the impossibility of supplying key parts under new international sanctions and restrictions.[34] As a major consequence, a number of self-described Iranian brands strived hard to replace similar Korean goods and products by assembling their essential components and small parts most of which apparently came from China, either directly or indirectly.[35]

In the car market, however, the situation was a little bit different. Before 2005 when the Iranian nuclear issue started to become a hotly debated topic in international politics, the French Peugeot and Renault were two foreign brands which had dominated Iran's automobile market. But the French companies dialed down significantly their car production in Iran in 2010 before leaving the Mideast country altogether in 2011. At the same time, the Chinese started to export cars to Iran from 2008 onward, and they could gradually increase their sale after 2011 in the absence of serious rivalry from major European auto brands. Trends in the car market, however, began to shift in 2015 when Iran and the 5+1 group agreed over the JCPOA according to which foreign companies were permitted to invest in Iran's industries, including the car industry.[36] Shortly, a number of major European corporations such as Germany's Volkswagen and France's Renault and Peugeot expressed their willingness to throw their capital and technology into Iran's rather bankable automobile market. Many potential Iranian customers simply demonstrated a wait-and-see attitude as soon as they heard about such happy news, causing panic among Chinese carmakers and their representative offices throughout Iran.[37]

Of course, the Chinese were still not the most popular automobile brands among Iranians as the car market in the Persian Gulf country had been dominated by Korean as well as Japanese brands since 2005.[38] Thus, an early marketing tactic for dealers of Chinese cars in Iran was to offer discounts as high as 25 percent to lure many potential customers. As it turned out, the Chinese proved to be sufficiently professional in dumping skills at least to help themselves maintain their minimum share of Iranian automobile market for the time being. The pendulum, however, swung back once again to largely favor Chinese automobile brands when the United States abandoned the Iranian nuclear deal and soon dialed up a slew of international sanctions against Tehran.[39] The famous European car companies had not reentered Iran's car market, while the domineering auto brands from South Korea and Japan had to also leave the country, one way or the other, because the Trump administration moved at a brisk pace to reinstate all previous sanctions and even add more crippling penalties and restrictions targeting Iranians. It was now a propitious time for the Chinese to consolidate their emerging automobile empire throughout the Middle Eastern country.[40]

Non-Oil Exports: Capitalizing on East Asian Markets

In 1978 or one year before the Islamic Republic's advent to power, Japan was the largest export market for Iran, though crude oil constituted a lion's share of Iranian exports to the East Asian country then.[41] In the same year, the United States was receiving some 12 percent of Iran's exports before its share shrank to just 5 percent by 1984. Washington eventually banned any formal imports from Iran in 1987, forcing the Persian Gulf country to diversify over time its export destinations after losing one of the top foreign markets for its non-oil products.[42] A great deal of Iranian non-oil exports comprised of some sought-after products such as saffron and carpet as well as pistachio and other dried fruits all of which were expected to find their way into right markets under right policy and marketing strategy. But a major stumbling block was that the Islamic Republic, despite pretending to the contrary from time to time, relied largely on its crude oil revenues and paid very little attention to promote non-oil exports. The Mideast country continued to remain by and large an oil-based system, and its potentially resourceful economy lost lots of propitious opportunities to diversify in the long run.[43]

But things had to change when Iran's crude oil exports encountered serious international restrictions in the wake of the nuclear controversy. Non-oil products could now help Iran earn some foreign exchange, and partially make up for the country's growing trade imbalance vis-à-vis its commercial partners. Japan, and to some extent South Korea, had previously received some of Iranian non-oil goods, but it was now China that became the largest target market for the export of non-oil products. Iran strived to coax the Japanese and South Koreans into accepting more cargos of Iranian non-oil products, but its efforts were of no avail because Japanese and Korean markets had traditionally been closed to foreign goods, especially non-Western products. But China turned out to be more receptive to Iran's demand, agreeing to increase gradually its non-energy imports from the Middle Eastern country.[44] By 2015, therefore, China was the final destination for more than a quarter of Iran's non-oil products, motivating many Iranian businesses to increasingly capitalize on the rising East Asian country's promising huge markets in the long haul.[45]

As late as early 2019, China was still the biggest market for Iran's non-oil exports before Washington's withdrawal from the nuclear deal upended both the scope and major destinations for Iranian non-oil products.[46] For all the policy cul-de-sac of the so-called "resistance economy" championed primarily by powerful conservative circles in the Islamic Republic, Iran was now more than any time dependent on exporting non-oil products as a means to shore up its rapidly dwindling reserves of foreign exchange.[47] Instead of China and other East Asian countries, however, the neighboring countries, Iraq in particular, became the largest markets for Iran's non-oil exports.[48] From Qatar to Russia and from Afghanistan to Turkey, Iran's surrounding neighborhood and adjacent territories were courted to import a larger share of Iranian products. In short, Iran's exports to Iraq grew at least five-fold more than its total non-oil exports to Europe, and Baghdad virtually replaced Beijing as the most favorite place to sort out all the financial transactions related to Iranian exporters of non-oil goods.[49]

NOTES

1. James M. Lindsay, "Trade Sanctions as Policy Instruments: A Reexamination," *International Studies Quarterly*, Vol. 30, No. 2 (1986), pp. 153–173.
2. Philip Shehadi, "Economic Sanctions and Iranian Trade," *MERIP Reports*, No. 98 (July–August 1981), pp. 15–16.
3. "Japan–Iran Relations (Basic Data)," *Ministry of Foreign Affairs of Japan*, September 2012.
4. Iran and Japan established their official diplomatic relationship in 1929. "Iranian, Japanese Envoys Call for Promoting Friendly Ties," *Mehr News Agency*, April 3, 2021.
5. "Korea in Dilemma over US Request for Sanctions against Iran," *Korea Times*, December 6, 2011.
6. "Don't Rush to Join Additional US Sanctions on Iran," *The Hankyoreh*, December 12, 2011; "SMEs to Take a Hit if Iran Bans South Korean Imports," *The Hankyoreh*, June 28, 2012; and "Iran Sanctions Eased, Relief for S. Korean Economy," *Korea Energy Economics Institute*, January 1, 2014.
7. "Barname kore jonoobi baray saderat 80 milyard dollari be Iran to 2025" [South Korea Plans to have $80 Billion Exports to Iran by 2025], *IRNA*, May 11, 2016.
8. "60% of Iranian Imports From 5 Countries," *Financial Tribune*, February 21, 2017.
9. "Iran–China trade can reach $100b," *Iran Daily*, January 18, 2017; "China Backs Iran Trade Plan," *Global Times*, September 26, 2018; and "Tejarat Iran va china nesf shod" [Iran–China Trade Halved], *Abrar-e Eghtesadi*, March 2, 2019, p. 7.

134   S. AZAD

10. "Iran's Foreign Trade Hits $65.5b," *Trend News Agency*, March 10, 2021; and "China and Iran Sign 25-year Agreement to Expand Ties," *Financial Times*, March 27, 2021. In 2020, China's two-way trade with Arab countries was around $240 billion or approximately 13 times more than its bilateral trade with Iran. "China Shares Wisdom for Middle East Stability," *China Daily*, March 29, 2021.

11. "Agar roohiye jihad va shahadat gostaresh yabad gerayesh be shargh va gharb rakht barkhahad bast" [If Jihad and Martyrdom Spirit Broadened Inclination toward the East and the West Would Pass Away], *Iran*, November 12, 2018, p. 2.

12. "Western Media Aren't Telling You the Truth about Iran," *The Wall Street Journal*, October 12, 2021.

13. "Zarbe sangin kore jonoobi be eghtesad Iran" [Heavy Punch of South Korea to Iran Economy], *Farhikhtegan Daily*, December 2, 2018, p. 8; and "Varedat kala jaigozin bazgasht arz daderati" [Importing Goods Replaces Retuning Exports Money], *Eskenas Newspaper*, April 17, 2019, p. 1.

14. "Motalebat nafti Iran va kore jonoobi ba kala tahator mishavad" [South Korea's Debts for Iran Oil to be Bartered with Goods], *Abrar-e Eghtesadi*, December 2, 2018, p. 1.

15. "Iran dar astanye douran 'naft dar barabar kala'" [Iran on the Cusp of 'Oil for Goods' Era], *Ebtekar News*, July 3, 2018, p. 2. Among all "oil for goods" schemes, there was an "oil for train" proposal by China in 2017, requiring Iran to supply oil to China in exchange for getting Chinese help to improve and extend its railways system through transferring China's technology. At that time, Iran possessed upwards of 13,000 km railways, and the Mideast country was planning to add at least another 9000 km, requiring significant finance and technology a large part of which could be supplied by China. "Pishnahad chin be Iran; naft dar moghabel ghatar" [Chinese Offer to Iran; Oil for Train], *Tabnak*, August 28, 2017.

16. "Ba dastoor dolat: Faghat az keshvarhai ken aft Iran ra bekharand kala vared mikonim" [Government Instructed: We Import Goods only from Countries Which Buy Iran Oil], *Abrar-e Eghtesadi*, July 5, 2018, p. 4; and "61 darsad varedat dar dakhel ghabel toolid ast" [61 Percent of Imports could be Produced Domestically], *Farhikhtegan Daily*, August 28, 2018, p. 8.

17. "Khoon chini dar raghay Iranian?!" [Chinese Blood in Iranian Arteries?!], *Tabnak*, October 5, 2015; "Bazaar shesh milyard dollari" [A $6 Billion Dollar Market], *7 Sobh*, June 19, 2016, p. 1; and "Naft midahim kalay namatloob roosi vared mikonim" [We Give Oil and Import Undesired Russian Commodity], *Aftab-e Yazd*, December 3, 2017, p. 2.

18. "Bazaar khodrohay varedati Iran dar ekhtiyar koreiha" [Iranian Market of Imported Cars in the Hands of Koreans], *Etemad Daily*, June 22, 2016, p. 5.

19. "LG, Samsung, Daewoo Worry about Fallout from Iran Sanctions," *Korea Times*, August 12, 2010; "Korea's Mark on an Expectation-defying Iran," *Korea Herald*, August 10, 2011; and "Che kesani koreiha ra gostakh kardand?" [Who Made Koreans Insolent?], *Kayhan*, July 28, 2020, p. 2.

20. "Sood varedat 5 barabar tolid ast" [Profit from Imports Five-fold more than Production], *Javan*, October 23, 2017, p. 1; "'Sood varedat' 200 darsad va sood tolid 5 ta 20 darsad" ['Imports Profit' 200 Percent and production profit 5–20 Percent], *Eghtesad-e Meli*, May 28, 2018, p. 9; and "Hame mikhahand varedkonande shavand" [Everyone Wants to Become Importer], *Vatan Emrooz*, June 23, 2018, p. 1.

21. Iranian customers were ultimately bearing the brunt of all costs and expenses paid to import any type of foreign products. Although sanctions had made the final cost of foreign products around 10 to 30 percent higher, still it was Iranian shoppers who had to eventually pay for all the tariffs demanded by the government for letting in imported products. As a case in point, if a Hyundai car was worth only $20,000 outside Iran, an Iranian customer would end up paying, on average, $47,200, including the actual tariff of 129 percent, to purchase that automobile somewhere inside Iran. "Yek namayande" Mafiay khodro vagheiyat darad" [One MP: Automobile Mafia is Real], *Tabnak*, October 8, 2014; "Toyotai 75 millioni chera 170 million tooman?" [Why is a 75 Million Toyota 170 Million Tooman?], *Asr Iran*, May 29, 2015; "Varedkonandegan khodro bejay sood 10 darsadi 100 darsad sood mibarand" [Car Importers Make 100 Percent Profit Instead of 10 Percent], *Kayhan*, October 16, 2017, p. 4; and "Edameh tahrimha be nefe sanat khodrosazi ast: Khatar tatili ghetesazan va verood chiniha" [Continuation of Sanctions Favors Auto Industry: Parts Makers Face Shut Down If Chinese Come], *Seday Eslahat*, April 7, 2021, p. 7.

22. "Sanat pooshak Iran be dalil varedat dar hal naboodi ast" [Iran's Textile Industry is Dying Because of Imports], *Kayhan*, February 23, 2017, p. 4; "Sanat va tolid keshvar ghofl shodeast" [National Industry and Production Locked], *Resalat*, February 19, 2017, p. 1; and "Naboodi eshteghal ba varedat enhesartalabane" [Employment Destroyed by Monopolized Imports], *Tejarat News*, September 14, 2017, p. 1.

23. "Chin hamchenan bazigardan asli bazaar tejari Iran" [China Still Major Player of Iranian Trading Market], *Abrar-e Eghtesadi*, February 27, 2017, p. 7.

24. "Tahator kala ba chin nahaishod" [Bartering Goods with China Finalized], *Akhbar-e Sanate*, November 24, 2019, p. 3.

25. "Rahbari bazaar khordo dar dast chiniha" [Leadership of Car Market in the Hands of Chinese], *Akhbar-e Sanate*, December 26, 2018, p. 8; "Jaygozini chiniha bejay koreiha dar 'sanat lavazem khanegi'" [Chinese Replacing Koreans in 'Home Appliances Industry'], *Eghtesad-e Meli*, August 26, 2019, p. 6; and "Tamigh enhesar bazaar mobile Iran baray chiniha" [Chinese Monopoly over Iran's Mobile Market Gets Tighter], *Arman Meli*, July 7, 2020, pp. 1, 4.

26. "China Shares 25% of Iran's Imports," *Trend New Agency*, June 30, 2015; and "Chin va emarat mabda nimi az kalahay veredati Iran" [China and UAE Source for Half of Goods Imported to Iran], *Mardomsalari*, August 2, 2020, p. 1.

27. "Ahmadinejad 700 milyard dolar sarf eshteghal chiniya kard!" [Ahmadinejad Spent $700 Billion on Job Creation for Chinese!], *Abrar-e Eghtesadi*, April 26, 2015, pp. 1, 2; and "Dolat Rouhani dobarabar Ahmadinejad az chin kala vared kard" [The Rouhani Government Imported Chinese Goods Twice more than Ahmadinejad], *Fars News Agency*, July 5, 2016.

28. "Negarani bakhsh khosoosi az edamye hojoom chiniha" [Private Sector Worried about Continuous Invasion of Chinese], *Jahan-e Sanat*, November 6, 2016, p. 7; and "Sayyad irani dar kam ezhdahay chini" [Iranian Fisher in the Clutches of Chinese Dragon], *Ghanoon Daily*, August 14, 2018, pp. 1, 3.

29. "Poshtpardeh vrood kargaran chini be Kerman" [Behind the Entrance of Chinese Workers to Kerman], *Aftab-e Yazd*, June 17, 2015, p. 1; and "Hatta ye shenavar chini dar abhay Iran vejood nadarad!" [Not Even a Single Chinese Ferry in Iran Waters!], *Kelid Newspaper*, August 27, 2018, p. 4.

30. "Abhay Iran dar tour mahigiran chini" [Iranian Waters Overrun with Chinese Fishers], *Hamdeli Daily*, August 11, 2018, p. 1; "Zeddonaghizgooyi masoulan irani dar mored hozoor chinihay mahikhar!" [Contradictory Statements of Iranian Officials Regarding the Presence of Chinese Fish-eaters], *Aftab-e Yazd*, August 27, 2018, p. 4; and "Kashtihay chini abhay Iran rat ark konand" [Chinese Ships Should Leave Iranian Waters], *Abrar News*, February 20, 2019, p. 1.

31. "Mahigiran chini baray Iran karmikonand" [Chinese Fishers Work for Iran], *Jahan-e Sanat*, September 6, 2018, p. 10.

32. "Varedkonandegan khodro bejay sood 10 darsadi 100 darsad sood mibarand" [Car Importers Make 100 Percent Profit Instead of 10 Percent], *Kayhan*, October 16, 2017, p. 4.

33. "Kore jonoobi bedoon America gedakhanei mesl kore shomali ast" [Without America, South Korea would be a Beggar House like North Korea], *Mostaghel Newspaper*, July 28, 2020, p. 1.

34. "Khorooj LG va Sansung az bazaar Iran" [LG and Samsung Left Iran Market], *Servat*, February 15, 2020, p. 2; and "Kore hich ghete lavazem khanegi be Iran ersal nemikonad" [Korea does not Send any Home Appliances Parts to Iran], *Aftab-e Eghtesadi*, February 25, 2020, p. 1.

35. "Chin az tahvil ghateat yadaki khodro be Iran khoddari mikonad" [China Refuses to Deliver Auto Parts to Iran], *Aftab-e Eghtesadi*, July 1, 2019, p. 2; and "Jaygozini chiniha bejay koreiha dar 'sanat lavazem khanegi'" [Replacing Koreans by Chinese in 'Home Appliances'], *Eghtesad-e Meli*, August 26, 2019, p. 6.

36. "Sanat Iran zir charkh khodro chini" [Iran's Auto Industry under the Wheel of Chinese Car], *Aftab-e Yazd*, December 6, 2014, p. 1; and "Vorood khodrohay taiwani be bazaar khoro Iran" [Taiwanese Cars Entered Iran's Auto Market], *Azarbaijan Daily*, June 30, 2020, p. 2.

37. "Emarat darvazeh vorood khodrohay chini be Iran" [UAE the Gateway of Chinese Cars to Iran], *Tabnak*, February 9, 2015; and "'Golden Age of Chinese Cars over in Iran'," *Press TV*, August 2, 2015.

38. "Mobareze akharin Samurai ba koreiha dar khiyabanhay Tehran" [Battle of Last Samurai with Koreans on Tehran Streets], *Jam-e Jam Daily*, August 27, 2016, p. 1; and "Sanat khodroo dar dastandaz chini" [Auto Industry in Chinese Bump], *Khorasan News*, July 3, 2019, pp. 1, 14.

39. "Araqchi: Afzoon bar 1500 tahrim bayad laghv shavad" [Araqchi: More than 1500 Sanctions Must be Removed], *Ettelaat*, April 11, 2021, p. 2.

40. "Dar gheibat khodrohay bakeifiyat varedati, bazaar khordo be kam chiniha" [As Imported Cars of High Quality are Absent, the Automobile Market Serves the Chinese], *Eghtesad Melli*, October 16, 2018, p. 11.

41. Miyagawa, p. 148.

42. Eyler, pp. 185–186.

43. Rudi Matthee, "'Neither Eastern nor Western, Iranian': How the Quest for Self-Sufficiency Helped Shape Iran's Modern Nationalism," *Journal of Persianate Studies*, Vol. 13, No. 1 (2020), pp. 59–104.

44. A.I. Salitskii, Zhao Xin, and V.I. Yurtaev, "Sanctions and Import Substitution as Exemplified by the Experience of Iran and China," *Herald of the Russian Academy of Sciences* Vol. 87, No. 2 (2017), pp. 205–212.

45. "Esteghbal chin az mahsoolat keshavarzi irani" [China Welcome Iranian Agricultural Products], *Tejarat News*, September 26, 2016, p. 5; and "Saderat gheirnafti keshavr be 47 milliard dollar resid" [Iran's Non-oil Exports Reached $47 Billion], *Ettelaat*, April 2018, p. 1.

46. "Chin, nakhostin moshtari kalahay irani" [China, First Customer of Iranian Goods], *Tafahom News*, October 19, 2016, p. 2; and "Divar boland chin maghsad 25 darsad az saderat gheirenafti Iran" [Great Wall of China Destination for 25 Percent of Iran's Non-oil Exports], *Afta-e Eghtesadi*, December 31, 2019, p. 1.

47. "Namgozari sal 1397 be onvan 'hemayat az kalay irani'" [Naming 1397 Year of 'Supporting Iranian Good'], *Aftab-e Yazd*, April 3, 2018, p. 1; and "Suzuki savar mishavim va az kalay irani hemayat mikonim!" [Drive Suzuki and Support Iranian Commodity!], *Aftab-e Yazd*, April 5, 2018, pp. 1, 2.
48. "Keshvarhay hamsaye maghsad 75 darsad saderat az Iran hastand" [Neighboring Countries Destination for 75 Percent of Iran Exports], *Roozgar*, February 28, 2021, p. 5.
49. "Tehran–Baghdad 5 barabar Iran–europa" [Tehran–Baghdad 5 Times More than Iran–Europe], *Farhikhtegan Daily*, September 17, 2018, pp. 1, 8; and "Jaigozin shodan aragh bejay chin dar tejarat khareji" [Iraq Replacing China in Foreign Trade], *Hadafeco*, February 25, 2019, p. 1.

CHAPTER 8

Not Impervious to Pressure: Teetering Technology Transfer

Spoke in the Wheels of Industrialization: Insatiable Demands for Technology

For all its glaring faults and shortcomings, the Pahlavi monarchy is globally identified as the architect of Iranian modernization and industrialization programs in the twentieth century. By the time a fairly stable flow of oil revenues was utilized to help some more ambitious projects of industrialization move through the gears, Iran had carried out for several decades a slew of massive modernization and economic development plans throughout the country. When the average rate of economic growth was upwards of 10 percent during the fourth five-year plan (1968–1973), top Iranian leaders were fired with enthusiasm, vowing to turn their Middle Eastern country into "a second Japan" and one of the top great powers by the end of the century.[1] The Shah's final five-year plan (1973–1978), moreover, contributed greatly to various progressing development and industrialization schemes all of which increased stupendously Iranian demands for foreign expertise and technology as machinery, metal, and chemical products were now a bulk of Iran's imports from the developed and industrialized nations such as Japan.[2]

When the Shah was overthrown and a hodgepodge coalition of Islamist fundamentalists and leftists took over in early 1979, almost all of critical developmental and industrial projects ground to a standstill. The leftist forces were soon either marginalized or largely kicked out of the political

© The Author(s), under exclusive license to Springer Nature   139
Switzerland AG 2022
S. Azad, *East Asia and Iran Sanctions*,
https://doi.org/10.1007/978-3-030-97427-5_8

system, while the core ideology of the triumphant fundamentalists was essentially unsympathetic to modernization without having any serious intention to abandon in total the pending economic development and industrialization projects. The new ruling system's political abracadabra and economic hocus-pocus had already put a spoke in the wheels of the Iranian industrialization juggernaut, but what compounded the situation was the cataclysmic Iran–Iraq War of 1980–1988 which practically nipped in the bud a great part of previously hard-earned achievements in different economic and industrial fields.[3] To cap it all, the existing and future regime of sanctions and international restrictions were to deal a knock-out blow to the prospects of revitalized industrialization and double-digit economic growth in Iran.

Despite the Islamic Republic's indifference to competitive industrialization and economic progress, and regardless of all corrosive impacts of lengthy military conflict with Iraq and international sanctions, however, the flow of foreign technology and industrial products to Iran was never interrupted over the past several decades. And no matter how much some top officials of the Islamic Republic preached fervently about some unworkable and dysfunctional credos such as self-sufficiency and "resistance economy," successive conservative and reformist governments often tried to keep various infrastructure and development projects going through close cooperation with resourceful foreign companies. If a Western contractor abandoned its Iranian projects because of sanctions or other reasons, the government would move to find an agreeable and qualified Eastern replacement. Just in case that Eastern business also turned its back on the project, a relatively competent domestic company would take over after the government assured it to bring in, by fair means or foul, all the required foreign technologies to just get things done.[4] On top of that, for decades Iranian citizens of every bent had developed good taste for fine stuff and technologically advanced products, providing the ground for the rise of a vast and bankable market fed largely by foreign technologies, including those produced by East Asian states.[5]

Technological Cooperation: Prescribed or Proscribed by Politics and Culture

Having themselves jumped through all sort of hoops and hurdles to acquire their required technology, the developed states of East Asia have conventionally been reticent about sharing their technological accomplishments with other nations. Even when these Asian latecomers had the will to transfer to other regions part of their industrial knowhow and technological knowledge, international alliance politics often played an indispensable role in the scope and size of their collaborations. When Saudi Arabia shifted its diplomatic allegiance from Taipei to Beijing in the early 1990s, for example, technological cooperation continued to form a linchpin of Taiwan's connections to the Arab country in the absence of formal political relationship between Riyadh and Taipei. Likewise, Japan has elevated its level of technological ties with the UAE in recent years, assisting the tiny Mideast country to launch "the first Arab space mission to the Mars" in July 2020.[6] The same Japan, however, had to say sorry to the United States after its Toyota Corporation had sold a car to the Iranian embassy in India in 2017.[7]

Aside from politics, a sense of cultural affinity or cultural difference has generally influenced the way many companies from East Asia have teamed up with their host nations in other countries, especially those located in non-Western regions such as the Middle East. South Korean companies are, for instance, famous for taking with them their own cultural mores and business practices when they decide to throw their capital and technology on a major project in a Middle Eastern environment. They even behaved in rather similar fashion when a large crowd of Korean contractors went to the region for the first time in the 1970s to carry out infrastructure projects there. That was, therefore, no coincidence why in late 2015 during a meeting with officials from Iran's Ministry of Industry, Hyundai Motors expressed its willingness to assemble automobiles in the Persian Gulf country under one precondition: working independently. The Korean managers present at the event had reportedly asserted that since Iran had a significantly different working culture, they could not engage in joint projects with Iranian carmakers, preferring to invest in the business separately through purchasing or setting up an auto factory.[8] Interestingly, Koreans had demonstrated such a rather haughty attitude at a time when they were among the underdogs because Iran and the 5+1 group had already agreed upon the nuclear deal, and a large number of well-known Western and Eastern automakers had announced that they were prepared to invest in the Mideast country.[9]

In sharp contrast to the foregoing examples, culture was hardly an important matter in Iran's technological relationship with North Korea and China, while politics turned out to be very instrumental in the nature and scope of the Islamic Republic's connections to both East Asian countries in the field of technology over the past several decades.[10] It was international alliance politics that smoothed the way for close technological cooperation between Iran and its communist counterparts from East Asia in various sensitive projects involving conventional and unconventional armaments. In recent years, moreover, there have been a lot of reports about closer, wider, and relatively secretive Sino–Iranian technological collaborations related to cyber security and potentially other areas.[11] Part of their relevant objectives is going to be materialized through the implementation of the 25-year agreement which was signed in March 2021. As a case in point, in April 2021, an Iranian member of the parliament made it public that the 25-year strategic framework will help Iran buttress its digital authority over the Internet after emphasizing that "unfortunately, we do not have control over cyberspace, search engines, social media apps, and emails. It is out of our hands. It's important for us to rule over cyberspace with the cooperation of the Chinese."[12]

SANCTIONS IMPEDIMENTS: DISCONCERTING DUAL-USE TECHNOLOGIES

Major US sanctions targeting transfer of technology to Iran began with the Clinton administration's "dual containment" policy in the 1990s. More specifically, in 1996 the Iran–Libya Sanctions Act (ILSA), which was updated and renamed the Iran Sanctions Act (ISA) in 2006, aimed to dissuade foreign businesses, especially those of American allies and close friends around the world, from supplying technologies related to Iranian oil and gas projects aside from deterring them to invest financially in the Middle Eastern country.[13] As a matter of fact, a great deal of major bilateral agreements involving Iran and a top Western or Eastern investor had essentially something to do with capital injection or technology transfer to Iranian energy projects. The United States could thereby fend off the flow of foreign technology and capital to Iran by intimidating international companies particularly through its extraterritorial or secondary sanctions.[14] Regarding technology transfer to other important economic areas in Iran such as the auto industry, frightening a top international carmaker or its subsidiary company with American secondary sanctions could be even more effective.

After the Iranian nuclear program became a vexed issue in international politics roughly from 2005 onward, moreover, the existing problem of technology transfer to Iran deteriorated because the ensuing UN and US sanctions upped the ante by prohibiting foreign businesses from any economic, financial, and technological cooperation with those Iranian entities and individuals suspected to be helping the country's ongoing nuclear and missile programs. A critical matter was now about transferring to Iran any technology of dual-use nature which Iranians could exploit to advance their secret nuclear and missile projects. While it was relatively difficult to classify which type of technology or industrial tool could have a dual-use function and be potentially useful for the Iranian nuclear program, at least the United States came up with a good excuse to go after some uncooperative and recalcitrant foreign companies, accusing them of abetting Iranians to make headway in their nuclear and missile programs. It was, therefore, very disturbing and ruinous for an international electronic or chemical company to be charged with supplying certain technologies and tools to Iran's WMDs undertakings.

The quandary over shipping dual-use items to Iran was particularly detrimental to Japanese, South Korean, and even Taiwanese technological cooperation with Iran. These East Asian players all used to have considerable economic and technological relationship with the Persian Gulf country prior to the nuclear-related UN resolutions and US sanctions against Tehran. Those international penalties and technological restrictions, moreover, affected the level and scope of collaborations involving some Chinese companies and Iran. All of a sudden, those Chinese investors became very cautious with regard to their technological role in some Iranian projects, fearing that the United States would sanction them for their alleged complicity in Iranian nuclear and missile programs even when their infrastructure or industrial undertakings in Iran had absolutely nothing to do with military affairs. As it turned out, therefore, it was generally not risk-averse top East Asian corporations but some greedy small companies and individuals with an East Asian identity that were behind a number of reported and publicized cases involving the illegal transfer of dual-use technologies or similar industrial parts to Iran.[15]

Technology Transfer Through Joint Ventures

The early history of Iranian–East Asian technological cooperation through setting up a joint venture goes back to the 1970s under the Pahlavi monarchy. Two prominent cases were Iran–Japan Petrochemical Complex (IJPC) and a 50–50 joint refining venture between the National Iranian Oil Corporation (NIOC) and South Korea's Ssangyang Corporation.

After the regime of the Islamic Republic came to power in early 1979, both joint projects eventually went into a tailspin as the Japanese Mitsui abandoned IJPC, while the Korean Ssangyang took advantage of the chaotic situation in the post-Pahlavi Iran and paid a cheap sum of $20 million to the NIOC to acquire its 50 percent stake in the joint project.[16] After the Iran–Iraq War when Iran embarked upon reconstruction, moreover, the Persian Gulf country was again willing to engage in a number of joint projects with East Asian countries such as South Korea. In particular, Iran and the ROK cooperated over several major joint projects in the car industry roughly from the second half of the 1990s almost until the implementation of crippling UN and US sanctions concerning the Iranian nuclear controversy.[17]

When it became very difficult to initiate more joint projects with Koreans in different industrial fields due to sanctions and other international restrictions, Iran made several attempts to procure an entire Korean company—lock, stock, and barrel—for the sake of turning its advanced technology to its own advantage in the long run. In April 2010, for instance, Iran's Entekhab Industrial Group was picked out as the preferred bidder to purchase South Korea's Daewoo Electronics, which at the time was one of the top industrial brands in the East Asian country.[18] The final deal between Entekhab and Daewoo, which was anticipated by many observers to fetch roughly half a billion dollars, eventually failed largely because of disagreement over price as well as international sanctions. In the absence of advanced and more resourceful Korean companies, however, several major industrial projects in Iran formed joint ventures with Chinese companies in order to benefit from all the technological advantages which were previously supplied by their Korean partners.[19]

Like South Koreans, Chinese companies were predisposed to enter into joint ventures with Iranians primarily in the car industry. Iran enjoyed a large consumption market as well as a robust manufacturing foundation, and its decades-long history of auto industry rivaled that of South Korea's, whetting the Chinese latecomers' appetite for partnership with some leading Iranian automakers such as Saipa Corporation. As major international automakers such as French Peugeot, Japanese Toyota, and Korean Hyundai pulled out of Iran in the wake of international sanctions, major Iranian carmakers had little options but to engage in joint ventures with Chinese automakers such as Chery, Lifan, Brilliance Auto, and so on.[20] Through building joint partnership, Chinese companies had to supply auto parts and other required technologies, while their Iranian partners provided proper manufacturing infrastructure and a massive market of car customers. By 2019 when a used MVM became an affordable automobile for an average Iranian car buyer, Chinese automakers in Iran were already basking in popularity and high sales.[21]

HINGED ON: KNOWLEDGE-SHARING FOR MARKET SHARE

In the weeks and months that followed signing and implementing the JCPOA, many top Iranian officials across several economic and industrial sections, ranging from the Ministry of Industry to the Ministry of Oil, out of the blue moved the goalpost, demanding from the visiting Western and Eastern delegates to provide a roadmap detailing basically the level and scope of technology and technical knowhow they were going to share with Iranians after being permitted to invest in the Persian Gulf country.[22] Buoyed up by the prospect of tuning Iran into "the Germany of the Middle East" within a relatively short period of time, Iranian interlocutors made it a precondition for interested foreign entrepreneurs and companies to essentially localize their expertise and technology in order to be allowed to stay in Iran in the long haul.[23] Even some Chinese companies which were already active in the Mideast country faced comparable requests, obliging them to either upgrade their technologies and services or simply wait to be replaced by more willing and resourceful rivals from a Western or Eastern country.[24]

Seeing a glimmer of bright light at the end of the sanctions tunnel, therefore, several Japanese companies and institutions signed a number of knowledge-sharing agreements of sorts with Iran after promising to scale up their technological and industrial activities in the Middle Eastern country.[25] Such intention was actually demonstrated by some major Japanese corporations to supply to Iran certain big-ticket products of advanced technology. In July 2016, for example, Japan's Mitsubishi Heavy Industries entered into negotiations to sell to Iran's Aseman Air around 20 planes worth approximately $500 million, but it was not clear whether the estimated cost had to be paid through Iran's frozen assets in the East Asian country.[26] Besides Japan, South Korea showed its eagerness to sign a more number of technology transfer and knowledge-sharing agreements with Iran in a whole array of fields, including energy, manufacturing, agriculture, fishery, marine environment, and urban planning.[27] The two countries also kicked off a "technology exchange center" to better coordinate their joint educational, marketing, and knowledge-sharing activities.[28]

146   S. AZAD

Compared to their Japanese and South Korean competitors, the Chinese were above all a sitting duck and a target for a non-stop barrage of Iranian criticisms with regard to China's inferior technology and its products of generally subpar quality found throughout much of the popular markets in Iran. At the same time, major Chinese businesses active in the Mideast country tried, as widely anticipated, to stand on moral high ground by asserting that they had already done their own heavy lifting in terms of proving Iran with its technological requirements in the absence of other international companies. Because of their proven service and loyalty, they now expected to be offered with more bigger and bankable projects by Iran, while insisting that they would carry out their assigned Iranian undertakings by taking advantage of the latest methods and newfangled technologies they possessed. In sum, Chinese investors expected to be given some sort of preferential treatments by claiming that their contribution to Iran was more than providing the Persian Gulf country with continuous cargos of suitable and affordable technologies in the heydays of international sanctions.[29]

Fledgling Startups: Finding a Platform for Publicity

Technology transfer and sharing technical knowhow did not have to be a one-way road for bringing East Asian achievements to Iran alone. In the same way that the Middle Eastern country was not just an exporter of crude oil and possessed a whole host of non-energy products to trade internationally, Iran after the conclusion of the nuclear deal in Geneva in June 2015 strived to turn as much as possible its increasingly growing technological connections to the outside world into a symbiotic relationship through which at least Iranian startups and nascent companies could find proper opportunities to flourish and become competitive internationally. Although knowledge production and wealth creation were the ultimate objectives of this rising trend in Iran, an immediate goal was to expose a more number of Iranian qualified companies and adept businesses to an international environment so that they hone their technological capabilities and professional skills. For now, internationalization in its broad applicability was not really a core objective; the whole process was to enhance technological foundations of Iranian companies in order to lessen partially the country's overdependence on foreign technology.[30]

Of course, Iran did not get that stage overnight, nor negotiating the JCPOA *per se* taught the Iranian government to have a high opinion of startups and pay serious attention to their technological requirements through smoothing the way for those young companies to boost their capabilities in a truly international atmosphere.[31] Since the late 1990s, the arrival of the Internet and some other critical technological innovations had captured the attention of a large crowd of Iranian graduates, inspiring them to set up their own technology-based business and over time turn it into a major company, at least domestically if not internationally. Making up some 40 percent of Iran's largest demographic bloc, therefore, the country's tech-savvy youth and graduates could make significant progress in many fields as diverse as computer software and hardware, biotechnology, nanotechnology, aviation, and so on. After all, the Iranian government and its institutions were among major beneficiaries of various technological accomplishments brought about by a slew of startups, and concluding the nuclear deal had certainly provided a better chance to help those fledging firms upgrade their technical knowhow, one way or the other.[32]

Despite some early rosy predictions, however, euphoria over gaining wider international access and opportunity was premature. Restricted international financial transactions remained in place, prohibiting startups as well as other Iran-based companies to purchase online their required technologies and educational materials. Likewise, they were prevented from selling their goods and services internationally through the Internet because it was impossible to sort out the relevant financial matters.[33] Instead of fostering better commercial and technological connections with Europe and other Western countries, therefore, Iranian startups as well as many of the country's internationally oriented businesses had to once again turn to Eastern nations, particularly China, for acquiring part of their required technologies in addition to benefiting from some other potentially good opportunities they could provide such as being introduced to a wider world through active participation in an international exhibition held somewhere in Shanghai or Beijing.[34]

NOTES

1. William Shawcross, *The Shah's Last Ride: The Story of the Exile, Misadventures and Death of the Emperor* (New York: Touchstone, 1989), p. 174.
2. Miyagawa, pp. 153–154.

148   S. AZAD

3. Later, some scholars claimed that the United States was a culprit behind the Iran–Iraq War by asserting that "the Carter Administration, with Zbigniew Brzezinski in the lead, encouraged and assisted Saddam Hussein in his invasion of Iran." Sasan Fayazmanesh, *The United States and Iran: Sanctions, Wars and the Policy of Dual Containment* (Abingdon and New York: Routledge, 2008), p. 27.

4. "Jahangiri dastoor dad: Iraniha jay chiniha" [Jahangiri Directed: Iranians Replace Chinese], *Shargh Daily*, June 18, 2017, p. 5.

5. "Iraniha faghat noavari va keifiyat mikhahand" [Iranians Want Only Innovation and Quality], *Tejarat News*, June 6, 2017, p. 1.

6. "Japan Launches First Arab Space Mission to Mars," *The Japan Times*, July 20, 2020.

7. "Barjam dar sandough aghab Toyota!" [JCPOA in Toyota's Trunk!], *Javan*, October 25, 2017, p. 1.

8. "Khodro moshtarek Iran va kore jonoobi dar rah bazaar" [Iran–South Korea Joint Automobile in the Way to Market], *Tejarat News*, November 30, 2017, p. 7.

9. "Korean Businesses Hasten Entry into Iranian Market," *Korea Herald*, February 29, 2016. After the JCPOA was concluded in 2015, there were also some talks about importing the American Chevrolet cars into Iran through South Korea playing an intermediary role. "Varedat rasmi khodroy americayi be bazaar Iran aghazshod" [Formal Importation of American Car to Iran Market Started], *Fars News Agency*, April 19, 2016.

10. "Iran, North Korea Sign Technology Agreement," *The Huffington Post*, September 1, 2012; "Iran, China Urge Closer Cooperation in Science, Technology," *Tasnim News Agency*, May 3, 2015; and "China and Iran to Strengthen Cooperation," *China Daily*, January 1, 2020.

11. "Hamkari ba chin baray filtering gostarde?" [Cooperation with China for Widespread Filtering?], *Aftab-e Yazd*, April 13, 2021, p. 4.

12. "Iran MP Implies China–Iran Deal Strengthens Regime's Internet Control," *Eurasia Review*, April 15, 2021.

13. Ryan, p. 109.

14. On December 7, 2018, Marco Rubio, a Republican senator in the US Congress, sent out a Tweet threatening Huawei, a giant Chinese company, with such secondary sanctions by demanding that "If Huawei has been helping violate US sanctions by transferring US technology to Iran they should be barred from operating in the US or from purchasing US technology."

15. "Taiwanese Firm's Nuclear Pieces Shipped to Iran," *Taipei Times*, January 9, 2010, p. 1; "US Worried over Taiwan's Exports to Iran: WikiLeaks," *Taipei Times*, June 12, 2011, p. 3; and "Tehran's Chinese Missile Man," *The Daily Beast*, September 6, 2014.

16. The Financial Times, *Financial Times Oil and Gas International Year Book* (London: Longman, 1983), p. 481.
17. "LG, Samsung, Daewoo Worry about Fallout from Iran Sanctions," *Korea Times*, August 12, 2010.
18. "Korea Pushing Ahead with Daewoo Sale to Iran," *Korea Times*, September 13, 2010.
19. "Tolid moshtarek dar Iran jaygozin varedat az chin mishavad" [Joint Production in Iran Replaces Imports from China], *Kasbokar News*, August 3, 2016, p. 3; and "Nimi az ghateat motenave lavazem yadaki khodro chini ast" [Half of Various Auto Parts Are Chinese], *Abrar News*, October 28, 2018, p. 1.
20. "Iran, China Carmakers Launch Joint Assembly Lines," *Global Times*, May 20, 2015.
21. MVM is a subsidiary of China's Chery and Iran's Kerman Motor.
22. "Sarmayegozari shart varedat khodro" [Investment Precondition for Car Imports], *Hamshahri*, December 3, 2016, p. 1.
23. "Zhapon va kore jonoobi gozinehay sharghi dar moghabel brandhay gharbi" [Japan and South Korea Eastern Options vis-à-vis Western Brands], *ILNA*, July 31, 2015.
24. "Sherakat ba iraniha, shart jadid vezarat naft baray kharejiha" [Partnership with Iranians, New Condition of Oil Ministry for Foreigners], *Iran*, January 26, 2021, p. 7.
25. "Signing of the Japan–Iran Investment Agreement," *Ministry of Foreign Affairs of Japan*, February 5, 2016; and "'Japan Seeking to Transfer Knowledge, Experience to Iran'," *Tehran Times*, December 25, 2016, pp. 1, 2.
26. "Iran's Aseman to Get Mitsubishi Planes," *Press TV*, July 20, 2016.
27. "Shahrsazan korei be Tehran miayand: Olgooy Seoul dar paitakht edari" [Korean City-builders Come Tehran: Seoul Model in Administrative Capital], *Donya-e-Eqtesad*, October 28, 2017, p. 7; and "Iran, South Korea Sign Agreement on Technology Transfer," *Xinhua*, December 12, 2017.
28. "Iran–South Korea Technology Exchange Center Inaugurated," *Tehran Times*, August 30, 2016, p. 1.
29. "Tamigh peivand Iran va chin" [Iran and China Deepen Ties], *Abrar-e Eghtesadi*, March 12, 2019, p. 1.
30. "Aghaz saderat mahsoolat daneshbonyan be chin" [Commencement of Exporting Knowledge-based Products to China], *Eghtesad-e Meli*, December 29, 2018, p. 11.
31. "Darhay Iran rooy zhaponiha baz ast" [Iran Doors Open to Japanese], *Abrar News*, December 22, 2019, p. 2; and "Berlin–Tokyo bejay Moscow–

pekan" [Berlin–Tokyo for Moscow–Beijing], *Jahan-e Sanat*, November 23, 2020, p. 2.

32. "Baz ham chinihay motaghalleb" [Again Chinese Cheaters] *Jahan-e Sanat*, June 2016, p. 2; and "Iran Eyes Tech Cooperation with China amid US Sanctions," *Global Times*, November 15, 2019.

33. "Foreign Sanctions on Iran Expected to Continue for 4–5 Years: Senior Official," *Xinhua*, December 11, 2020.

34. "Sherkathay irani dar namayeshgah chin be jahan moarefi mishavand" [Iranian Companies Introduced to the World at China Exhibition], *Aftab-e Eghtesadi*, November 11, 2019, p. 1.

CHAPTER 9

Arms Embargoes: Military and Security Adjustment

To Bottle Genie: Arms Embargoes and Military Impediments

Unlike economic sanctions which are generally broad and encompass a wide range of issues and areas, military sanctions or arms embargoes are more specific and clear-cut, aiming on the whole to destroy or deter a target country's military capabilities. Considered as a form of "smart sanctions," arms embargoes put a stop to normal and uncomplicated supply of standard or conventional armaments and military equipment to a militarily sanctioned country.[1] As the case of Iran has signified during the past four and half decades, moreover, arms sanctions may not be only about fending off the flow of conventional armaments from international weaponry markets to a target country; arms embargoes could also be applied to neutralize or delay that country's quest for acquiring any type of nuclear, chemical, and biological weapons (also known as WMDs) or missiles for their delivery. Similar to the Trump administration's "most biting sanctions ever" against Iran after Washington's withdrawal from the JCPOA in May 2018, therefore, international military sanctions against the Persian Gulf country, at least those arms restrictions imposed by the US-led West, have long zeroed in on curbing the sale of both conventional and unconventional weapons to the regime of the Islamic Republic.[2]

Basically, the first US measure with regard to arms sanctions against Iran took place on November 8, 1979, when the Carter administration

© The Author(s), under exclusive license to Springer Nature Switzerland AG 2022
S. Azad, *East Asia and Iran Sanctions*,
https://doi.org/10.1007/978-3-030-97427-5_9

151

put off the transfer of some $300 million worth of military spare parts which the Middle Eastern country under the Shah had purchased and paid for duly. During the follow-up Iran–Iraq War of 1980–1988 and in sharp contrast to what the scandalous Iran–Contra divulged, it was the official policy of the United States and its Western partners not to sell any weapons to Iran, though the Americans had given green light to their friends and allies around the world to supply to Iraq as much as arms they wished. The next serious US move concerning arms sanctions against Iran came about in April 1992 when the American Congress passed the Iran–Iraq Arms Non-Proliferation Act which essentially banned the supply of whatever good and technology useful to develop Iran's WMDs or missile capabilities. As counterintuitive as it came into view then, the United States had previously imposed such strict types of military sanctions against Baghdad after Saddam Hussein invaded and occupied the neighboring tiny sheikhdom of Kuwait.[3]

Later, the Clinton administration's "dual containment" policy upped the ante by recognizing Iran as the biggest threat to US national interests in the greater Middle East region. From now on, the United States drew a parallel between Iranian military capabilities and its "unacceptable" behaviors in the Middle East, pushing for more international penalties in general and arms sanctions in particular to contain Tehran.[4] China under Jiang Zemin was, for instance, bludgeoned into relinquishing its growing nuclear and missile cooperation with Iran. After the Iranian nuclear program became a hot topic of international politics roughly from 2005 onward, however, the Middle Eastern country came under the severest forms of international arms embargoes. Aside from the relevant UN sanctions which precluded its member states from giving "advanced offensive weapons systems" to Tehran, the United States carved out its own unilateral sanctions to prevent a "nuclear Iran" at any cost. To avert an Iranian "breakout capability" and "bottle its nuclear genie," therefore, all US-drafted military sanctions and non-military penalties now aimed to forbid the shipment of any goods and services to Iran which could help Iranians advance their nuclear and missile capabilities.

Although many experts and pundits believed that Iran's military power had been greatly exaggerated and even a "nuclear Iran" would not be really a menacing danger to US vested interests in the Middle East and beyond, however, many American top politicians used to often put a spotlight on expanding Iranian threat to the United States and its allies here and there.[5] In particular, the Trump administration took the rhetoric of Iranian military threat to new heights by drawing a bead on the Islamic Revolutionary Guard Corps (IRGC). In April 2019, the United States under Trump singled out publicly the IRGC and its Quds Force as a Foreign Terrorist Organization (FTO), targeting a linchpin of the present armed forces of the Persian Gulf country. More important, the American move was the first time when Washington officially recognized a major part of another country's military as a terrorist entity. In September 2019, the United States also sanctioned the Central Bank of Iran (CBI) after accusing it of providing the IRGC and its Quds Force with billions of dollars.[6]

To evaluate, decades of international arms embargoes were certainly detrimental to Iran's overall fighting power and military ambitions. As a country that once was one of the major purchasers of armaments in the world, the lack of access to key arms markets in the West put Iran in serious difficulty, thwarting the country's ability to even procure some urgent spare parts for its old weapons let alone to keep abreast of recent military technologies and defense innovations. Coupled with crippling economic penalties and financial restrictions, arms sanctions obviously kept Iran behind some of its arch-regional rivals in certain vital military areas such as aerial power.[7] For all those impediments, however, Iran could almost always find a way to obtain its required armaments and muddle through. As a matter of fact, the Middle Eastern country was more successful in procuring its essential conventional weapons and munitions, while its rather surreptitious quest for possessing nuclear and missile capabilities was a road to myriad troubles and misfortunes.

CONVENTIONAL ARMS AND MILITARY DEALS: EAST ASIAN INVOLVEMENT

In contemporary history of arms trade, the United States has so far remained as the top exporter of weapons and munitions to Iran despite the fact that Washington has not engaged in any reported arms deal with Tehran excepting what happened between the two countries under the sensational Iran–Contra revelation in the 1980s. In the period between 1950 and 1979, the United States shipped to Iran some $24.94 billion worth of arms, while Washington also sold about $64 million weapons to the Persian Gulf country based on their Iran–Contra collusion from 1984 to 1986. Prior to 1979, moreover, Iran engaged in significant arms deals with other Western countries, especially Britain, but after 1979 such arms trades were sporadic and largely stealthy.[8] Under the Islamic Republic,

East Asia emerged gradually as a major market for procuring Iran's conventional military requirements, though Russians often continued to claim for the largest share of Tehran's unceasing arms imports from the 1990s onward. At least during the Iran–Iraq War of 1980–1988, all East Asian players, excluding Japan, found a good chance to engage in overt and covert arms trade with Iran.

Basically, North Korea was the first East Asian country which engaged in arms business with Tehran as soon as the Iran–Iraq War broke out in September 1980. The internecine conflict in the Middle East was like manna from heaven, making it easy for the reclusive communist state to emerge as a major supplier of armaments to Iran by 1982. Based on some estimates, in 1982 North Korea could ship to the Mideast country some $500 million to $2 billion worth of weapons, accounting for around 40 percent of Iran's total arms imports in that year alone. Part of the wide difference in the reported statistics could be attributed to the fact that the DPRK was simultaneously playing the role of a conduit for the Soviet Union and especially the communist China both of which desperately needed to hide as much as possible their ongoing arms trade with Tehran at that very sensitive time in international politics.[9] The Iran–Iraq War experience, however, brought a lot of political capital for North Korea in military and political circles of the Islamic Republic, persuading the two countries to maintain their rather close cooperation in military as well as in other areas after the war conclusion in 1988.[10]

Besides North Korea, there were two other small players from East Asia that could have a cameo yet critical role in the Iran–Iraq War: South Korea and Taiwan. But unlike the DPRK which supplied arms exclusively to Iran, the ROK and Taiwan strived to sell weapons both to Tehran and Baghdad after declaring officially their neutral position toward the two warring parties in the Middle East. Based on what later was unearthed concerning the Iran–Contra affair, moreover, South Korea had also apparently played an intermediary role for other big arms exporters, the United States in particular, shipping to Iran some of the preferred types of Western weapons or their replacement parts.[11] Similar to South Korea, Taiwan was then producing US weapons under license, but diplomatically Taipei was not really in a comfortable position to expand its arms trade during that Middle Eastern mayhem. Still, Taiwan's rather insignificant share of arms deals with Iran, which was handled mostly through private middlemen, was of great boon to the Persian Gulf country then, and that was no coincidence why some controversial aspects of Taipei–Tehran arms trade continued to make headlines several decades after the Iran–Iraq War was over.[12]

In comparison to its East Asian neighbors, however, China turned out to be a larger and relatively more loyal stakeholder in Iranian, and generally Middle Eastern, trade in armaments. By the mid-1980s, China managed to get involved directly in the shipment of weapons to Iran and place itself virtually as the top arms supplier to Tehran in spite of serious pressures by the United States to curtail its sale of arms and munitions to the Persian Gulf country. At the same time, China was an important arms partner of Iraq, supplying some $3 million worth of armaments to Baghdad in the first half of the 1980s alone.[13] Based on some estimates, the East Asian power could sell approximately $12 billion worth of weapons and military equipment to Baghdad and Tehran during the Iran–Iraq War as both warring Mideast countries eventually received about 74 percent of China's total arms deal with the entire third world from 1980 to 1987.[14] The Iran–Iraq War's experiences, moreover, provided China with a lot of invaluable lessons, expediting Beijing's success as one of the top global exporters of armaments and munitions to the region and beyond in the following decades.[15]

After the Iran–Iraq War, however, there happened to be lots of ups and downs both in the nature and scope of Chinese military engagement and defense cooperation with Iranians. Much of the fluctuation in Sino–Iranian arms trade had to do with a changing nature of Beijing–Washington relationship over the past several decades as China was prepared to often exploit its politico-economic as well as military and technological connections to Tehran as a bargaining chip in some of its quid pro quo deals with the United States.[16] Apart from the US factor, since the Middle East became the largest international market for China's arms exports, Beijing by and large needed to walk on eggshells trying to balance its military, and even its political and economic, ties with different antagonistic partners across the region. At least with regard to trade in conventional arms, nonetheless, the prospect for Iranian–Chinese military relations seemed bright from the moment the UN arms embargoes on Tehran expired on October 18, 2020.[17] The two ancient partners have also vowed to deepen their military and defense cooperation in lockstep with what the 25-year agreement between Beijing and Tehran stipulates.[18]

Oscillating Nuclear and Missile Liaison: Direct and Indirect Collaboration

The Iranian nuclear program is an old project harkening back to the 1950s when the Shah embarked upon this ambitious development plan in close cooperation with the United States and some other Western countries. To help the promising project move through the gears, Iran established the Atomic Energy Organization in 1974 and its generous budget was increased to roughly $1 billion by 1976.[19] Coincidently or not, it was around this time when two other American allies, South Korea and Taiwan, came under tremendous US political arm-twisting and even economic sanctions to do away with their construction of nuclear reprocessing plants. In fact, South Korea in 1975–1976 and Taiwan in 1976–1977 both were sanctioned by the United States to give up permanently their nuclear processing schemes.[20] Koreans were also pressed hard by Washington to call off the arrangement to buy a nuclear plant from France.[21] It was, therefore, much easier for Americans and Western Europeans to walk away from their commitments to Iran's nuclear program with impunity once the Pahlavi monarchy was overthrown and the Islamic Republic occupied the Persian Gulf country's strategic heights of power in early 1979.

At the beginning, the Islamic Republic did not take the nuclear program seriously, and it took some time before Tehran decided to resume the work by relying on Moscow as the biggest foreign stakeholder in the project for decades to come. China also got involved in the nuclear program, but by the second half of the 1990s Beijing moved essentially to terminate its nuclear collaboration with Tehran in tandem with the growing Sino–American entente under Jiang Zemin and Bill Clinton. In September 1995, for instance, China put off an agreement to ship to Iran two 300-MW nuclear reactors before Beijing made it public in November 1996 that it was going to call off the sale of a uranium conversion facility to the Middle Eastern country. In 1997 and following a sort of quid pro quo deal between Jiang and Clinton, China basically put an end to its nuclear cooperation with Iran, aiming to maintain its quickly improving partnership with the United States and be regarded as a "mature great power" or a "responsible stakeholder" by demonstrating in practice its corresponding nonproliferation commitments and obligations.[22]

By the time the US-led West put the spotlight on the Iranian nuclear program around 2004–2005, therefore, China was twice cautious not to be associated in any way with Iran's controversial nuclear project. Diplomatically, China threw its armchair quarterbacking behind Iran's legitimate rights to capitalize on its nuclear program for civilian purposes, but Beijing also jumped on the bandwagon voting in favor of the UN resolutions authorizing a slew of punitive international sanctions against Iranians over their ongoing nuclear program. After the 18-month international negotiations between Iran and the 5+1 nations, including China, led to the signing of the JCPOA in June 2015, however, the East Asian power was officially given a critical role in the Iranian nuclear program to serve as the primary liaison between Iran and an international working group created to redesign and reconstruct the Arak heavy water reactor in order to bring down its output of plutonium.[23] But after the United States quit the nuclear deal, China was again unwilling to play a leading role in the working group, fearing potential American displeasure and sanctions. At the same time, China's continuous shirking and foot-dragging in redesigning the Arak reactor angered some Iranian officials who publicly criticized China and questioned its genuine commitments to a successful implementation of the JCPOA.[24]

For all its official apathy toward the Iranian nuclear program since the late 1990s, China was constantly accused of having contributed to Iran's nuclear project directly or indirectly one decade after another. More specifically, a number of Chinese companies and individuals were charged with assisting Iran to advance its nuclear program through supplying Tehran with various sensitive components, parts, dual-use technologies, and so on. Some of those Chinese businesses were suspected to be affiliated with the People's Liberation Army, and their involvement in the Iranian nuclear as well as missile programs was thought to be mostly about gaining lucrative commercial benefits rather than helping Iran out of any political and ideological incentive. Additionally, some major port cities across China as well as Hong Kong and even Taiwan were occasionally suspected of becoming a transshipment hub of sorts, making it possible for Iranians or their foreign middlemen to transfer to Iran part of their required nuclear materials and technologies.[25]

With regard to Iran's missile program, China's direct and indirect role followed a trajectory relatively similar to its involvement in the Persian Gulf country's nuclear program. Compared to China, however, North Korea turned out to be a larger stakeholder in Iran's missile undertakings as if Beijing and Pyongyang switched their roles in the Iranian nuclear and missile programs so that China played a bigger part in advancing the nuclear project, while North Korea contributed more to the missile undertaking.[26] The DPRK's involvement in the Iranian missile projects was also a lengthy collaboration dating back to the heydays of the Iran–Iraq War in the 1980s, and Pyongyang scaled back its missile cooperation mostly when Tehran was short of sufficient cash to proceed with its new missile undertakings. Unlike China and all other East Asian players, moreover, North Korea's missile and its possible nuclear collaborations with the Middle Eastern country over the past several decades were all about the reclusive communist regime of the DPRK and its will; there was absolutely no North Korea company, nor there was any ambitious and greedy North Korean individual who wished to quickly make a mint by providing Iranians with some desired missile technology or nuclear expertise.

In essence, Iran's missile program goes back to the 1980s, and this ambitious plan, similar to the nuclear project, was initially very dependent on importing required materials and technologies from foreign countries such as North Korea. After testing successfully North Korea's Scud-B missiles against Iraq in the final stages of the Iran–Iraq War, in the 1990s Iran decided to purchase from the DPRK a more number of the 300 km-range Scud-B missiles as well as some of its 500 km-range Scud-C missiles which the Mideast country later named Shahab-1 and Shahab-2 missiles, respectively. Around mid-1990s, Iran opted for purchasing Pyongyang's medium-range No-dong missiles which Tehran renamed Shahab-3 and tested it in 1998. Shahab-3 enjoyed a maximum range of around 900 km, but Iran wished to develop it into an intercontinental ballistic missile (ICBM). By the time the Persian Gulf country was hit with heavy-handed sanctions over the nuclear controversy, Iran had already made significant progress in terms of improving the range of Shahab-3, naming its longer range versions as Ghadr-1, Sajjil-1, Sajjil-2, and so on.[27] In all likelihood, Iran and North Korea shared their relevant knowledge and technology while trying to develop their own ICBMs, and that is a reason why the two countries agreed to resume their missile cooperation when Iranians decided, probably sometime in the second half of the 2010s, to make additional progress in their missile program.[28]

In Sync with the Zeitgeist: Going After New Security Challenges

Although arms embargoes and military sanctions were instrumental in compelling Iran to increasingly tilt toward East Asia for securing its defense requirements both in conventional and unconventional areas, the continuation of those international impediments and restrictions also played an important role in persuading the Middle Eastern country to extend, and even expand, its long-lasting military cooperation with East Asian nations, especially China, into various recent security challenges which matter to both sides, including extremism, terrorism, drug smuggling, piracy, cyber security, and so on.[29] Since a great deal of new security problems had something to do with contemporary geopolitical, economic, and technological developments, particularly Iran and China shared a lot in common with regard to varied sweeping ramifications which these modern challenges may bring about, convincing the two countries to incorporate over time such concerns into their broader military and security areas of bilateral collaborations. As far as Iran was concerned, however, cyber security was of the utmost importance, and probably no country other than China in the world could better help the Islamic Republic to dominate its cyber space thoroughly amid rising domestic tensions caused by international sanctions and other problems.[30]

First and foremost, the cyber realm is a universe unto itself, and in recent decades all governments across the world have allocated lots of financial and human resources to define and wield their own version of cyber security. In particular, countries such as China and Iran have been very cognizant of such imperative, striving to carve out and implement their rules and regulations regarding the Internet and its astonishingly boundless space. The two countries have, moreover, developed somehow identical policies and measures to control their cyberspace, ranging from restricting access to some popular global social media such as Facebook to blocking connection to dissident groups' websites. These commonalities gradually pushed Iran and China to increasingly enhance their cyber collaborations through paying more attention to cyber security in different military and defense deals they agreed upon in more recent years.[31] The 25-year strategic agreement between Beijing and Tehran was, for instance, one of such critical bilateral accords in which expectations over cyber security cooperation reached new heights.

Despite the fact that the Iranian government's cyber capabilities have expanded substantially in recent years, some news reports following the signing of the 25-year agreement signified that particularly some conservative forces in the Islamic Republic had already pinned much hope on China to wield more power over cyberspace by taking advantage of relevant Chinese experiences and technologies. Some Iranian lawmakers even talked about Tehran's firm resolve to "rule over cyberspace" through close cooperation with China, though they did not provide any important details on how the 25-year agreement would help the Islamic Republic to tighten its grip on the levers of influence and power in the Internet.[32] Such rather provocative expectations and comments, however, had a lot of potential to deal a knock-out blow to China's fairly limited soft power among many liberal and open-minded Iranians who have long harbored grudges and suspicions against Beijing's growing military and security collaborations with the Islamic Republic.[33]

Sino–Iranian Joint Naval Drills

Perhaps no aspect of Sino–Iranian military and defense cooperation turned out to be more public and assertive than their collective naval exercises. Both countries had their own rationale to participate willingly in several rounds of naval drills which were a sure-fire way of thrusting them into the limelight of media and policy circles around the world. Commensurate with its rising political and economic power in world affairs, China had already capitalized substantially on its naval power, and its military strength in general, in order to develop its capability to operate in far-flung waters. Since a capable Chinese navy was to partly serve its national priority of vouchsafing a sustainable supply of energy resources from the Persian Gulf, no country other than Iran in the region was a better choice to help China demonstrate its growing naval assertiveness.[34] For its part, Iran was under crippling international sanctions, including arms embargoes, and engaging in collaborative naval drills with China was thereby a powerful way for Tehran to show it to the world that the country was still politically and militarily confident and determined. Bilaterally, such joint exercises could provide Iran with a lot of new experiences from China's naval modernization, as a part of its broader military modernization, over the past several decades.[35]

Iran and China commenced their high-profile naval drills in September 2014 when two Chinese ships, a missile destroyer and a frigate, berthed at the Iranian port of Bandar Abbas. They arrived in Iran for a "friendly visit" after an Iranian flotilla had sailed to the Chinese port of Zhangjiagang in 2013.[36] The naval forces of the two countries then took part in joint exercises for four days, but their collaborative move captured less national and international attention as compared to what happened during their next joint naval drills.[37] It was in December 2019 when Iran and China upped the ante by participating in a trilateral naval drill with Russia. It was the first time that "the three continental powers" were partaking in a flashy and conspicuous naval maneuvering. Although Iran, China, and Russia scheduled another joint naval drills for mid-February 2021, however, their collective naval exercises in December 2019 set international media and press abuzz with a flurry of news stories and articles concerning what the three countries were doing in the Sea of Oman then.

In the view of some media outlets, the joint maritime move of the "Eastern triangle" was a bold show of force and assertiveness by the "top foes" of the United States at a sensitive time when Washington under Trump had also assembled its naval coalition from many like-minded countries, except Japan and South Korea, to display their resolve and unity vis-à-vis Iran through taking part in exercises in the Persian Gulf and the nearby waters. Moreover, Iran overplayed the naval event after the Middle Eastern country's navy commander declared that "the era of American invasions in the region is over." In particular, some conservative Iranian media and press interpreted the Islamic Republic's first joint military drill with two great powers as "a clear message to the United States and its allies" now that Washington had tried to further isolate Tehran with a similarly multilateral naval maneuvering in the region.[38] Whether or not the Sino–Iranian–Russian joint naval drills in December 2019 were the dawn of "an emerging Eastern coalition" as some conservative forces in Iran proclaimed with a whiff of optimism, at least the "Western coalition" in the placid waters of the Persian Gulf had long been put together by the United States, though its turns and twists were largely subject to changing regional and international circumstances.[39]

Keeping Both Sides Happy: Japanese and Korean Naval Presence in the Persian Gulf

In the wake of the US withdrawal from the JCPOA in May 2018 and Iran's subsequent threats to disrupt the flow of oil from the Persian Gulf if Tehran was not allowed to export its own crude oil, the Trump administration attempted to form the International Maritime Security Construct (IMSC) as a US-led naval coalition to assure a safe and sustainable supply of energy through the Strait of Hormuz. As late as July 2019, the United States intensified its relevant diplomatic campaign after Trump dispatched his National Security Advisor, John Bolton, to Japan and South Korea to ask them join the IMSC by contributing their own naval units.[40] For Washington, the whole maritime initiative was about sending a strong political message to Tehran, while for many top political officials in Tokyo and Seoul, the very US request was déjà vu all over again. It was during the Kuwaiti crisis of 1990–1991, and more critically in the run-up to the Iraq War of 2003, when Washington's pressures on both East Asian countries to send their military forces to a combat zone in the Middle East had triggered serious political crises in Japan and the ROK, including widespread anti-war demonstrations in Tokyo and Seoul.[41] This time, the United States again faced similar resistance to have its two East Asian allies on board.

From a Japanese point of view, the crux of the problem was about the retreat of the United States from Iran's nuclear deal which Japan supported from the beginning and remained faithful to even after Trump quit it.[42] In spite of the so-called bromance between Donald Trump and Shinzo Abe, therefore, Japan opted to stay outside the US-led IMSC by launching independently its own naval operation; a prudent move not to antagonize Washington, but it could also satisfy Iranian officials who had already objected to any formal Japanese and South Korean participation in the US-created anti-Iran naval coalition.[43] More important, Japan decided not to include the Strait of Hormuz in its self-determining naval operation, and only use a destroyer and a patrol aircraft to collect information in the Persian Gulf which supplied a bulk of Japan's imported crude oil. Outside the Persian Gulf region, the Japanese maritime activities were to concentrate largely on the Gulf of Oman, the northern part of the Arabian Sea, and the Gulf of Aden as a focal point of anti-piracy missions by several countries, including the ROK.[44]

Taking a leaf out of Japan's book, South Korea insisted that it was not going to officially join the US-initiated IMSC. South Koreans had a similar reasoning that quitting the JCPOA by the Trump administration was the main cause of new tensions between Washington and Tehran, arguing that "we cannot become an enemy of Iran" by formally joining the US-led IMSC.[45] In January 2020, therefore, the South Korean government of Moon Jae-in made it public that the ROK's Cheonghae Unit was going to expand its naval operation from the Gulf of Aden to cover the Gulf of Oman and the Persian Gulf. Since July 2019, moreover, South Korea had been taking advantage of the political capital of Oman, Muscat, as its naval unit's primary port of call to coordinate its maritime activities in the region.[46] In spite of what was announced officially, however, South Korea like Japan strived hard not to let its naval forces operate unnecessarily in the Strait of Hormuz, and only when the IRGC seized the Korean oil tanker, MT Hankuk Chemi, in early January 2021, its Cheonghae Unit was dispatched temporarily to the Iran-controlled strategic straits.[47]

NOTES

1. Eyler, p. 17.
2. Andrew Parasiliti, "After Sanctions, Deter and Engage Iran," *Survival: Global Politics and Strategy*, Vol. 52, No. 5 (2010), pp. 13–20.
3. Ryan, p. 109.
4. Hossein Alikhani, *Sanctioning Iran: Anatomy of a Failed Policy* (London and New York: I.B. Tauris Publishers, 2000), pp. 66–67.
5. During one of the televised debates of the 2012 presidential elections campaign in the United States, for instance, when Mitt Romney, Republican nominee, was asked to mention the single biggest threat facing US national security, he answered "a nuclear Iran." Cited from: Paul R. Pillar, "The Role of Villain: Iran and U.S. Foreign Policy," *Political Science Quarterly*, Vol. 131, No. 2 (summer 2016), pp. 365–385.
6. "U.S. Tiptoes through Sanctions Minefield toward Iran Nuclear Deal," *Reuters*, May 17, 2021.
7. Juneau.
8. Michael Brzoska, "Profiteering on the Iran–Iraq War," *Bulletin of the Atomic Scientists*, Vol. 43, No. 5 (June 1987), pp. 42–45; and "Iran az che keshvarhai aslahe kharide?" [Which Countries did Iran Purchase Arms from?], *Tabnak*, June 2, 2016.
9. Adam Tarock, *The Superpowers' Involvement in the Iran–Iraq War* (Commack, NY: Nova Science Publishers, 1998), pp. 73, 93.

164   S. AZAD

10. Azad, *Looking East*, pp. 12–14.
11. "U.S. Ambassador to South Korea under Scrutiny of Iran–Contra Probe," *Associated Press*, July 31, 1991.
12. As a case in point, in 1981 a Taiwanese company owned by Wu Fu-jeou brokered an arms deal between Iran and Taiwan. In order to sort out the financial issue of the arrangement, the Central Bank of Iran (CBI) asked a British bank to wire some $15 million to a joint banking account held at Taiwan's Chang Hwa Bank under the names of three Iranian citizens representing the government of Iran. But when the three people dropped by the bank to collect the funds, they were told that three other individuals had already withdrawn the money after apparently handing over proper documentation. Iran filed a lawsuit against the Taiwanese bank in 1997, demanding Chang Hwa Bank to return the funds and its interest, but it was to no avail. Taiwanese courts turned down the suit, and after it ended up in the supreme court of Taiwan on appeal, the Iranian legal action failed for another time "on the grounds that a 15-year statute of limitations for the case had expired." For more details, see: "Iran Loses Lawsuit in Taiwan over Arms Scam," *New Straits Times*, October 25, 2014; and "Rad darkhast vezarat defae Iran az yek bank taiwani" [Lawsuit by Iran Defense Ministry against Taiwanese Bank Rejected], *Tabnak*, October 25, 2014.
13. John Calabrese, "China and Iraq: A Stake in Stability," in P.R. Kumaraswamy, ed., *China and the Middle East: The Quest for Influence* (New Delhi: Sage Publications, 1999), pp. 52–67.
14. Richard F. Grimmett, *CRS Report for Congress: Trends in Conventional Arms Transfers to the Third World by Major Supplier, 1980–1987* (Washington, D.C.: Congressional Research Service, Library of Congress, May 9, 1988), p. 52.
15. Bates Gill, "Chinese Arms Exports to Iran," *Middle East Review of International Affairs*, Vol. 2, No. 2 (May 1998), pp. 55–70.
16. "United States Should Derail Prospects for an Iran–China Alliance," *The Heritage Foundation*, October 6, 2020.
17. "US Dumped at UN Security Council with Iran Sanctions," *Global Times*, August 17, 2020; and "US versus the World on 'Snapback'," *Taipei Times*, September 20, 2020, p. 5.
18. "Velayati: Iran be donbal gostaresh ravabet nezami ba chin ast" [Velayati: Iran after Expanding Military Relations with China], *Asr Iran*, June 8, 2015; "Movafeghatname hamkarihay nezami Iran va chin emza shod" [Iran–China Agreement on Military Cooperation Signed], *Ettelaat*, November 15, 2016, p. 2; and "Will China Strengthen Iran's Military Machine in 2020?" *The National Interest*, January 16, 2020.
19. Nephew, p. 28.
20. Hufbauer et al., pp. 24–25, 60.

9 ARMS EMBARGOES: MILITARY AND SECURITY ADJUSTMENT 165

21. "Seoul Officials Say Strong Pressure Forced Cancellation of Plans to Purchase a French Nuclear Plant," *The New York Times*, February 1, 1976, p. 11.
22. Evan S. Medeiros, *Reluctant Restraint: The Evolution of China's Nonproliferation Policies and Practices, 1980–2004* (Palo Alto, CA: Stanford University Press, 2007), 59–64, 82, and 101–103.
23. After Iran started to implement the nuclear deal, Japan offered Tehran a $2.2 million in the name of "nuclear safety cooperation." To help Iran implement the JCPOA perfectly, Japan also announced its inclination to dispatch Japanese nuclear experts to the Middle Eastern country, and provide support to improve its relevant human resources through field training courses and other programs. Tokyo's friendly approach toward Tehran after concluding the nuclear deal, moreover, buoyed up Iranian officials to think about purchasing nuclear reactor from Japan. "The 'Implementation Day' of the Final Agreement on the Iranian Nuclear Issue: Statement by Foreign Minister Fumio Kishida," *Ministry of Foreign Affairs of Japan*, January 17, 2016; "Salehi: Amadeh kharid reactor hastei az zhapon hastim" [Salehi: Ready to Buy Nuclear Reactor from Japan], *Asrar Daily*, September 14, 2016, p. 3; and "Japan to Offer $2.2 Million to Iran for Nuclear Safety Cooperation," *Kyodo*, December 8, 2016.
24. "China Criticized for Arak Project Delays," *Financial Tribune*, February 9, 2017; and "Glayeh shaded Salehi az kondi chiniha" [Salehi Gripes Harshly about Chinese Slowness], *Aftab-e Yazd*, January 31, 2019, pp. 1, 15.
25. Daniel Salisbury and David Lowrie, "Targeted: A Case Study in Iranian Illicit Missile Procurement," *Bulletin of the Atomic Scientists*, Vol. 69, No. 3 (2013), pp. 23–30; and "US Accuses Former HK Official of Breaking Iran Sanctions," *Financial Times*, October 4, 2018.
26. In December 2020, in a controversial speech given at Imam Housein University, which is affiliated with the IRGC, the former commander of the IRGC, Mohsen Rezai, said when he was the IRGC's *numero uno*, "he made an agreement with North Korea, and if it had been implemented, Iran would have now been at the highest point of its nuclear success and ahead of its missile capability." Without providing any details regarding his nuclear agreement with the DPRK, Rezai added that "Iran will not forgo its nuclear knowledge no matter what the United States and Israel wish simply because nuclear knowledge is itself independent from other industries and can be a great asset in ocean transportation, medicine, energy security, agriculture, and some other major industries." He also emphasized that "taking advantage of all such potentials are very dear to us even though we may decide to abandon for now the use of nuclear technology for defensive purposes." "Mohsen Rezai: Tavafogh ba kore shomali amal-

iati mishod dar gholeh bolad hastei boodim" [If Agreement with North Korea Implemented We Could Reach the Nuclear Summit], *Afkar*, December 7, 2020, p. 2.

27. George Lewis and Frank von Hippel, "Limitations on Ballistic Missile Defense—Past and Possibly Future," *Bulletin of the Atomic Scientists*, Vol. 74, No. 4 (2018), pp. 199–209.

28. "Sokhangooy vezarat khareje: Hamkari Iran va kore shomali edame peida mikonad" [Foreign Ministry Spokesman: Iran–North Korea Cooperation Continues], *Aftab-e Yazd*, October 19, 2017, p. 1; and "Iran and North Korea Resumed Cooperation on Missiles, UN Says," *Bloomberg*, February 9, 2021.

29. "Iran, China to Strengthen Defense Cooperation," *Tehran Times*, May 5, 2014; "Syasat rahbordi Iran dar hamkari nezami ba chin" [Iran's Strategic Policy in Military Cooperation with China], *Hemayat*, November 15, 2016, p. 2; and "Hamkari nezami bolandmoddat Iran va chin" [Long-term Military Cooperation of Iran and China], *Iran*, November 15, 2016, p. 2.

30. "Maghamat arshad nezami va syasi chin va roosiye dar Tehran" [Top Military and Political Officials of China and Russia in Tehran], *Ettelaat*, November 13, 2016, p. 1; and "Iran, China Sign Defense Cooperation Deal," *Tehran Times*, November 15, 2016, pp. 1, 2.

31. "Tehran–Beijing Relations not to be Affected by Intl. Issues," *Mehr News Agency*, January 25, 2021.

32. "Iran MP Implies China–Iran Deal Strengthens Regime's Internet Control," *Eurasia Review*, April 15, 2021.

33. "Iran: Chinese-made Armored Anti-riot Trucks, Equipped with Plows, May Arrive in Tehran," *Los Angeles Times*, January 1, 2010; "Iran Plans Its Own Sanitized Internet with Chinese Help," *Voice of America*, July 31, 2013; and "Safar vazir amniyat omoumi chin be Tehran" [Chinese Minister of Public Security Visits Tehran], *Jahan News*, April 20, 2016.

34. Cole, p. 133.

35. "United States Should Derail Prospects for an Iran–China Alliance," *The Heritage Foundation*, October 6, 2020.

36. "China and Iran's Historic Naval Exercise," *The Diplomat*, September 23, 2014.

37. "Iran, China to Stage Joint Naval Drill," *Tasnim News Agency*, September 21, 2014; and "China and Iran to Conduct Joint Naval Exercises in the Persian Gulf," *The New York Times*, September 21, 2014.

38. "Payam sarih mosallas sharghi be America" [Clear Message of Eastern Triangle to America], *Khorasan News*, December 28, 2019, pp. 1, 16; and "Razmayesh sharghi" [Eastern Drill], *Hamshahri*, December 28, 2019, p. 2.

39. "Europa sharik dozd ast" [Europe is the Partner of Thief], *Kayhan*, October 22, 2017, p. 1; and "Razmayesh etelaf sharghi moghabel etelaf gharbi" [Drill of Eastern Coalition before Western Coalition], *Mardomsalari*, December 28, 2019, pp. 1, 2.
40. "S. Korea has little to Lose by Withdrawing from GSOMIA," *The Hankyoreh*, July 25, 2019.
41. Azad, *East Asia's Strategic Advantage in the Middle East*, pp. 55–58.
42. "Abe: Japan Supports Iran Deal," *The Jerusalem Post*, May 3, 2018; "Concerned about Escalating Iran–U.S. Tensions, Japan Offers to Work with Tehran as Minister Visits," *Kyodo*, May 16, 2019; and "Japan Urges Iran to Take 'Constructive Approach' to Biden Overtures," *Nikkei Asia*, March 11, 2021.
43. "Japan Briefs Iran on Plan to Send Forces to Middle East," *The Asahi Shimbun*, December 21, 2019.
44. "Iran's Rouhani Welcomes Japan Opt-out of U.S.-led Naval Mission in Gulf," *The Asahi Shimbun*, December 22, 2019.
45. "S. Korea Tries to Appease both US and Iran with Strait of Hormuz Deployment," *The Hankyoreh*, January 22, 2020.
46. "Anti-piracy Unit's Mission Expanded to Include Hormuz Strait near Iran," *Korea Herald*, January 1, 2020; and "Iran Expresses Concerns with S. Korean Deployment to Strait of Hormuz," *The Hankyoreh*, January 22, 2020.
47. "Cheonghae Unit Sent to Strait of Hormuz after Iran Seizes S. Korean Oil Tanker," *Arirang TV*, January 5, 2021; and "Seoul Moves Warship Away from Hormuz Strait amid Negotiations over Seized Tanker: Source," *Yonhap News Agency*, January 18, 2021.

CHAPTER 10

Cracks in the Ivory Tower: Academic and Cultural Repercussions

Unstoppable Brain Drain

One of the main characteristics of modern Iranian society is the mass emigration of its talented and educated people to other societies, especially developed and affluent Western countries. Although this pitiful phenomenon started during the reign of the Shah, the political ascendancy of the Islamic Republic turned emigration into a zeitgeist of talents and gifted graduates from all walks of life. For obvious reasons, the system which the triumphant Islamists established in Iran after the fall of the Pahlavi monarchy in the early 1979 as well as the ensuing internecine military conflict with the neighboring Iraq played a crucial role in the personal decision of many brilliant and skillful Iranians to leave their country en masse in the late 1970s and during the 1980s. However, certain visionary yet catastrophic measures of the newly established Islamic Republic such as the "cultural revolution" as well as the cataclysmic Iran–Iraq War eventually came to an end, but the caustic current of Iranian brain drain never dwindled to a trickle. Quite to the contrary, the situation steadily worsened one decade after another, intensifying the wave of talent exodus as the Middle Eastern country's faltering educational system was increasingly producing more graduates and postgraduates nearly in all academic areas.

Over the past several years, Iran has constantly ranked number one among developing countries in terms of brain drain and an incessant departure of its talented and skillful graduates. Excluding the recent

© The Author(s), under exclusive license to Springer Nature
Switzerland AG 2022
S. Azad, *East Asia and Iran Sanctions*,
https://doi.org/10.1007/978-3-030-97427-5_10

169

invasion of coronavirus which somehow slowed down the previous wave of talent departure from Iran, the overall situation got exacerbated by a confluence of several corrosive developments, including the aggravation of international sanctions, deepening economic stagflation, and a substantial devaluation of Iranian currency, rial.[1] Real statistics are often hard to come by with regard to the exact number of trained and accomplished Iranians who leave their country permanently, but it is widely estimated that by and large each year some 150,000 people among Iranian graduates and experts decide to go abroad forever. Some sources have reported that on average 180,000 graduates leave Iran per annum.[2] Whether the real figure is 150,000 or 180,000, however, the impact of Iranian brain drain has been truly catastrophic in some scientific and technological fields. In 2017, for instance, it was reported shockingly that out of 150 math geniuses only one top-notch mathematician had remained in Iran.[3]

Economic and social costs of brain drain for the Persian Gulf country were equally mind-blowing. Based on most calculations, the large-scale exodus of educated and gifted segments of Iranian population costs the country, on the whole, some $50–60 billion annually. Given the fact that under the two-term government of Hasan Rouhani (August 2013–August 2021) the entire export of Iranian crude oil was less than $100 billion, $50–60 billion would be indubitably a large fortune to be squandered gratuitously.[4] Still, it would be rather difficult to estimate various long-term economic and financial implications of losing, on a continuous basis, a large crowd of schooled and skillful citizens. Sizing up all relevant social and cultural consequences of extensive brain drain would be even more difficult and complicated. But it cannot be denied that when a melting pot society like Iran was deprived of a large pool of its "real good genes" in the wake of massive departure of talents and gifted people, the present as well as future generations all would be condemned to pay a hefty price, one way or the other.[5]

Iranian Universities and the Triple Whammy

First and foremost, Iranian universities and research institutions have been blighted by brain drain for more than half a century. Although brain drain is a rather universal predicament and even academic institutions in many industrialized countries such as Germany and South Korea have long been afflicted with the exodus of their talents and gifted graduates, however, the Iranian quandary over an incessantly mass exit of its top-notch citizens has been both deep-seated and more consequential. Unlike some other countries which have struggled with a similar problem but at the same time have benefited greatly from the so-called phenomenon of knowledge circulation in various ways, moreover, an overwhelming majority of the Iranian talents who left their country permanently have essentially served their newly adopted societies much more than they could contribute to the scientific progress and economic wellbeing of their fatherland (i.e., Iran). On top of that, their personal success and professional accomplishments often compounded rather than alleviated the brain drain crisis in Iran because their usually intriguing stories, as a role model of sorts, generally encouraged a more number of bright students and capable scholars to emigrate at an earlier possible time.

Sanctions turned out to be the second blight that brought about tremendous repercussions for Iran's academic institutions and research centers over a course of more than four decades. Economically and financially, sanctions made it very difficult to appropriate sufficient funds for educational and research purposes. Not only academic studies and research projects were badly underfunded, scholars and researchers were often paid meager salaries barely enough to make ends meet. In fact, sanctions-induced economic woes as well as a substantial devaluation of the Iranian currency, rial, had corrosive impacts on education and research in Iran more than met the eye. In 2019, for instance, some 900 university professors simply quit their jobs and left the country chiefly for economic reasons after roughly 250,000 rials could buy only one US dollar.[6] Some two years earlier, an American dollar was equivalent to around 33,000 rials, but the Trump administration's withdrawal from the nuclear deal and the ensuing crippling sanctions literally made the Iranian national currency worthless within a short period of time. All aspects of university life in Iran were to be soon affected correspondingly; from the real purchasing power of professors' salaries to allocating funds for international exchanges.[7]

Educationally and scientifically, sanctions created a whole array of troubles for international collaborations involving Iranian universities and their foreign partners. In the wake of blocked international financial transactions, it was simply hard for Iranian scholars and researchers to purchase their required equipment and materials from other countries, pay the requested fees to publish an article or attend an international conference, book accommodations before taking part in an international scientific event, and so on.[8] More important, Iranian scholars and students often encountered serious impediments concerning their visa applications for many Western countries, the United States in particular. Such restrictions reached their pinnacle in 2017 when the Trump administration's travel

172   S. AZAD

ban prohibited Iranian citizens from entering the United States. Additionally, Trump's draconian decree even made travel to the United States more difficult for those Western scientists and students whose passports had been stamped by the government of Iran, dealing another devastating blow to academic and research cooperation between Iranian academic institutions and their willing partners in many industrialized and developed countries.[9]

More specifically, international sanctions targeted some Iranian academic institutions and scientists for their allegedly cooperation with Iran's nuclear program and missile projects. Even the government of Japan provided and uploaded on the Internet its own rather long list of the Iranian universities and research centers which Tokyo regarded as a risk for nuclear proliferation and missile development.[10] Shahid Beheshti University was, for instance, sanctioned by the European Union (EU), Canada, and Australia after the EU charged it with conducting "scientific research relevant to the development of nuclear weapons." In the same way, Malek Ashtar University came under UN, US, and EU sanctions because of its alleged contribution to the Iranian nuclear program.[11] On the whole, it appeared that Washington had an ex to grind not to sanction a more number of high-profile Iranian universities such as Sharif University of Technology which had long benefited the United States enormously as a significant number of its top-notch students often ended up at a prestigious American university upon graduation.

Lastly, the third whammy has something to do with Iranian universities' hidebound orientation toward international educational exchanges and research collaborations. By and large, the Islamic Republic has long regarded universities and research centers as a potential target for foreign intelligence agencies and their domestic collaborators. As a corollary to that, the relevant Iranian institutions have drafted certain rules and regulations to prevent universities from becoming a likely den for spies whenever there is going to be an important international exchange between an academic body in Iran and its partner from another country, especially when that foreign country is a powerful and influential Western nation such as the United States. Such obstacles have sometimes discouraged some competent and motivated Iranian scholars and researchers to engage in substantial educational and research collaborations with their foreign counterparts. Likewise, just in case a joint educational program or research project was originally proposed by foreign academic institutions, their initiatives could simply encounter significant bureaucratic red tape in Iran at any stage throughout the process.

ATTENTION TO EAST ASIAN ACADEMIC INSTITUTIONS

Since the Islamic Republic's Weltanschauung was viscerally anti-West fraught with standoffish attitudes toward Western social mores, the system which it brought into being in Iran strived to minimize formal cultural as well as intellectual relationship between Iranians and Western societies through academic institutions. "Islamization of universities" was an official policy of the Islamic Republic, aiming to promote an Islamic way of thinking and living among Iranian students by turning their back on Western ideas and values. Still, academic and intellectual connections between Iranian universities and Western countries survived the onslaught of anti-West forces as more and more academic departments throughout the country continued to remain highly dependent on teaching textbooks and materials produced originally in the West. Additionally, in various academic disciplines a significant number of faculty members and researchers who themselves had already studied and trained at a Western university contributed substantially to the dynamics of scholastic and intellectual interactions involving academic institutions in Iran and Western countries.[12]

Despite a relatively dominant role of Western ideas and theories in scientific and intellectual life of Iranian universities, however, attention to East Asian academic bodies began to grow in lockstep with impressive economic and technological developments in the region. Japan, for instance, became a first destination in East Asia for a new generation of Iranian students who applied to study at a top Japanese university instead of going to a Western European or North American institution of higher education. Even the Iranian government sent to Japan a significant number of Iranian students on scholarship to major in certain scientific and technological disciplines at major Japanese universities and research institutes.[13] By early years of the twenty-first century, moreover, South Korean and Chinese universities gradually emerged as an attractive alternative for a growing number of Iranian students and researchers who wanted to pursue their educational objectives abroad in the midst of a growing tendency among political as well as academic institutions in Iran to speak highly of East Asian scholastic and scientific achievements during the past several decades.[14]

Part of that recognition had to do with a rapidly improving ranking of East Asian universities among the world's top academic bodies for education and research. More and more universities in East Asia were overtaking some rather well-known and popular Western universities and colleges, while an increasingly bigger number of East Asian scientists and scholars were continuously capturing highest global awards and prizes in sciences, economics, literature, and so on. Such swift developments in international ranking and status of East Asia's educational bodies and scientists appeared more intriguing and inspiring when Iranian universities and colleges also paid serious attention to their own comparative standing vis-à-vis academic institutions from other regions, especially the greater Asian continent. It would be even more captivating and consequential when some Iranian and East Asian universities could occupy the same international slot based on their updated educational and scientific rankings. This situation could thereby galvanize the two sides into action by signing different agreements on joint academic and research collaborations favorable to them.[15]

Another equally important factor was undeniably the continuation and intensification of international sanctions and restrictions which pushed more Iranian universities and research institutes toward unprecedentedly better interactions with academic and research bodies as well as with corporations and businesses in East Asia. After all, universities and research centers could play an instrumental role in smoothing the way for transferring some required technologies and scientific knowhow from East Asia to Iran in addition to improving the overall knowledge of Iranians about various aspects of East Asian societies.[16] In particular, after the Iranian government concluded the nuclear deal in June 2015, for about three years a number of South Korean and Chinese corporations demonstrated their inclination to engage in some technological cooperation with certain Iranian universities and research centers with the hope of boosting their profile in Iran and capturing a better share of its rather profitable markets as a reward for their technological contribution to the Persian Gulf country.[17]

Belated Establishment of East Asian Studies Programs

Compared to Iranians, East Asian states turned out to be more successful in terms of commencing earlier their academic studies and research undertakings about various political, economic, and cultural aspects of Iran, and generally Middle Eastern societies. In tandem with their rising interests in the Middle East, the Japanese embarked on some Iranian studies a short while after they established their official diplomatic ties with Iran more than nine decades ago. More important, the first oil shock of 1973–1974 was a watershed in pushing Japanese, as well as South Korean, political and academic circles to subsequently appropriate more generous funds and train adequate human resources for carrying out more critical studies on Middle Eastern countries, especially Iran.[18] Later, China joined the race, but it was basically the increasingly expanding interests of East Asian countries in Iran and other parts of the Middle East that upped the stakes of their relevant academic and research rivalry, leading to a whole array of national initiatives; from inaugurating academic departments to launching specialized journals on Iranian, and Middle Eastern, studies.[19]

Unlike Japan, however, it was long overdue when Iran laid the groundwork for some serious academic studies on the East Asian country. As early as 1987, Tehran University, as a leading academic body in Japanese studies in Iran, offered Japanese as a second optional foreign language for interested Iranian students. In September 1994, the top Iranian university eventually offered BA (Bachelor of Arts) degree in the Japanese language and literature. In the period from 2008 to 2010, Tehran University also accepted students for MA (Master of Arts) degree in the Japanese linguistics, but due to some problems, including insufficient applicants, the university put the program on hold for some five years before it was offered again from 2015 onward. A few years ago, moreover, a different college at Tehran University launched an MA program in Japanese studies with the aim of focusing more on political and economic characteristics of modern Japanese society, though the accepted students were required to have a sufficiently prior knowledge of the Japanese language.[20]

Concerning China, Shahid Beheshti University became one of the first Iranian academic institutions of higher education that launched the department of Chinese language in 1996 after signing an agreement with Shanghai University of International Studies which simultaneously commenced its own program on the Persian language and literature. In

January 2009, another Tehran-based university accepted to host the first branch of Confucius Institute in Iran before Tehran University moved to offer a BA degree in the Chinese language in late 2015.[21] Given China's swiftly growing political and economic clout in world affairs and particularly its expanding multifaceted relationship with Iran and other Middle Eastern countries, therefore, Iranian universities were very late in establishing their own distinctive educational and research programs on the East Asian great power. After all, it was only in April 2019 when the first academic center for Chinese studies in Iran was inaugurated at a Tehran-based university in order to carry through more comprehensive research about contemporary China.[22]

In sharp contrast to all belated Japanese and Chinese programs, Koreans studies in Iran continue to remain in a state of dormancy. No major Iranian university has so far set up its own program of the Korean language, and such apathy has certainly played a part in a relatively poor situation of Korean studies in the Persian Gulf country, though the overall situation of Korean studies in most of other Middle Eastern societies is hardly better. In fact, since 2006 successive South Korean ambassadors to Tehran made a request, to no avail, to Tehran University to offer a BA program in the Korean language at its college of foreign languages where the Japanese language was already being taught for many years. In order to curry favor with the administrators at Iran's top university, Korean Foundation was prepared to partially share the burden by providing some funds and a number of language instructors. For all its luckless and futile attempts in coaxing Iranians into kicking off a Korean studies program at a leading Iranian university, nonetheless, South Korea turned out to be surprisingly and relatively more successful than other East Asian players in advancing its cultural diplomacy in the Middle Eastern country.[23]

In Lieu of Public Diplomacy: One-Way Cultural Representation

As far as contemporary relationship between East Asian countries and Iran, or generally the Middle East, is concerned, culture was rarely treated as an end in itself. A great deal of bilateral cultural initiatives and culture-related activities were carved out and implemented by governments without any active participation of non-state players. State institutions and public officials happened to be the dominant, and most of the time the only, players that could assume some cultural roles as circumstances required. More important, culture and cultural programs were to ultimately serve certain political and particularly economic objectives simply because immediate politico-economic goals were too important to be sacrificed for the sake of achieving long-term cultural ideals and ambitions. Based on such general characteristics, therefore, it was no coincidence why a politically isolated and economically sanctioned Iran became a potentially fertile ground for the promotion of East Asian culture, while the Iranian culture was less successful in making inroads into East Asian societies after the Islamic Republic's advent to power in early 1979.

In the 1980s, political relationship and especially procuring arms requirements were all that mattered in Iran's connections with East Asia. The region was not also a right place to give publicity to the Islamic Republic's ideological agenda and cultural values. Because of Iran's growing distance from the West and Western cultural imports, for much of the 1980s and 1990s Japanese cultural products, including classic drama serials, received a lot of attention in Iran in lockstep with a rising popularity of Japan's manufactured goods among Iranians. Under the presidency of Mohammad Khatami (1997–2005), Tehran's visionary project of "dialogue among civilizations" essentially aimed to open a new chapter of diplomatic and political relationship between Iran and Western countries under some high-sounding cultural and intellectual abstractions. Despite their appearance in many relevant conferences and dialogue forums organized by Iran or an international organization, East Asian societies were not really a major obsession of Tehran's highly publicized plea for civilizational exchanges during that hectic period of "political reform and cultural discourse" in the Persian Gulf country.[24]

In the following period (roughly from 2006 to 2015) that coincided with sundry UN and US sanctions against Iran in the wake of its nuclear enrichment program, the Korean wave (*Hallyu*) found a unique opportunity to unprecedentedly mesmerize a rather large crowd of Iranian citizens. It was also the pinnacle of South Korea's economic presence in Iran epitomized by an omnipresence of Korean brands and goods throughout Iranian markets. Of course, none of these abrupt cultural and economic developments was taking place quite naturally. Essentially, as a result of some bartering agreements between Tehran and Seoul, large volumes of Korean manufactured goods had been imported into Iranian markets and required a magic marketing ploy of sorts. That was why *Hallyu* came to the rescue; from Iran's top public broadcasting to the Iranian embassy in

178   S. AZAD

Seoul and from major Korean companies to the Korean embassy in Tehran all were mobilized out of the blue to give promotion to a number of *Hallyu*'s historical dramas and their top actors and actresses among Iranians.[25]

Similar to the experience of Japanese technological goods and cultural products in Iran during the 1980s and 1990s, therefore, the rise and decline of *Hallyu* in Iran followed the trajectory of Korean economic presence in the Mideast country. Thus, the publicity for *Hallyu* serials in Iran's public media outlets just dwindled to a trickle once the ROK's famous companies left the country and Korean brands and goods were quickly replaced by Chinese products. But so far the Chinese culture has not stepped in the same route previously taken by Japan and South Korea in Iran. Probably a major reason was that Korean goods and *Hallyu*'s cultural products were still very popular among Iranians several years after China had become Iran's top trading partner. Under the newly signed 25-year strategic deal between Iran and China, however, the two countries have agreed to boost their cultural interactions.[26] But it is not yet clear what aspects of culture will receive more attention, and whether or not any forthcoming Sino–Iranian cultural relationship will be truly reciprocal and different than what Iran had already come across with regard to cultural engagement with Japan and South Korea.

NOTES

1. "Iran's Big Crisis: The Price of Chicken," *Bloomberg*, August 7, 2012; "Barkhi bankha 400 hezar khane kharidand!" [Some Banks Purchased 400,000 Houses], *Seday Eslahat*, July 28, 2018, p. 1; and "Bashgah keshvarhay tahte tahrim" [The Club of Sanctioned Countries], *Sobh-e Emrooz*, July 29, 2020, p. 2.
2. "Saderat rayegan nokhbe" [Free Exports of Talent], *Shahrvand*, January 23, 2018, p. 5; and "Khorooj saliyane 150 hezar nokhbe az keshvar" [Exodus of 150,000 Talents Annually], *Arman Daily*, June 23, 2018, p. 9.
3. "Az 150 nokhbe ryazi 1 nafar dar Iran mande ast" [Out of 150 Math Geniuses One Individual Left in Iran], *Arman Daily*, September 16, 2017, p. 2.
4. "Khorooj 50 milyard dollar, ba mohajerat tahsilkardegan" [$50 Billion Drained with the Migration of Educated People], *Tabnak*, August 23, 2014; and "Farar maghzha 300 barabar latme balatar az jang" [Damage from Brain Drain 300-fold more than War], *Arman Meli*, January 21, 2021, p. 7.

10 CRACKS IN THE IVORY TOWER: ACADEMIC AND CULTURAL... 179

5. "Zhenhay khoob miravand" [Good Genes Leave], *Arman Daily*, December 13, 2017, p. 4; and "Zhen khoobhay vaghei az keshvar miravand" [Real Good Genes Leave the Country], *Bahar Daily*, August 26, 2019, p. 2.
6. By October 2021, the value of Iranian currency further depreciated as one US dollar valued more than 280,000 rials.
7. "900 ostad dar sal 98 az Iran kharej shodand" [900 Professors Left Iran in Year 98 (2019)], *Mostaghel Newspaper*, March 7, 2021, p. 2.
8. Toni Feder, "Sanctions on Iran Slow Science, Slam a Scientist," *Physics Today*, Vol. 63, No. 8 (2010), pp. 22–25.
9. Richard Stone, "Renewed Sanctions Strangle Science in Iran," *Science*, Vol. 361, No. 6406 (September 7, 2018), p. 961.
10. The list is in the Japanese language and can be accessed through the website of Japan's Ministry of Economy, Trade, and Industry (METI) at https://www.meti.go.jp/english/press/2020/pdf/0508_002a.pdf.
11. "The Academic Pipeline to Iran's Nuclear Program," *Iran Watch*, May 29, 2020.
12. Barry Rubin, *Paved with Good Intentions: The American Experience and Iran* (New York: Oxford University Press, 1980), p. 137; and "Az daneshgahay gharbi enkar, az iraniha esrar" [Western Universities Deny, Iranians Insist], *Farhikhtegan Daily*, November 13, 2018, p. 1.
13. "Chin va zhapon do maghsad daneshjooyan bursiye" [China and Japan Two Destinations for Students on Scholarship], *Tabnak*, November 17, 2014.
14. "Taiwan Academician Wins Khwarizmi Award," *Taiwan Today*, December 2, 2015; and "Vazir omour khareje Iran va rais daneshgah pekan didar kardand" [Iran Foreign Minister Met President of Beijing University], *IRNA*, December 6, 2016.
15. "Seud daneshgahay sharghi" [Eastern Universities Climb], *Farhikhtegan Daily*, October 21, 2018, pp. 1, 2.
16. "Iran, China to Further Research Cooperation," *Mehr News Agency*, May 3, 2015; "Iran, S Korea to Boost Academic Coop.," *Mehr News Agency*, October 19, 2016; and "Peking University to Host Seminar on Iranian Studies," *Tehran Times*, October 28, 2016.
17. "Iran, China Discuss Scientific, Academic Coop.," *Mehr News Agency*, December 6, 2016; and "Samsung Opens Tech Centre with Iran University," *Telecompaper*, April 25, 2017.
18. "Hangug-e 'tehelanro' ilan-e 'seoulro' saenggin kkadalgeun?" [What is behind 'Tehran Road' in Korea and 'Seoul Road' in Iran?], *Chosun Ilbo*, May 2, 2016.

19. Shirzad Azad, *East Asian Politico-Economic Ties with the Middle East: Newcomers, Trailblazers, and Unsung Stakeholders* (New York: Algora Publishing, 2019), pp. 136–139.
20. "Raizan farhangi Iran dar zhapon: Zhapon pishro dar motaleaat Iranshenasi ast" [Iran's Cultural Attaché in Japan: Japan a Leading Country in Iranian Studies], *IRNA*, April 8, 2021.
21. "Avvalin shoebeh moasseh Confucius dar Iran goshayesh yaft" [First Branch of Confucius Institute Opened in Iran], *Hamshahri Online*, January 14, 2009; and "Reshteh zaban va adabiat chini dar daneshgah Tehran rahandazi shod" [Chinese Language and Literature Major was Launched at Tehran University], *Tehran University*, December 19, 2015. Currently, there are more than 548 Confucius Institutes in more than 154 countries, including Turkey, Lebanon, and the UAE in the Middle East region. "Confucius Institute Eyed at Saudi College," *Global Times*, June 10, 2019.
22. "Nakhostin markaz motaleaat chin dar Iran rahandazi shod" [First Center for Chinese Studies in Iran Launched], *IRNA*, April 15, 2019.
23. Azad, pp. 75–77.
24. United Nations Educational, Scientific and Cultural Organization (UNESCO), *Dialogue among Civilizations: The Round Table on the Eve of the United Nations Millennium Summit* (Paris: UNESCO, 2001).
25. Azad, *East Asia's Strategic Advantage in the Middle East*, pp. 141–143.
26. "Peiman 25 sale rahbordi shir va ezhdaha" [25-Year Strategic Pact of Lion and Dragon], *Javan*, June 25, 2020, p. 1; "Pact with Iran Gives China a Foothold in the Middle East," *The Times*, March 29, 2021; and "Iran–China Agreement Indicates Economic and Cultural Cooperation," *Trend News Agency*, March 29, 2021.

CHAPTER 11

Looking East or Looking Elsewhere: Fault Lines of International Orientation

THE POLITICS OF (DIS)PROPORTIONALITY: "MUGGING MULLAHS OR PULVERIZING PEOPLE?"

In criminology or criminal law, for justice to be met, proportionality needs to be taken as a sacrosanct principle, signifying that punishments and penalties must be "proportionate in their severity to the gravity" of offenses and crimes committed. In other words, the more serious a crime was, the more acute a punishment would be meted out.[1] By such an unambiguous yardstick, it seems that sanctions, and particularly international economic sanctions, are a realm of injustice and cruelty. In the wake of sanctions, often an overwhelming majority of a country's citizens undergo tremendous pressures, sometimes fatally, for crimes they never committed or for policies they had absolutely no control over. Although the so-called smart sanctions or targeted sanctions have tried to partially rectify this grave problem, however, no shrewd regime of international sanctions and restrictions has ever succeeded in mitigating their ubiquitous negative externalities.[2] More precisely, many sanctions scholars have long warned that when such penalties and restrictions were forced universally, they would in all likelihood predispose most of the citizenry of a country under sanctions to a lot of harms, economically and politically.[3]

In terms of economic ramifications, sanctions simply lead to humanitarian crises, causing massive poverty and high levels of inequalities in all economic and social standards. In fact, the most susceptible segments of a

© The Author(s), under exclusive license to Springer Nature Switzerland AG 2022
S. Azad, *East Asia and Iran Sanctions*,
https://doi.org/10.1007/978-3-030-97427-5_11

sanctioned society are the biggest casualties of sanctions because they enjoy much less, if any, economic and social protections. It is also this highly vulnerable group whose education and health are badly affected by sanctions. Politically, sanctions usually give strength to standpattism and authoritarianism at the cost of democracy and civil liberties, though sizing up political repercussions of sanctions is normally more difficult than measuring their economic implications.[4] After all, sanctions hurt the middle class as the backbone of democracy and liberal values, and once the middle class was weak it would be much easier for the dominant political class to further restrict civil liberties and bring almost all opposition forces to their knees. In this sense, an authoritarian system may just take advantage of sanctions and morph into a full-fledged dictatorship.[5]

Given the foregoing assertions, there happened to be wide discrepancies between what Iran sanctions intended to achieve and what they brought about in practice. In principle, the greatest number of crippling international sanctions, including the Trump administration's "strongest sanctions in history," were imposed on Iran because of its nuclear program over which more than 99 percent of Iranians had no say whatsoever. Most of the non-nuclear sanctions had also something to do with the charges of sponsorship of terrorism or human rights abuses by the regime of the Islamic Republic; allegations which had certainly no connection to the mentality or behaviors of the greatest number of Iranian citizens. For many years, therefore, the largest number of Iranians were subject to unprecedented international pressures and restrictions for some allegations and wrongdoings in which they had played no role at all. What added insult to injury was that Iranian citizens were quite hapless to do anything about those charges for which they had been punished terribly by the entire world, while their political system, as the culprit, could survive the flood of savage international sanctions virtually unscathed.[6]

To say the Islamic Republic could escape sanctions scot-free would be an understatement; international sanctions greatly empowered the theocratic system as well as its stalwart supporters and their families. Economic sanctions were to essentially deprive the Islamic Republic of enough funds to finance its nuclear and missile programs, but as Robert Gates put it in his book, *Duty*, even an active Iranian brigade general in Iraq was financially powerful enough to grease Iraqi lawmakers' palm with $250,000 to persuading them into voting against the extension of US forces bill.[7] Sanctions were, moreover, supposed to bring about some fundamental changes in Tehran's security and foreign policy priorities, but officials of the Islamic Republic constantly kept themselves busy with counterclockwise policy behaviors, including injection of money to the central bank of

Syria lest its total bankruptcy, bankrolling the construction of a nuclear reactor for Syria by North Korea, handing out wads of cash to the "martyred families" of Islamist militant groups in Lebanon and other places, etc.[8]

For all their ruinous consequences for average Iranians, international sanctions and restrictions were a bona fide bonanza for officials of the Islamic Republic and their families in so many other ways. More than 5000 of their mollycoddled kids could live in the United States; among them children of those notorious hostage takers who had occupied the US embassy in Tehran in 1979.[9] In the same way, economic sanctions or other international restrictions were no obstacle for many other family members of the ruling elites who could live and study in an expensive European country largely at the cost of the public budget.[10] Of course, many of those officials or their families who had opted to live in Iran had embarked on a royal lifestyle by benefiting from all the trappings of wealth and luxury.[11] Some of them could even carry an additional American passport or green card while serving as a cabinet minister or a subaltern administrator.[12] That was then no coincidence why when such a nouveau riche ended up serving as the Islamic Republic's top representative to the World Bank, he could afford to purchase a $700,000 house in the Washington D.C. area.[13]

THE CHARADE OF SMART SANCTIONS: FROM EMPIRE-BUILDERS TO ASYLUM-SEEKERS

While sanctions were a gift from heaven for the ruling elites of the Islamic Republic and their families, they brought about myriad terrible consequences for average Iranians "comparable to war" as if the country's innocent citizens had been made a scapegoat for the clerical regime's ambitious agendas and policy behaviors at home and abroad. On the whole, warlike sanctions had little chance to devour Iranians without Washington functioning as battering ram for their execution.[14] Perhaps the United States never had a real plan to go to war with the Islamic Republic, but even if Americans had ever carved out a serious roadmap for their intended war with Tehran, sanctions would have made it superfluous, and only thing they needed was, in the words of Woodrow Wilson, to apply "this economic, peaceful, silent, deadly remedy and there will be no need for force." As some observers and critics pointed out, a good number of trigger-happy lawmakers in the US Congress were essentially hell-bent on "hitting not only the core of the Iranian regime but also the Iranian people" primarily through applying more doses of international sanctions and penalties.[15] As John Bolton asserted in his book, *Surrender Is Not an Option*, "sanctions without pain are not sanctions at all," and that was why the prime goal of this zealot group of American politicians and their ilk in other Western countries was to inflict more pain on irreproachable Iranians by heaping them with sundry sanctions over a course of more than four decades.[16]

The facts simply spoke for themselves, and that was the best way to reckon that waging sanctions against average pitiful Iranians turned out to be anything but "a promising struggle."[17] In a rich land endowed with cornucopia of natural wealth, international sanctions, coupled with the political system's incompetency, sank one-third of the entire population into the abyss of absolute poverty, and some 6 percent or close to five million of those wretched people were living in a state of constant hunger and destitution.[18] Some Iranian newspapers and media outlets were also no longer abashed to splash across their front-page, citing politicians that "we have 60 million poor people receiving subsidies."[19] As an inexorable consequence of sanctions, moreover, Iran joined the jinxed club of "top 10 depressed countries in the world," and that was why many of its cursed and downhearted citizens had virtually turned their back on everything; from abandoning their own cultural values and traditions to deserting the political system's pooling stations opened for another sham and rigged elections.[20]

Meanwhile, emigration or leaving Iran en masse was another reliable barometer of worsening socio-economic conditions of Iranians in the wake of sanctions. Compounded by some other political and cultural constraints created by the Islamic Republic, international sanctions and restrictions made many Iranian citizens lose any hope for a better future in Iran, setting their sights on emigration as the only recourse to chase their shattered dreams somewhere else.[21] The gloomy outcome was not brain drain alone; capital flight and beauty exodus were also part of the doleful phenomenon because many of those who left permanently were among the smartest, richest, and prettiest people whom the country had given birth to.[22] Still, for a good number of those individuals who were leaving Iran in search of a different life abroad, the road ahead was not the primrose path; the shortcut to their personal fulfillment and happiness was basically strewn with boulders and littered with thorny shrubs. Some of them were simply willing to risk their life stepping up to the plate at any cost; from sneaking illegally into a coveted Western territory to applying for a refugee status in a third country. In sum, for the people whose ancestors were ruling over a large empire extending from Baghdad to Bombay less than three centuries ago, it was unbecoming that major international institutions were now "warning about the wave of Iranian refugees to Europe."[23]

From Yakuza Recruitment to Olympic Blues: Iranian Ordeals in East Asia

For many Iranians who opted for living in a foreign country either temporarily or permanently, sanctions and their troublesome implications were not constrained to Iran's sovereign borders; they often had to struggle with sanctions culturally and intellectually no matter if they had managed to escape them economically. In other words, Iranian migrants and travelers usually encountered their own "glass ceiling" in the new societies they chose to deal with. The crux of the problem was that the world's mainstream media and press were generally putting a spotlight on certain policies and behaviors of the theocratic system of the Islamic Republic, influencing negatively the way an average citizen of a foreign country viewed Iran and average Iranians. This rather partisan and prejudiced approach often caused less problems in the societies that were diverse racially and open-minded politically such as Canada, Australia, New Zealand, the United States, and some Western European countries; the popular places which happened to be the top destinations for a majority of Iranian migrants.

Some other foreign territories which Iranians entered over the past several decades, however, were not that heterogeneous and unprejudiced. Japan and South Korea were prime examples among such societies which had historically been isolationist fraught with standoffish attitudes toward whatever foreign. Despite decades of state-sponsored internationalization and social diversification, the liberal-oriented governments in Japan and the ROK could hardly make a substantial dent in the whole edifice of racial homogeneity and cultural provincialism in both developed and industrialized countries. More important, these societies did not have much broad international exchanges with Iran, and their overall image and impression of contemporary Iranians were to be influenced ineluctably by what major international press and media outlets broadcast about the Middle Eastern

186 S. AZAD

country and its government's policies. As a consequence, Iranians in Japan and South Korea could end up facing plenty of discrimination and mistreatment part of which had to do with international sanctions and limitations.

Concerning Japan, the experience of large-scale travel by Iranians to the East Asian country took place in the 1980s and early 1990s when the Japanese economy was truly booming and required a lot of foreign labor force. Since 1974, Iranians did not need visa to visit Japan, and the Iran–Iraq War of 1980–1988 and the follow-up economic and social upheavals forced tens of thousands of Iranian males to fly to Japan for work. In April 1992, the Japanese government suddenly abolished the visa waiver program for Iran, creating a lot of troubles for a large crowd of Iranians who wanted to continue working in Japan legally. The Japanese move was obviously self-serving; Japan had scraped the visa requirement for Iranians in 1974 to benefit from Iran's economic boom in the aftermath of the first oil shock, but it reinstated visa in 1992 to partially deal with some deteriorating economic conditions at home after taking advantage of cheap and abundant labor force from some other countries, including Iran, during the 1980s and early 1990s. The Japanese economic bubble had already burst, and it was time for the national government in Japan to restore trust and confidence in a panicked and anxious citizenry partly by clamping down on certain unfortunate groups of foreigners, including Iranians, who were regarded as visa overstayers and illegal immigrants.[24]

The government's campaign, however, terrified many Japanese employers who were by and large very satisfied with work performance and productivity of their Iranian employees. Iranian workers, including some of those who were staying in Japan on a valid visa, now found it rather difficult to find a job. Struggling to make ends meet, they looked like sitting ducks and could easily fall prey to any trap.[25] Hundreds of them were seduced and attracted by Japanese women as a marriage partner, while a good number of others were recruited by Japan's notorious mafia, Yakuza, though in some cases the apparently lovely Japanese wife herself turned out to be a trained Yakuza member as well. Working for Yakuza, many Iranians were then used as a front to engage in some illegal and criminal activities, including selling fabricated telephone cards, distributing narcotics, and pimping.[26] For obvious reasons, a good number of those luckless Iranians ended up in Japan's dreadful prisons, suffering many years of mistreatment and torture at the hands of their merciless jailors. Some of them simply could not make it and lost their life at a detention center or jailhouse in Japan while still crying that they had absolutely no clue what they were really doing before being rounded up by the Japanese police.[27]

With regard to South Korea, a collectively painful experience for Iranians occurred during the 2018 Winter Olympics held in the ROK's Pyeongchang on February 9–25. In the opening ceremony, Samsung refused to give its gift smartphones to the participating Iranian athletes by excusing international sanctions against Iran. The incident was immediately covered widely by almost all media outlets and press across the world, creating bad feelings among Iranians at home and abroad. It was a time when Samsung had an annual income of $2.7 billion from Iran's bankable mobile market alone, making many Iranians to question how the giant Korean company was so sensitive about the Iran-related sanctions in South Korea but it paid no attention to those sanctions while benefiting greatly from Iranian markets.[28] In addition to lodging formal protests by the Iranian government, some newspapers in Iran also called for boycotting Samsung products, putting additional pressures on Koreans to backtrack soon by handing over their smartphone presents to the Iranian sports team.[29]

Some three and half years later, however, another unpleasant incident involving two Korean and Iranian athletes proved that international politics could even influence major sports events and the way athletes behaved toward each other. The new incident took place at the 2021 Summer Olympics hosted by Japan in Tokyo on July 23–August 8. After Javad Foroughi, an Iranian marksman, won a gold medal in the men's 10-meter air pistol, Jin Jong-oh, a six-time Olympic medalist shooter who now failed to even make it past the qualification stage in Tokyo, objected to the International Olympic Committee (IOC) by saying in front of reporters "How can a terrorist win first place (at the Olympics)? That's the most absurd and ridiculous thing."[30] The Iranian athlete had reportedly some affiliation with the IRGC, although it had little to do with his agreeable sporting performance at the Tokyo Olympics. The disappointed Korean medalist was later forced to apologize for his "inappropriate comments," but the whole episode made it clear for the umpteenth time that sanctions and international constraints against Iranian citizens had universally inescapable implications more than met the eye.[31] For many Iranians who were then living in East Asia or other parts of the world, the incident also evoked some memories of being harassed by similar libelous statements and slanderous remarks no matter if they, unlike Foroughi, had no relationship with the Islamic Republic and its institutions.

A Litmus Test of Ties: The Coronavirus Crisis and "Humanitarian Assistance"

In the midst of grappling with ubiquitous repercussions of the reinstated international sanctions, Iran was hit out of the blue with a new mysterious plague of dubious origin, coronavirus or COVID-19. This perplexing plight was a universe unto itself, turning the sanctioned country into one of the most infected places on the earth and the worst affected country in the entire Middle East region. COVID-19 had already affected more than four million Iranians leading to more than 95,000 deaths among a population of 80 million by August 2021 when China, as the reportedly source country of the deadly virus, had experienced only some 95,000 affected cases with less than 4700 deaths out of a population of more than 1.3 billion people.[32] By this time, almost every two minutes one ill-fated Iranian was dying of the coronavirus pandemic as nearly all highly transmissible variants of COVID-19 found their way into the Persian Gulf country uncannily and speedily.[33] The situation had reached the point of no return, and it was time for East Asian countries to once again rekindle their Tehran connections which had recently been hamstrung due to Trump's sanctions diktats.[34]

South Korea was among the first countries which raised the issue of "humanitarian trade" with Iran after it was badly invaded by the coronavirus pandemic. Since the United States had exempted the supply of food, medicine, and other humanitarian items to Iran, the ROK essentially wanted to take advantage of "humanitarian exports" to the Middle Eastern country to give a boost to its international trade which had been partially contracted in the wake of COVID-19.[35] After receiving special permission from Washington, South Korea dispatched to Iran some $500,000 worth of medicine for hereditary diseases in late May 2020.[36] Since Iran and the ROK could not easily settle their bilateral dispute over some $7 billion Iranian frozen funds in Seoul, it took more than another year before South Korea shipped to Tehran through the COVAX facility roughly 700,000 doses of Oxford AstraZeneca vaccine which had been manufactured by the Korean company SK Bioscience. As compared to its East Asian rivals, therefore, South Korea remained rather reserved and stingy throughout the pandemic, unwilling to offer much technical help or emergency medical equipment free of charge.[37]

Unlike South Korea, Japan was appreciated publicly by different officials and institutions of the Islamic Republic for its "good assistance" during the pandemic, though there was not much details about all types of support and relief Tokyo provided. Most probably Japan had also facilitated some sort of financial mechanism through which Iran could make use of its frozen assets abroad to purchase all medical requirements including vaccines to fight coronavirus.[38] To do so, the Japanese government had certainly been given the green light by the United States to sort out the relevant financial matters involving the trade in medical stuff between Iran and other countries. In July 2021, moreover, 2.9 million doses of Japan's AstraZeneca vaccine in three separate batches arrived in Iran through the COVAX facility.[39] While Japanese officials, including a top Japanese diplomat at Japan's embassy in Tehran, announced that their government had donated the AstraZeneca vaccines to the Middle Eastern country, some officials in Tehran told reporters that those vaccines had been acquired with the help of Iran's Ministry of Health and the central bank, indicating that the country had actually paid for them.[40]

As widely expected, however, China turned out to be far more successful than Japan in capitalizing on COVID-19 to get closer to Iran. From early months of the pandemic, several consignments of Chinese medical donations arrived in Tehran, containing masks, coronavirus diagnostic kits, vaccines, etc.[41] The East Asian power, moreover, emerged as the largest trading partner of Iran in terms of selling its Sinopharm COVID-19 vaccines to Iranians as almost 75–80 percent of the vaccines which Iran imported came from China. Officials in both countries acknowledged that China had additionally donated over ten million doses of the Sinopharm vaccines to Iran to help the country curb the infectious disease as quickly as possible.[42] More important, the political aspect of such Sino–Iranian synergies received more attention internationally as well as domestically. The Iranian government took a leading role throwing its full support behind China's policies and measures with regard to the coronavirus pandemic at a trying time when some Western countries, including the Trump administration in Washington, were accusing Beijing of manufacturing the deadly disease in the first place and falsifying its related information and data. In return, China's close cooperation with Iran throughout the pandemic buoyed up many Iranian conservatives who regarded Beijing more reliable than Western countries and asked for deepening ties with the East Asian country in lockstep with the recently-signed 25-year strategic agreement.[43]

THE LOOKING-EAST APPROACH AND ITS DISCONTENTS

For many proponents of the looking-East orientation in Iran, especially those powerful conservative forces affiliated with the Islamic Republic's security and ideological institutions, the East is an alternative to and a replacement for the West. By and large, they are anti-West and particularly anti-American, and their deep animosity toward the West played an instrumental role in fostering closer connections between Tehran and major Eastern powers such as China. Some of them even claim that the US-led sanctions had nothing to do with the departure of the Shah and the follow-up seizure of the US embassy in Tehran because Iran had been boycotted by the West, technologically in particular, even under the Pahlavi monarchy. In their view, the United States had no intention to industrialize Iran despite its apparently close and friendly relationship with the Shah, forcing the ambitious king to import second-hand heavy industries from the Soviet Union and its satellite states in Eastern Europe. The real nature of American, and generally Western, commercial interactions with the Shah was thereby, as they argue, superficial and exploitative based on importing vital raw materials from Iran and selling unproductive consumerist goods and armaments to the Persian Gulf country.[44]

On the contrary, advocates of looking-East assert that the East happened to be a more helpful and reliable partner. More specifically, the Trump administration's withdrawal from the nuclear deal supplied grist to the mills of the anti-American zealots in the Islamic Republic, providing their gotcha mentality with a new justification to raise the rhetoric of "Western unreliability" another notch.[45] Focusing particularly on the Sino–Iranian relations during the Iran–Iraq War and sanctions, such supporters of good ties with the East warn that Tehran should never forget those friendly countries of tough days which came to its assistance at a time when the West was spearheading a global coalition to harm Iranians in every possible way. They think that Iran should not replace China with Western powers simply because the West was the power of the past while China is going to be the power of the future. More important, many of those pro-Eastern forces believe that the United States will not remove all Iran sanctions and penalties any time soon, making it very necessary for Tehran to stay in good terms with Beijing in order to overcome any likely economic and technological impediment caused by the US-led West.[46]

Beyond sanctions, some diehard supporters of looking-East claim that Iran's alliance with the Eastern powers such as China and Russia would contain Western policies and checkmate any American hostile move against the Islamic Republic.[47] It is a close partnership among these three Eastern powers, as they predict with a heady optimism, that "can shake the walls of the White House," compelling the United States, and the West in general, to stop interfering in many domestic affairs of other nations.[48] They think that part of this critical objective could be achieved through the Sino–Iranian 25-year strategic agreement which, in their view, will reduce American power and influence in the Middle East, if not beyond. That is why, as they argue with self-assurance, the United States and its close allies here and there worry too much about the 25-year deal because they do not want Iran to become another China through taking advantage of Chinese capital and technology and turning its currently flatlining economy into another powerhouse in the greater Middle East region.[49]

In more practical terms, some champions of the looking-East orientation call for Iran's serious contribution to the materialization of an "Eastern century." Arguing that Iran was historically the cultural capital of the East, this group of pro-Eastern campaigners maintain that by and large the classical Iranian empires had prop-Eastern proclivities, and the present-day Iranian system should not be any exception to that general pattern. The proponents of the East also pay more attention to Iranian deep legacy in many Asian cultures exemplified by Iran's footprint in the Chinese language, religion, and customs.[50] For this reason, they think that Iran and China need to carry forward their millennia-old connections now that the Chinese government has tried to bring back a lot of the archaic memories through its gigantic project of reviving the ancient Silk Road (i.e. the BRI). Feeling particularly nostalgic about cultural and commercial interactions in ancient times through the famous road, these protagonists favor all-out support for the Chinese initiative which they think would also help Iran to strengthen its civilizational links to all societies that were previously part of the Silk Road.[51]

Opponents of the East-leaning approach, however, have their own arguments concerning how Iran should think up the nature and scope of its relationship with other major countries, including Eastern powers. On one hand, they do not reject the necessity of engaging in economic and technological interactions with Eastern nations as long as such bilateral connections are symbiotic and benefit both sides. They also acknowledge that Iran can learn a lot of invaluable lessons from the trajectory of economic development and industrialization in some Eastern societies such as Japan and South Korea.[52] For all their liberal and pro-West tendencies, this group of critics sometimes become rather sentimental with regard to Iran's relatively unsuccessful quest for economic growth and industrialization as compared to what happened to the Japanese and Korean societies in contemporary history. That is why they think that Iran should take a leaf out of the strategic book of Japan and the ROK by concentrating more on productive economic and technological activities rather than squandering its huge potentials on some visionary political and ideological slogans.[53]

On the other hand, these antagonists strongly oppose any Iranian preference and commitment to the so-called Chinese development model which they think does not suit Iran's politico-economic and cultural characteristics at all.[54] On the whole, they are not in favor of taking China and Russia as a model in political or economic terms, while arguing against developing close political and strategic connections between Iran and those two powers.[55] Additionally, these looking-East sceptics point out that any form of political and economic dependence, including dependency on the East, is basically terrible, and submission to China and Russia is really not the proper way for the Islamic Republic to fight back the United States and other major Western powers. Likewise, Iran's membership in the Shanghai Cooperation Organization (SCO), as they assert, would not be any different for Tehran than its accession to the North Atlantic Treaty Organization (NATO) because "falling in an Eastern pit is simply as dreadful and consequential as getting stuck in a Western pit."[56]

Finally, opponents of the looking-East approach are very critical toward the 25-year strategic agreement which they believe does not secure Iran's national interests sufficiently. Since the Sino–Iranian deal has been formulated under crippling international sanctions, as they contend, the Chinese government could essentially dictate the terms and disregard Iran's long-term interests otherwise they really did not need to be secretive and reticent about the contents of their agreement.[57] Enumerating some of China's anti-Iran behaviors in the heydays of international sanctions against Tehran, moreover, these sceptics insist that China does not have a good record in the past, and it should not be trusted with regard to all those economic and technological promises it has made in the 25-year agreement. In their view, the crux of the problem is that Beijing has so far treated Tehran more like an economic customer than a true political ally, and as long as China continued to behave in similar fashion, it would be a great mistake for Iran to put all of its strategic eggs in the Chinese suspicious basket.[58]

NOTES

1. Andrew von Hirsch, *Censure and Sanctions* (New York: Oxford University Press, 1996), pp. 6, 29.
2. Mathew Craven, "Humanitarianism and the Quest for Smarter Sanctions," *European Journal of International Law*, Vol. 13, No. 1 (2002), pp. 43–61.
3. Pape.
4. Ronald Wintrobe, "The Tinpot and the Totalitarian: An Economic Theory of Dictatorship," *The American Political Science Review*, Vol. 84, No. 3 (September 1990), pp. 849–872; and Dursun Peksen and A. Cooper Drury, "Economic Sanctions and Political Repression: Assessing the Impact of Coercive Diplomacy on Political Freedoms," *Human Rights Review*, Vol. 10, No. 3 (September 2009), pp. 393–411.
5. "Sanctions Cripple Iran's Middle Class, not the Regime," *Foreign Policy*, August 2, 2012; "Sanctions: War by other Means," *Financial Times*, March 31, 2014; "4 Myths about the Iran Sanctions," *The National Interest*, July 10, 2015; and "The US Sanctions on Iran are Causing a Major Humanitarian Crisis," *The Nation*, January 21, 2020.
6. Erica S. Moret, "Humanitarian Impacts of Economic Sanctions on Iran and Syria," *European Security*, Vol. 24, No. 1 (2015), pp. 120–140.
7. Gates, p. 236.
8. "Safir Iran dar lobnan: Iran be khanevade har shahid felistini 7 hezar dollar komak mikonad" [Iran Ambassador to Lebanon: Iran Gives $7,000 to the Family of Every Palestinian Martyr], *Asr Iran*, February 25, 2016.
9. "Mohammad Gharazi: 5 hezar aghazadeh irani dar America sekoonat darand va dolarhay mardom ra bordehand" [Mohammad Gharazi: 5000 Children of Iranian Officials are Residing in the United States and Have People's Dollars], *Mostaghel Newspaper*, May 2, 2021, p. 2.
10. "Tahsi 4000 aghazade dar englis" [4000 Children of Officials Studying in England], *Seday Eslahat*, February 29, 2018, p. 1; and "Panj hezar aghazade dar America zendegi mikonand" [5000 Children of Officials Living in America], *Seday Eslahat*, November 17, 2020, p. 1.
11. "Shah raft vali zendegi shahane edame darad" [Shah Left Iran but Royal Life Goes on], *Ghanoon Daily*, February 6, 2019, p. 1.
12. "Hozoor 198 modir dotabeiyati dar badanye dolat" [198 Managers with Dual Citizenship in Executive Branch], *Asr-e Iranian*, May 21, 2018, pp. 1, 2; and "Ettelaat migooyad barkhi vozara tabeiyat amerikai darand: Modiran amrikai!" [Intelligence Says Some Ministers have American Nationality: American Managers!], *Seday Eslahat*, May 21, 2018, p. 1.
13. "Kharid khane 700 hezar dollari dar America az sooy namayande Iran dar bank Jahani!" [House Worth $700,000 in America Purchased by Iran's Representative to the World Bank!], *Kayhan*, May 28, 2019, p. 11.

14. Robert D. Blackwill, and Jennifer M. Harris, *War by Other Means: Geoeconomics and Statecraft* (New York: The Belknap Press of Harvard University Press, 2016), p. 58.
15. Willem van Kemenade, "China vs. the Western Campaign for Iran Sanctions," *The Washington Quarterly*, Vol. 33, No, 3 (2010), pp. 99–114.
16. Bolton, *Surrender is not an Option*, p. 336.
17. Michael Jacobson, "Sanctions against Iran: A Promising Struggle," *The Washington Quarterly*, Vol. 31, No. 3 (2008), pp. 69–88.
18. "33 darsad jamiyat Iran dar 'faghr motlagh'" [33 Percent of Iran Population in 'Absolute Poverty'], *Roozgarma*, April 8, 2018, pp. 1, 7; "40 darsad jamiyat keshvar zir khatte faghr" [40 Percent of the Country's Population under Poverty Line], *Eghtesad-e Meli*, May 14, 2019, pp. 1, 2; and "Hoghoogh mardom be rial ast amma hazineha be dollar" [People's Salary in Rial Their Costs in Dollar], *Emrooz (Today Online)*, May 19, 2021, p. 2.
19. "Irani boodan sakht ast!" [Hardship of Being Iranian!], *Seday Eslahat*, December 8, 2018, p. 6; and "60 million faghir yaranebegir darim" [We have 60 Million Poor People Receiving Subsidies], *Mostaghel Newspaper*, February 23, 2021, p. 1.
20. "Iran dar miyan 10 keshvar afsorde jahan" [Iran among Top 10 Depressed Countries in the World], *Tejarat News*, June 3, 2018, p. 10; "Bohran eghtesadi mardom ra bejanham andakhte ast" [Economic Crisis Has Pitted People against Each Other], *Eghtesad-e Pooya*, February 3, 2020, p. 1; and "Dar barkhi shahrha tanha yek darsad dar entekhabat dordovvom majles sherkat kardand" [In Some Cities only One Percent Participated in the Second Round of Parliamentary Elections], *Mostaghel Newspaper*, September 16, 2020, p. 1.
21. "Ahmadinejad Says Enemies Destroy Iran's Rain Clouds—Reports," *Reuters*, September 11, 2012.
22. "2 hezar milyard dollar sarmayeh iraniyan kharejneshin" [$2000 Billion Wealth of Iranian Expats], *Asr Iran*, June 13, 2015; "Saliyane 150 hezar nokhbe az Iran miravand" [150,000 Talents Leave Iran Annually], *Bahar Daily*, August 7, 2018, p. 1; and "Mohajerat mahyane 500 parastar az Iran" [500 Nurses Emigrate from Iran Every Month], *Asia News*, April 12, 2021, p. 1.
23. "Hoshdar sazeman melal darbare moj panahjooyan irani be Europa" [UN Warning about the Wave of Iranian Refugees to Europe], *Abrar News*, September 12, 2018, p. 2.
24. In the period between 1980 and 1993, more than 54,000 Iranians traveled to Japan, accounting for more than 5 percent of all foreigners who had visited the East Asian country in those years. By 1999, still some 14,516 Iranians were living in Japan, and 7304 people or half of them were staying there illegally. A decade later, however, the total number of the registered

Iranians in Japan fell to around 5000 people. Robert S. Yoder, *Deviance and Inequality in Japan: Japanese Youth and Foreign Migrants* (Bristol, UK: The Policy Press, 2011), pp. 101–103.

25. Kevin J. Cooney, *Japan's Foreign Policy Maturation: A Quest for Normalcy* (London and New York: Routledge, 2002), p. 127.

26. Hiromasa Mori, "Foreign Migrant Workers in Japan: Trends and Policies," *Asian and Pacific Migration Journal*, Vol. 4, No. 2–3 (1995), pp. 411–427.

27. "Mohakeme dolat zhapon ba shekayat ghahraman koshti Iran, joziyat 11 sal shekanje dar zendan" [Japanese Government on Trial by Iranian Wrestling Champion's Complaint, Details of 11-Year Torture in Prison], *Mehr News Agency*, June 11, 2013.

28. "Koreihay soodjoo" [Profit-seeking Koreans], *Shahrvand*, February 10, 2018, p. 2.

29. "Iran: Samsung must Apologize for Gift Ban against Athletes," *Press TV*, February 8, 2018; and "Tahrim mahsoolat Samsung kamtarin pasokh be raftar tahghiramiz kore jonoobi" [Boycotting Samsung Products the Minimum Response to South Korea's Humiliating Behavior], *Kayhan*, February 8, 2018, pp. 1, 10.

30. "Jin Jong-oh Criticizes IOC over Iranian Gold Medalist," *Korea Times*, July 29, 2021.

31. "Shooter Jin Jong-oh Apologizes for 'Terrorist' Comment," *Korea Times*, August 1, 2021.

32. "Iran Sees Highest Daily Virus Case, Death Counts in Pandemic," *AP*, August 8, 2021.

33. "Iran Says One Person Dying of COVID-19 Every Two Minutes," *Reuters*, August 9, 2021.

34. Other countries and regions also got involved. In 2021 alone, for instance, the European Union (EU) offered Iran some 15 million euros to spend on the most vulnerable inhabitants in the country, including some 3.65 million Afghans living in the Persian Gulf country. According to the EU, Iran had received over 76 million euros of such special reliefs in the period from 2016 to 2021. "Humanitarian Aid: EU Mobilises €22 Million to Support Most Vulnerable in Iran and Pakistan," *European Commission*, July 12, 2021.

35. "S. Korea, Iran Agree to Launch Working Group on Humanitarian Trade," *Yonhap News Agency*, August 2, 2020.

36. "Korea to Export $500,000 Worth of Hereditary Disease Medicine to Iran," *Korea Times*, May 28, 2020.

37. "Mahigiri koreiha az ab gelalood" [Koreans Fishing from Muddied Waters], *Tejarat News*, June 11, 2020, p. 1.

38. Long before the coronavirus pandemic, Japan had probably played a critical role in facilitating some financial transactions between Iranians and

196 S. AZAD

third parties. At some point, for instance, Korean businesses could sort out their payment issues with Iran through Japan. "'Iran Sanctions Won't Hurt Korean Exports'," *Korea Herald*, February 8, 2012.

39. "New Batches of Sputnik, AstraZeneca Vaccines Imported," *Tehran Times*, July 30, 2021; and "Iran Receives 3rd Batch of AstraZeneca COVID-19 Vaccine from Japan," *IRNA*, July 31, 2021.

40. "Iran Thanks Japan for Covid Vaccines," *Tehran Times*, July 24, 2021.

41. "Zhongguo xiang yilang juanzeng 25 wan zhi kouzhao" [China Donates 250,000 Masks to Iran], *Xinhua*, February 26, 2020.

42. "75 ta 80 darsad varedat vaccine Iran az chin ast" [75–80 Percent of Iran's Imported Vaccines Come from China], *ILNA*, July 18, 2021.

43. "Na be gharb, bale be shargh" [No to West, Yes to East], *Mostaghel Newspaper*, October 1, 2018, p. 2; "Hamahangi Tehran va pekan dar zeddiyat ba Trumpism" [Tehran and Beijing Coordination in Opposition to Trumpism], *Roozan News*, February 20, 2019, pp. 1, 3; and "Iran Hardliners Claim China is Serving Islam by Suppressing Uyghur Muslims," *Radio Farda*, August 4, 2020.

44. "Ghabl az enghelab ham dar mavared mohemmi tahrim boodeim" [We had also been Sanctioned in Certain Important Areas before Revolution], *Raja News*, December 1, 2014.

45. "Rahbord sharghi" [Eastern Approach], *Ghanoon Daily*, February 20, 2019, pp. 1, 2; "Rahzanan 'jaddeh abrisham'" [Bandits of 'Silk Road'], *Quds Daily*, July 9, 2020, p. 1; and "Bonbast teorik" [Theoretical Dilemma], *Vatan Emrooz*, July 29, 2020, pp. 1, 2.

46. "Dour Asia dar haft rooz" [Around Asia in Seven Days], *Hamshahri*, May 18, 2019, p. 2; and "Gharadad ba chin kahesh feshar Americast" [Deal with China is to Reduce American Pressure], *Arman Meli*, July 30, 2020, p. 1.

47. "America aramesh shargh Asia ra baray atashafroozi dar gharb Asia mikhahad" [America Wants Peace in East Asia to Make Trouble in West Asia] *Siasat Rooz*, June 24, 2018, p. 1; and "Razmayesh moshtarek daryaei Iran, roosiye va chin payami az daryay Oman baray America" [Joint Naval Drill of Iran, Russia and China a Message for America from the Sea of Oman], *Kayhan*, December 28, 2019, p. 1.

48. "Tamin amniyat Asia ba komak Iran va chin" [Securing Security of Asia with the Help of Iran and China], *Tejarat News*, November 16, 2016, p. 1; and "Mosalas Tehran, Mosco, pekan batelosehr tamam doshmanihay gharb ast" [The Triangle of Tehran, Moscow, and Beijing Checkmates All Western Enmities], *Kayhan*, January 24, 2018, p. 1.

49. "Asgaroladi: Jai chiniha r aba hich keshvari avaz nemikonim" [Asgaroladi: We do not Replace Chinese with any other Country], *Tafahom* News, May 25, 2016, p. 1; and "Gharb negaran tabdil shodan Iran be yek chin digar

ast" [West Worries Iran Become another China], *Etemad Daily*, May 12, 2020, pp. 1, 4.
50. "Iran payetakht farhangi shargh ast" [Iran is the Cultural Capital of the East], *Javan*, June 18, 2019, p. 6; and "Mehdi Safari: 6 sal pish bayad ba chin gharardad mibastim" [Mehdi Safari: We Would Have Singed Agreement with China 6 Years Ago], *Asr Eghtesad*, August 25, 2020, p. 1.
51. "Farhang va tamaddon tarikhi noghteye ettesal Iran va chin" [Culture and Historical Civilization Linking Iran and China], *Servat*, May 18, 2019, p. 1.
52. "'Arj' biarj; 'Samsung' porarj!" ['Arj' Disrespectable; 'Samsung' Respectable!], *Shahrvand*, April 4, 2018, p. 4; and "Kore jonoobi ra asan azdast nadahim" [Let not Lose South Korea Easily], *Jahan-e Sanat*, January 6, 2021, p. 1.
53. "Eghtesad Iran 6 barabar shod eghtesad kore jonoobi 34 barabar" [Iran Economy Grew Six-fold and South Korean Economy 34-fold], *Arman Daily*, October 14, 2017, p. 9; and "Zhapon chegoone modern shod va ma nashodem" [How Japan Modernized and We Did not], *Aftab-e Yazd*, January 3, 2018, p. 1.
54. "Olgooy tosye chin dar Iran shekast mikhorad" [Chinese Model of Development Fails in Iran], *Arman Daily*, November 12, 2017, p. 1; and "Diktatory chin potansiyel tahdid jahani ra darad" [Chinese Dictatorship Has Potential to Threaten the World], *Mostaghel Newspaper*, April 20, 2020, pp. 1, 3.
55. "Khanjarhay ashna: Safir pishin Iran dar sazman melal be 'kharidar' migooyad china, roosiye va hend ghabel etemad nistand" [Familiar Daggers: Foremer Iran Ambassador to UN Tells 'Kharidar' China, Russia and India are not Trustworthy], *Kharidar Daily*, July 11, 2018, p. 1; and "Chin va roosiye mokhalef hal moshkelat Iran va America hastand" [China and Russia Oppose Settling Iran and America Disputes], *Mardomsalari*, September 14, 2020, p. 9.
56. "Risk sherakat ba ezhdahay sorkh" [Risk of Collaborating with Red Dragon], *Sobh-e Emrooz*, July 19, 2020, p. 1.
57. "Bastan gharardad ba chin dar dourye tahrim khatast" [Singing Contract with China during Sanctions is Mistake], *Arman Meli*, April 5, 2021, pp. 1, 11.
58. "Chin Iran ra sharik strategic nemidanad" [China is not Considering Iran Strategic Partner], *Mostaghel Newspaper*, July 15, 2020, p. 1; "Chin Iran ra moshtari midanad; na mottahed" [China Regards Iran Customer; not Ally], *Arman Meli*, July 22, 2020, p. 1; and "Iran bazandeh sanad rahbordi ba chin khahad bood magar anke chin ham taahodati bedahad" [Iran Would be the Loser of the Strategic Document with China Unless China Gave Some Commitments], *Mardomsalari*, August 5, 2020, p. 1.

CHAPTER 12

The Empire Strikes Back: Circumventing Sanctions

REPRISAL: "DOCTORATE IN BYPASSING SANCTIONS"

Over the past several decades, Iran made a really big name in the world of sanctions not only for being a top target of some lasting and extensive regimes of international sanctions but also in terms of finding ways to deal with those harmful penalties and crippling restrictions. In fact, from around mid-November 1979 when the United States commenced its sanctions against Tehran, the Islamic Republic had to learn to cope with all detrimental effects of never-ending international impediments and boy-cotts.[1] As a relatively big and populous country, Iran simply could not afford to stand idle because stakes were too high and the country had too much resources at its disposal to fight back sanctions. By the time the Trump administration ditched the nuclear deal and reinstated all Iran sanctions with additional punitive measures in 2018 and 2019, the Persian Gulf country already knew all the ropes in evading almost any type of international obstacle and restriction. Such mastery was also confirmed in April 2019 by the then Foreign Minister, Mohammad Javad Zarif, who bragged rather self-righteously that "we have earned a doctorate in bypass-ing sanctions."[2]

Iran's proficiency and sophistication in going around sanctions brought about one long-term advantage and two short-term disadvantages. Its benefit or reward had essentially something to do with mastering the "knowledge of sanctions" and coming to terms with all negative and nasty

© The Author(s), under exclusive license to Springer Nature   199
Switzerland AG 2022
S. Azad, *East Asia and Iran Sanctions*,
https://doi.org/10.1007/978-3-030-97427-5_12

consequences of being boycotted by all rich and resourceful countries across the world. After all, it is a golden age of sanctions, and even democratic and industrialized societies sometimes levy substantial sanctions and hurting restrictions against each other. The existence of sanctions and penalties among close political allies and friendly economic partners has hardly been regarded as an anomaly either.[3] Learning how universal sanctions work and muddling through their restrictive ramifications were to thereby give Iranians a leg up over their peers and rivals in the Middle East and beyond. Getting past sanctions in every possible way was, moreover, about honing marketing skills and building new international connections informally, and all such invaluable assets would be of great use to Iranians under normal circumstances when international sanctions and restrictions against their country are lifted entirely.[4]

Concerning disadvantages, the first downside was that the sanctions-busting devices and measures were rarely, if at all, cheap or free of charge. In September 2016, the governor of the CBI revealed that some 15 percent of the cost for Iran's foreign trade had gone to the pockets of the middlemen that played a part in sidestepping sanctions.[5] As another confirmation, in April 2021 Abbas Akhondi, a former cabinet minister, made it public that the Islamic Republic had spent virtually $400 billion to bypass sanctions.[6] Dodging different types of sanctions and international restrictions certainly required different costs, but when some sets of sanctions were comprehensive and pretty stringent in nature, Iranians had to allocate higher expenses to get rid of them.[7] Before the CBI was sanctioned and international financial transactions between the Middle Eastern country and the outside world were banned, for instance, Iran could transfer $50 million through the international banking system at a maximum cost of $30–40, but after international financial sanctions were levied against Tehran, the same transaction required up to $4 million or some 7–8 percent of the total value of the whole business.[8]

As a corollary to the first drawback, the second disadvantage was about corruption on a scale never seen before. Over time, the crucial mandate of evading sanctions led to the creation of a vast empire which extended its tentacles virtually into every important business in every part of the world. From developed and democratic countries to developing and authoritarian societies, rapacious corporations and greedy individuals came out to play a part in the gigantic network of bypassing sanctions and international restrictions against Iran. Wrongdoing and corruption were part and parcel of the business because the whole process was ultimately about going around laws and regulations, sewing up the loopholes, offering bribes, favoritism, nepotism, etc.[9] On top of that, a great deal of all corrupt practices in the process were never discovered, and those players who had a role to play in dodging sanctions were sometimes rewarded rather than prosecuted because the criminal was to be treated as a hero in the same way that a terrorist of one society could be regarded as a freedom fighter by another community.[10]

MIND-BOGGLING METHODS: FROM CONVENTIONAL TO AMBASSADORIAL

The invisible empire of sanctions-busters consisted of a large group of individuals and businesses working in different parts of the world. Iranians themselves were certainly the backbone of this titanic network, but a big crowd of foreigners, including foreign governments as well as their companies and private citizens, contributed tremendously to achieve its ultimate objective; going around sanctions. The stakeholders were truly multinational; from Asia to Africa and from the Middle East to Latin America, a slew of businesses and individuals from every walk of life got involved. There were also many Western businesses and individuals among them, willing to play a role in facilitating some sanctions-busting measures conducted by themselves or third parties through taking steps to conceal those dealings which were intended to benefit Iran, one way or the other. Regarding the foreign participants, some were acting out of politico-ideological reasons, while most of them engaged in the risky business for pure economic interests because the task often paid handsome dividends.

Meanwhile, there were a number of critical areas which did not entail any well-thought sanctions-busting initiative. As an energy-rich country with huge potentials in some other areas, Iran could not be sanctioned in certain fields. Unlike Japan and Germany during World War II or North Korea in the post-Cold War era, Iran possessed sufficient energy resources and was not a proper target for foreign oil embargoes, though the country's temporary yet avoidable dependence on gasoline imports proved to be a source of trouble more than a decade ago.[11] The Middle Eastern country could also supply its own electricity requirements, and its self-sufficiency in agricultural products only required some heavy lifting domestically. In the heydays of international sanctions and restrictions against Iran, therefore, sanctions-busting boiled down to selling oil and bringing in oil revenues. It was the critical period when the colossal coalition of domestic and foreign resources needed to be mobilized in order to export one additional cargo of crude oil and return back its income in every possible way.

To supply more crude oil, perhaps an easy and less expensive method for Iran was to use its own tankers or rented vessels to transport petroleum to foreign destinations.[12] To overcome some relevant restrictions on maritime transportation, the ship sailing on the high seas had to make recourse to certain deceptive behaviors, including changing its automatic identification system (AIS), ship-to-ship transfers, and any other practice to hide the true nature of its transactions. These methods were among some basic techniques long practiced by some sanctioned countries such as North Korea to keep their maritime foreign trade going.[13] To carry through their "secret sale of oil," moreover, even top Iranian officials acknowledged that they were taking advantage of some "other ways." After an OPEC meeting in Vienna in June 2018, for instance, when the then Iranian Oil Minister, Bijan Namdar Zanganeh, was pressed to explain what he meant by "other ways," he said "I cannot describe these other ways....If the United States administration knows what we are going to do, they will block us."[14]

Probably those peculiar ways had something to do with the disguising practices used by some of Iran's top oil customers, especially China, to evade international sanctions. Although it was an open secret that China was handling a great deal of its oil trade with Iran through Bank of Kunlun which inevitably came under American financial penalties, the East Asian power had to manage part of its unofficial oil imports from the Persian Gulf country through taking advantage of intermediaries in the same way that it could supply gasoline to Iran in 2009.[15] From Iraq and Kuwait in the Middle East to Malaysia and Vietnam in Southeast Asia and from Russia and Kazakhstan in Central Asia to Sri Lanka and Bangladesh in South Asia, these third parties could essentially smooth the way for Chinese oil companies to "falsely rebrand" Iranian crude oil and ship it to somewhere in mainland China.[16] It was then no coincidence why some in the Iranian media were surprised that China could astonishingly buy eight million barrels of Iranian crude oil even without registration by Iran's customs.[17]

Returning back the revenues made by exporting oil was, however, more important than selling crude oil itself. It became a Herculean task after the CBI was put under stringent sanctions, making it impossible to use the international banking system for conducting financial transactions involving Iran and other countries. Aside from Iranians, even foreign entities with considerable power and immunity like embassies encountered similar problems with regard to transferring into Iran their required financial budget. In a speech delivered at a business gathering in July 2016, for instance, South Korea's ambassador to Tehran revealed that his embassy still had to bring in its funds through smuggling six months after Iran started to implement the JCPOA.[18] Likewise, a number of Iranian officials later made it public that before the nuclear deal was agreed in June 2015, the country was bringing in part of its oil incomes using mules.[19] They also confessed that the CBI had to use motor ferry to carry oil dollars from the Persian Gulf which turned out to be very vital when Iran could bring in part of its oil money through bartering.[20]

FROM DUBAI TO HONG KONG: THE "WHITE KNIGHT" MEETS THE "WHITE GLOVE"

Aiming to cash in on international sanctions and penalties levied against Iran, a number of intermediary port cities emerged over time as major players to bypass those restrictions. As a warehouse for international commerce, or an entrepôt trade, some of these transshipment hubs, especially Dubai and Hong Kong, could be of great use for sanctions-busters from Iran and other parts of the world either directly or via third countries. The importance of these port cities grew by leaps and bounds particularly when certain international sanctions created a lot of troubles, ranging from fuel to insurance premium issues, for Iranian ships or ships and vessels from other nations which were going to dock at Iranian ports. Over the past several decades, moreover, the United States and some other Western countries took serious legal actions against many companies and individuals active in these port cities for their alleged roles in circumventing international sanctions against Tehran. Iran was also accused by Washington almost constantly for taking advantage of these cosmopolitan hubs to go around sanctions.[21]

Concerning Dubai, this former den of pirates became important overnight as soon as the United States commenced its sanctions against Iran in late 1979. For example, US exports to the UAE increased surprisingly four-fold within a month from some $100 million in January 1980 to roughly $400 million in February.[22] A bulk of what Americans shipped to the UAE then ended up in Iran, and this practice continued, *mutatis mutandis*, by 1997 when the Clinton administration issued Executive Order 13,059 to legally prevent US businesses to engage in indirect trade with Iran and thereby dodge the relevant sanctions through the tiny Arab country.[23] Both before and after Clinton's EO, however, Dubai was widely used by businesses from across the world, East Asians in particular, to bypass sanctions and sell their products and services to Iran sometimes at a mark-up. Even many Western companies which were not willing at all to do any business with Iran by using Dubai, were often prepared to trade with businesses which were based in that port city legally.

Of course, the West had for long turned a blind eye to what was really going on in Dubai despite Washington's bravado in 1997. It was also a way to prop up the port city, and the UAE in general, for Middle Eastern citizens as well as for expatriate professionals and workers from other parts of the world. As a consequence, many Iranian businesses moved to Dubai and some other port cities of the UAE, paving the ground for large-scale commercial interactions between Iran and the UAE in spite of all reportedly political antagonism between the two Persian Gulf countries. From importing highly expensive foreign products to bringing in suitcases full of dollars, they had skin in the game and turned Dubai into a true white knight for their various sanctions-busting activates.[24] Through their legally registered companies in Dubai and other UAE cities, they could also engage in business virtually with the rest of the world.[25] In some cases, their international business and sanctions-busting trade had to go through a willing third party located, for instance, in Iraq and Turkey in the Middle East or Honk Kong and Singapore in Asia.[26]

The impact of Hong Kong, however, had a lot to do with an overall role of Asians in neutralizing some harsh and hurting implications of Iran sanctions.[27] As a truly international venue for conducting free trade, Hong Kong was used by mainland China for certain subterranean trade with Iran even before its ultimate sovereignty was handed over to Beijing in 1997. Turning the gigantic commercial hub into a "white glove" of sorts, China managed to use the port city for shipping to Tehran some cargoes of sensitive materials which could be exploited for Iran's chemical and nuclear programs.[28] That was why from the 1990s through 2020, the United States and some other European nations such as Britain charged many Hong Kong-based businesses and individuals for their sanctions-busting practices beneficial to Iranians. As a case in point, in 2020 the United States put sanctions on several companies in Hong Kong, accusing them of "falsifying documents and engaging in other deceptive practices" basically to facilitate transactions with the Islamic Republic of Iran Shipping Lines (IRISL) and its subsidiaries. Some of those businesses had also strong connections to the mainland, but the allegations against them were mostly about helping the sanctioned-IRISL and its ships to berth at Hong Kong ports even if the Iranian vessels had engaged in no illegal trade using the port city as a conduit.[29]

THE SHADOWY MAFIA: "SMUGGLING BROTHERS" ARE IN CHARGE

Sanctions-busting initiatives and measures were not to meet various requirements of the Iranian citizenry alone; serving some special interests was also a critical part of the practice. In fact, the establishment of the Islamic Republic quickly led to the formation of a number of conglomerates which managed overtime to reportedly dominate some 50 percent of the country's economy. Currently, Iran's private sector is greatly affected by the power and influence of these economic giants because they are well-connected with strong lobbies in every major political and security organ of the Islamic Republic.[30] Besides these semi-governmental monopolies, some key institutions of the Islamic Republic, particularly the IRGC, opted to engage in many economic activates as soon as the Iran–Iraq War of 1980–1988 ended. Coupled with other special interests, these new economic players and resourceful groups were destined to dominate a lot of commercial dealings in both the public and private sectors. Their enormous vested interests, moreover, dragged them increasingly into sanctions-busting practices almost in every legal and illegal method, including smuggling.

Basically, it was the former President, Mahmoud Ahmadinejad, who was the first top official of the Islamic Republic to talk about some illegal imports of foreign products by those powerful economic forces that were not accountable to the government in any way. During a speech given at a national conference in July 2011, Ahmadinejad singled them out by using the term "smuggling brothers," signifying their deep involvement in circumventing sanctions through their own rather peculiar devices.[31] In December 2017, additionally, the Islamic Republic's chief prosecutor dropped the bombshell by telling reporters that some officials as well as their children and relatives were involved in smuggling.[32] Such entrenched economic practices were to be certainly facilitated by their political and security connections, giving them a strong say in Iran's domestic and foreign affairs. That was then no coincidence why the former Foreign Minister, Mohammad Javad Zarif, in a leaked recording in April 2021 criticized, albeit mildly, their corrosive impacts on Iranian foreign and diplomatic practices.[33]

As another evidence, part of that conflict of interests in Iran's politico-economic affairs surfaced in 2016 when the government of Hasan Rouhani signed a deal with the ROK involving the building of ten new ships by Koreans for the Middle Eastern country. As soon as the news about the agreement was reported by the press, certain forces affiliated with the IRGC questioned the government's economic rationale behind offering the ship deal to South Korea, asserting that Iran possessed sufficient expertise and materials to produce those ships domestically (i.e. by some companies essentially owned by the IRGC). Almost all conservative media outlets also echoed the same argument, urging the government to cancel the deal with South Korea and give it to Iran's own companies.[34] After several days of such railing complaints and criticisms, the Vice-President, Eshaq Jahangiri, turned down such requests by announcing that the ship deal was basically for 2008 when the conservative government of Ahmadinejad paid more than 25 percent of the whole value of the agreement but the ensuing sanctions had made it impossible for Iran to clear the rest of the payment.[35]

Of course, if the deal had been about another Korean product which the IRGC-related companies could not produce themselves, they would not have raised any objection to it.[36] That was why Ahmadinejad's "smuggling brothers" got heavily involved in the bankable business of importing various types of foreign goods manufactured by South Korea and other Eastern and Western countries. They simply enjoyed their own special docks not controlled systematically by Iran's customs and mostly located in the country's southern ports, enabling them to bring in, often quietly and illegally, a whole array of foreign products from Dubai and other places in the Persian Gulf. But their sanctions-busting activities could go beyond such rather easy practices, involving some more intricate arrangements in close cooperation with their foreign collaborators. As a case in point, in 2014 a number of media outlets in the West reported that, based on some Western intelligence agencies, certain international financial transactions by the IRGC's Quds Force had been facilitated by China's financial institutions, though the Chinese foreign ministry repudiated such allegations frantically.[37]

Retaliating Trade War: A Role for "The Economic Paramilitary"

In July 2018, Iran's Oil Minister, Bijan Namdar Zanganeh, applied the term "trade war" to refer to the American sanctions measures against Tehran, indicating implicitly that it was justifiable for his country to use all resources at its disposal to fight back those US-led international penalties and restrictions.[38] The Islamic Republic had already embraced this approach when it had to deal with Saddam Hussein during the Iran–Iraq War of 1980–1988 when Iran had to rush into arms trade with the communist regimes of North Korea and China regardless of all ideological differences between Tehran and the political systems of Pyongyang and Beijing.[39] In the same way that fighting a shooting war could lead to destruction of some people and triumph of others, sanctions-busting struggles would have a lot of potentials to further impoverish some groups while smoothing the way for the rise of some nouveaux riches who played a part in dodging sanctions. This small coterie of hand-picked individuals, who could end up becoming some terrific tycoons or legendry criminals, may not have originally any political and ideological commonalities with the ruling elites, but they are still recruited for their perceived talent and competence in helping those elites bypass sanctions and muddle through.[40]

At least that was what happened in the second term of the Ahmadinejad presidency during which his government's sanctions-busting policies gave birth to the rise of two previously unknown figures both of whom came under criminal investigations. The first was a businessman named Reza Zarrab whose key role in the so-called gas-for-gold scheme between Iran and Turkey resulted in bilateral deals worth roughly $10 billion involving the two Middle Eastern countries in 2012 alone.[41] The second was Babak Zanjani, known in Iran as "the economic paramilitary" (*basiji eghtesadi* in Persian), who was hired by the Ahmadinejad government to skirt the American sanctions related to the sale of Iranian crude oil. Compared to Reza Zarrab's case, the sanctions-busting saga of Babak Zanja turned out to be far more complex and became the subject of hot public debates and court hearings for many years. His endeavors also entailed several countries, most of which were located in the greater Asian continent, and some of what he and his associates did in practice may remain shrouded in secrecy permanently.[42]

In order to help the Iranian government export more cargoes of its sanctioned oil, Babak Zanjani had basically taken advantage of a network of more than 60 businesses registered in the UAE, Turkey, and Malaysia. To sell more crude oil, he had managed to conceal the source of Iranian oil, making it possible to broker some 24 million barrels of oil to customers in India, Malaysia, Singapore, etc. Throughout the process, Zanjani could actually make a whopping $17.5 billion a bulk of which had been handed over to the CBI, the oil ministry, and IRGC. So far so good, but the problem was that some of the oil money which he had earned had not returned to Iran and had allegedly been misused by Zanjani himself. After being arrested, Babak Zanjani, who had been pitchforked from a humble seller of sheepskins into a high status of tycoon, was charged with the embezzlement of billions of dollars gained by the sale of Iranian crude oil.[43] For all his contradictory statements given in defense of his sanctions-busting practices, during a court hearing in June 2017 Zanjani claimed surprisingly that he still got 22 billion euros withheld in a bank in Tokyo.[44]

When Pain Is the Point, Porters Pull In

Compounded by sanctions, informal economy (also known as underground economy or black market) has long been a drain on Iran's economic system and its proper function. Real statistics are almost impossible to come by, but it is widely estimated that informal economy accounts for roughly one-third of the Iranian economy. For all its peculiar characteristics and role in busting sanctions, smuggling has become the building block of Iran's informal economy over the past several decades.[45] In December 2016, Vice-President, Eshaq Jahangiri, warned that "no country engaged in smuggling more than Iran," acknowledging the dire situation of this ruinous economic phenomenon.[46] More important, smuggling is not only about illegal imports of foreign products into Iranian markets; it does include exports as well.[47] Smuggling gasoline to Iran's neighboring countries, for instance, has been a professional business of many people for years, if not decades, because gasoline prices in those countries are much higher than Iran, enabling those people to make a living by smuggling their own country's heavily subsidized gasoline. Smuggling Iran's fertile soil to the Arab sheikhdoms of the Persian Gulf has also been another problem, though this type of smuggling has often received little national attention and scrutiny in comparison to what imports smugglers have been doing for decades.[48]

Generally, more than $20 billion bankable market of imports smuggling in Iran has been run by three groups. The first group, which pretty much epitomizes what Ahmadinejad called "smuggling brothers," has been the dominant player with strong security and legal protection. The second group includes many political and economic families as well as trusted individuals with special connections to the sinews of power and wealth in the Islamic Republic. They are the very people who can get the subsidized foreign currency from the government, import luxurious goods and products, and then bask in huge profits upon selling their imported stuff to Iranian customers at the market price of up to ten-fold higher.[49] Among this group, moreover, there happened to be some government officials and top bureaucrats who could take advantage of their position and import a lot of expensive Porsche and Maserati cars by the subsidized dollars which had originally been allocated for importing medicines for cancer patients.[50] For obvious reasons, any set of new stringent international sanctions and the subsequent drought of famous Western and Eastern brands and products from Iranian markets were essentially a gift from heaven for this fortunate group of well-connected smugglers.[51]

The third group, however, differs from the other two groups in many ways. A majority of the people in this group are often ordinary citizens who often choose smuggling as a temporary profession in order to make ends meet. They belong to the pool of the disadvantaged and innocent Iranians who have borne the brunt of sanctions and international limitations levied against their country for several decades. The people active in this group are better known as porters, but they also include individuals and families that may smuggle foreign goods by motor ferry and other means instead of carrying them on their back as porters normally do.[52] What porters often bring in from the neighboring countries are consumption goods and other less expensive items such as foods, cigarettes, home appliances, textiles, shoes, etc. While porters may profit from smuggling in the wake of escaping the government's tariffs and some other fees, they are, unlike the other two groups, very susceptible and often the first target of the state's occasional crackdown on smuggling and illegal imports of foreign goods.[53]

Notes

1. Carswell; and Christopher C. Joyner, "United Nations Sanctions after Iraq: Looking Back to See Ahead," *Chicago Journal of International Law*, Vol. 4, No. 2 (2003), pp. 329–332.
2. "Mohammad Javad Zarif: Doctorai dourzadan tahrimha ra darim" [Mohammad Javad Zarif: We Have Doctorate in Bypassing Sanctions], *Ebtekar News*, April 27, 2019, p. 1.
3. David S. Cohen and Zachary K. Goldman, "Like it or Not, Unilateral Sanctions Are Here to Stay," *AJIL Unbound*, Vol. 113 (April 2019), pp. 146–151.
4. "Yek rah khoob baray doorzadan tahrim!" [A Good Way for Bypassing Sanctions!], *7 Sobh*, February 15, 2020, p. 1.
5. "Rais bank markazi elam kard: 15 darsad hazineh tejarat khareji dar jib kaseban tahrim" [Governor of Central Bank Announced: 15 Percent of the Cost of Foreign Trade Go to the Pocket of Sanctions Middlemen], *Iran*, September 14, 2016, p. 5.
6. "Abbas Akhondi: 400 milyard dollar kharj 'doorzadan tahrimha' kardim" [Abbas Akhondi: We Spent $400 Billion on 'Bypassing Sanctions'], *Asr Iran*, April 22, 2021.
7. "Geroukeshi baray feroosh naft Iran" [Blackmailing for Selling Iran Oil], *Shargh Daily*, August 9, 2018, p. 5.
8. "Swift ra kheili geran dourmizadim" [We were Bypassing Swift at a High Cost], *Taadol Newspaper*, December 5, 2015, p. 1.
9. "Fasad be yeki az elzamat faaliyat tejari tabdil shod east: Iran; dargir ebtezal eghtesadi!" [Corruption Has Become an Imperative of Trading Activity: Iran; Stuck in Economic Sleaze!], *Abrar-e Eghtesadi*, July 12, 2018, p. 1; "Tahrimha behtarin bahane baray ekhtelas va rant" [Sanctions Best Excuse for Embezzlement and Rent], *Aftab-e Eghtesadi*, March 12, 2019, p. 1; and "Rant va fesad be esme dourzadan tahrimha" [Rent and Corruption in the Name of Bypassing Sanctions], *Eghtesad-e Pooya*, April 4, 2021, p. 2.
10. "Rais jomhoor: Be bahane tahrim gharat kardand" [President: They Plundered by Excusing Sanctions], *Shargh Daily*, February 14, 2016.
11. Bruce Cumings, "Rapprochement in Postwar History: Implications for North Korea," in Kyung-Ae Park, ed., *New Challenges of North Korean Foreign Policy* (New York: Palgrave Macmillan, 2010), pp. 205–222.
12. "Naftkeshhay irani tahrim ra dour mizanand" [Iranian Oil Tankers Bypass Sanctions], *Forsat Emrooz*, October 13, 2018, p. 3.
13. Richard L. Kilpatrick, Jr., "North Korea's Sanctions-Busting Maritime Practices: Implications for Commercial Shipping," *Chinese (Taiwan) Yearbook of International Law and Affairs*, Vol. 37 (2019), pp. 199–220.

14. "Iran doesn't Expect Oil Customers—Including Japan—to Get Sanctions Waivers," *The Japan Times*, June 23, 2018; and "Froosh makhfi naft" [Secret Sale of Oil], *Shargh Daily*, May 25, 2019, p. 1.

15. "China Sweats Iran Trade Ties," *Global Times*, September 30, 2009; "China Supplying Gasoline to Iran: Report," *Global Times*, September 24, 2009; and "Hajm bisabeghei az naft Iran be Dalian chin raft" [Unprecedented Volume of Iran Oil Went to China's Dalian], *Mostaghel Newspaper*, October 21, 2018, p. 5.

16. "Washington Warns Hong Kong to Watch for Vessel Carrying Iranian Oil," *CNBC*, May 29, 2019; "Tokyo; dariche mozakere va goshayesh eghtesadi" [Tokyo; Window to Negotiation and Economic Breath], *Hamshahri*, December 14, 2019, pp. 1, 4; and "Vietnam Laments U.S. Decision to Sanction Firm over Iran Trade," *Tehran Times*, December 18, 2020.

17. "Chin 8 million boshke naft Iran ra bedoon sabt dar gomrok kharid" [China Purchased 8 Million Barrels of Iran Oil without Customs Registration], *Servat News*, August 5, 2020, p. 5.

18. "Safir kore: Pool sefarat r aba ghachagh be Iran miavarim" [Korean Ambassador: We Bring to Iran Our Embassy Money through Smuggling], *Tabnak*, July 11, 2016.

19. "Mahane 2 milyard dollar kala va arz ghachagh mishavd" [$2 Billion Goods and Currency Smuggled Every Month], *Javan*, September 10, 2016, p. 12; and "Ghabl of barjam dollarha ba ghaterhay 25 milyoni vared keshvar mishod!" [Before JCPOA Dollars were Entered the Country by Mules Valued 25 Million Toomans], *Aftab-e Yazd*, February 5, 2017, p. 1.

20. "Jabye syah bank markazi Ahmadinejad: Ba ghayegh dollar miavardam" [Ahmadinejad's Black Box of Central Bank: I Was Bringing Dollar with Motor Ferry], *Arman Daily*, September 23, 2017, p. 1; and "Ba ghayegh motori az khalij fars pool miavardim!" [We Brought Money from the Persian Gulf by Motor Ferry!], *Aftab-e Yazd*, September 23, 2017, p. 15.

21. Salisbury and Lowrie; and Taylor.

22. Shehadi.

23. "Sanctions-busting is in Dubai's DNA," *The Guardian*, April 20, 2010.

24. "Iran Smuggles $1 Billion in Cash through Dubai, Turkey to Dodge Sanctions," *The Japan Times*, February 26, 2015; and "Moaven avval rais-jomhoor: Dolat ghabl 23 milyard dollar be Dubai va Istanbul bord" [First Vice-President: Previous Government Took $23 billion to Dubai and Istanbul], *Arman Daily*, August 31, 2016, p. 1.

25. "Sony: Sanctioned Iran Firms Got Gear It Sold Via Dubai," *The Japan Times*, June 29, 2013.

26. A foreign company could export its products to Iraq, and then those goods were to be re-exported to Iran. But Iraqis had to pay for those goods first

212 S. AZAD

before shipping them to Iran for their debts to Iranians incurred for importing electricity and other goods from Iran. This bartering system was a relatively convenient method to evade sanctions, while the two neighboring countries could settle some of their financial matters caused by the impossibility of doing international financial transactions between Iran and other nations. "Chin va torkye tahrimhay Iran ra ejra nemikonand" [China and Turkey not Implementing Iran Sanctions], *Javan*, July 30, 2018, p. 15; "Varedat vasetei kala az aragh" [Importing Intermediary Goods from Iraq], *Aftab-e Yazd*, September 16, 2020, p. 5; and "US Regulators Accuse Singapore Energy Trader of Iran Sanctions Breach," *Global Trade Review (GTR)*, November 4, 2020.

27. "Naghsh asiaiha dar kahesh asarbakhshi tahrim nafti" [Role of Asians in Cooling the Effectiveness of Oil Sanctions], *Tejarat News*, June 3, 2018, p. 1.

28. "China 'a Conduit' for Iran's Nuclear Programme," *South China Morning Post*, February 16, 2013; and Simon Shen, "Hong Kong–Middle East Relations: Chinese Diplomacy and Urban Development," *Israel Journal of Foreign Affairs*, Vol. 9, No. 2 (2015), pp. 253–266.

29. "Various Hong Kong Companies Caught Up in Iran Sanctions," *Hong Kong Trade Development Council (HKTDC)*, October 27, 2020.

30. "Nesf eghtesad keshvar dar ekhtiyar yazdah ghoul eghtesadi ast" [11 Economic Giants Control Half of the Country's Economy], *Tabnak*, May 8, 2019.

31. "Baradaran ghachaghchi" [Smuggling Brothers], *Radio Farda*, July 7, 2011.

32. "Dadsetan kol keshvar: Barkhi maghamat dar ghachagh sahm darand" [Iran Chief Prosecutor: Some Officials are Involved in Smuggling], *Jame-e Farda*, December 19, 2017, p. 1; and "Dadsetan kol keshvar: Barkhi maghamat va aghazadeha dar ghachagh sahimand" [Top Prosecutor: Some Officials and Children of Officials are Involved in Smuggling], *Bahar Daily*, December 19, 2017, p. 2.

33. "Iran's Foreign Minister, in Leaked Tape, Says Revolutionary Guards Set Policies," *The New York Times*, April 25, 2021; and "In Leaked Recording, Iran's Zarif Criticises Guards' Influence in Diplomacy," *Reuters*, April 26, 2021.

34. "Sakht 10 farvand keshti: Khodeman mitavanim, be koreiha nadahid" [Building 10 Ships: We Ourselves can Make it, Do not Give it to Koreans], *Kayhan*, December 12, 2016, p. 1; and "Rais jomhoor gharardad kharid kashti az kore ra laghvkonad" [President Should Cancel the Deal for Purchasing Ships from Korea], *Javan*, December 12, 2016, p. 12.

35. "'Hyundai' baray Iran 10 keshti va 6 tanker misazad: Gharardad bisabeghe ba ghool kashtisazi jahan" ['Hyundai' Builds 10 Ships and 6 Tankers for

Iran: Unprecedented Contract with the World's Shipbuilding Giant], *Iran*, December 10, 2016, p. 1; and "Posht pardeh gharardad Iran ba kashtisaz korei" [Background of Iran's Deal with Korean Shipbuilder], *Hamshahri*, December 13, 2016, pp. 1, 4.

36. "Gharardad kharid 10 keshti korei hezar milyard tooman pool beitolmal ra bebaddad" [Contract for Buying 10 Korean Ships Squandered 1,000 Billion Toomans of Public Funds], *Resalat*, January 28, 2017, p. 4.

37. "Chin hamkari mali ba sepah Quds ra takzib kard" [China Denied Financial Cooperation with Quds Force], *Tabnak*, November 18, 2014.

38. "In yek jang tejari ast" [This is a Trade War], *Etemad Daily*, July 8, 2018, p. 1.

39. "Ebraz rezayat majlis az moravedat miyan Iran va kore shomali" [Parliament Pleased with Iran–North Korea Interactions], *Aftab-e Yazd*, September 9, 2020, p. 5.

40. Jones, p. 45.

41. For more details on this case, see: "Iran's Turkish Gold Rush," *Foreign Policy*, December 26, 2013.

42. In March 2021, Vice-President Eshaq Jahangiri boasted that the government of Hasan Rouhani, unlike his predecessor, could also sell oil under American sanctions "without creating people like Babak Zanjani." "Bedoon dorostkardan Babak Zanjaniha va hadardadan yek dollar, naft ham frookhtim" [We also Sold Oil without Creating People like Babak Zanjani and Wasting a Single Dollar], *Iran*, March 7, 2021, p. 6.

43. "To This Tycoon, Iran Sanctions Were Like Gold," *The New York Times*, October 4, 2013.

44. "Eddeai jadid Babak Zanjani: Poolha dar Tokyo bank ast!" [Babak Zanjani's New Claim: Money are in Tokyo Bank!], *Kelid Newspaper*, June 19, 2017, p. 1.

45. "27.6 darsad eghtesad Iran gheirrasmi ast" [27.6 Percent of Iran Economy is Informal], *Tabnak*, November 8, 2015; "Eghtesad keshvar gereftar kalay ghachagh" [Iran Economy Grappling with Smuggled Goods], *Hemayat*, February 8, 2017, p. 16; and "60 darsad eghtesad Iran zirzamini edare mishavad" [60 Percent of Iran Economy Managed Underground], *Arman Daily*, May 28, 2018, p. 1.

46. "Hich keshvari be andaze Iran dargir ghachagh kala nist" [No Country Engaged in Smuggling More than Iran], *Shahrvand*, December 11, 2016, p. 1.

47. "Saderat peste dar dast mafia" [Pistachio Exports in the Hands of Mafia], *Jahan-e Sanat*, October 17, 2017, pp. 1, 12.

48. "Khak Iran hamchenan ghachagh mishavad" [Smuggling of Iran Soil Continues], *Jahan-e Sanat*, December 16, 2018, p. 12; and "Ghachagh khak" [Smuggling Soil], *Akhbar-e Sanat*, December 18, 2018, p. 1.

214   S. AZAD

49. "Manategh azad behtarin makan baray ghachagh kala va varedat biraviyeh ast" [Free Trade Zones Best Place for Smuggling Goods and Unwarranted Imports], *Kayhan*, October 31, 2017, p. 1; and "Chera afrad khassi emzai talai varedat darand?" [Why Certain Individuals Got Golden Signature of Imports?], *Farhikhtegan Daily*, April 19, 2018, p. 10.

50. "Mikhastand 75 keshti 'khodro va kalay lux' ra be esm daroo vared konand" [They Wanted to Enter 75 Ships of 'Cars and Luxurious Goods' in the Name of Drugs], *Tasnim News Agency*, August 3, 2013; and "Joziat jadid az varedat khodro ba arz daroo" [New Details about Importing Cars with Drugs Money], *Tabnak*, October 13, 2015.

51. "Tahrimha mafiay eghtesadi ra gostaresh dad" [Sanctions Expanded the Economic Mafia], *Tabnak*, April 6, 2015; and "Lobby ghavi ghachagh-chian" [The Strong Lobby of Smugglers], *Jahan-e Sanat*, July 25, 2016, p. 12.

52. "Bazaar shesh milyard dollari" [The $6 Billion Dollar Market], *7 Sobh*, June 19, 2016, p. 1; and "5 miliard dollar ghachagh kala dar tahlenjiha" [$5 Billion Smuggled Goods in Vessels], *Kasbokar News*, December 26, 2016, pp. 1, 8.

53. "Payan empratoori mobilhay ghachagh dar Iran" [The Empire of Smuggled Mobiles in Iran Over], *Kar va Kargar*, July 24, 2016, p. 16; "Faaliyat koolbaran ghanooni mishavad" [Activity of Porters to be Legalized], *Iran*, December 22, 2019, p. 1; and "Payan froosh lavazem khanegi ghachagh va taghallobi" [Sale of Selling Smuggled and Fake Home Appliances Over], *Iran*, February 16, 2020, p. 8.

CHAPTER 13

The West and the East on the Lookout: Tracking a Tangled Web of Sanctions-Busting

PERPETUALLY OBSESSED: THE UNITED STATES MONITORS THE WHOLE WORLD

Although sanctions scholars differ significantly with regard to the issue of sanctions effectiveness, they rather unanimously agree that implementing sanctions poses a whole array of challenges. The first major challenge starts with the sender or the nation which carves out sanctions against another sovereign country. Besides the problem of convincing its own citizens and businesses to abide by what those sanctions require in practice, the sender or the coercer needs sustainable political will and sufficient recourses to push perpetually for what its sanctions intend to achieve.[1] The second big challenge is related to other important international players whose understanding and cooperation would be instrumental to sanctions implementation. The sender's extraterritorial sanctions or secondary sanctions are certainly bound to interfere with political sovereignty and legal jurisdiction of other countries. Apart from a humongous task of persuading those nations to give up a lot of economic benefits and material rewards for the sake of sanctions success, moreover, the sender has to ineluctably present enough justifications when it fines their companies and imprisons their citizens for sanctions violations.[2]

Iran sanctions, therefore, entailed all those challenges for the United States. More important, Iran's own characteristics as well as the tangled skein of sundry Iran sanctions made their implementation far more

© The Author(s), under exclusive license to Springer Nature
Switzerland AG 2022
S. Azad, *East Asia and Iran Sanctions*,
https://doi.org/10.1007/978-3-030-97427-5_13

215

difficult. Unlike other sanctioned countries such as Cuba and North Korea, Iran happened to be a relatively giant landmass surrounded by 13 sovereign countries, both on land and sea, in addition to all benefits which the Middle Eastern country could get from its easy and permanent access to the Persian Gulf and the Caspian Sea. As a rather wealthy and resource-rich country, Iran's endowment with copious natural assets and geological advantageous made it less vulnerable in some areas. Iran also engaged in substantial commercial interactions with a vast throng of nations located in all the five continents, enabling it to diversify its trading partners and pivot from one region to another if circumstances required it to do so. On top of that, a fair number of Iran's international partners, including some great powers, were adamantly committed in maintaining their connections to the Mideast country primarily because of its political importance and strategic weight, providing Tehran with help and assistance while making the United States more frustrated in achieving its sanctions objectives.[3]

Meanwhile, the United States was partly responsible for complicating the implementation of the sanctions which it levied against Iranians over a course of more than four decades. It devised and issued different sets of sanctions targeting Iran under different pretexts, ranging from hostage taking to terrorism and from human rights violations to nonproliferation. Not only all those sanctions and penalties required myriad regulations and policy guidelines to carry through, Washington was hardly ever clear-cut about its ultimate goal of Iran sanctions. Different American administrations and political parties in Washington, moreover, sometimes demonstrated rather contradictory policy behaviors toward the Middle Eastern country, creating a lot of troubles for many other nations' Iran direction and their compliance with sanctions.[4] On some issues, for instance, a Republican-dominated US Congress often followed an uncompromising and unilateral American approach and thereby tied the hands of a sitting Democrat president who essentially favored diplomacy and multilateralism in dealing with Iran and its relevant sanctions.

Implementing sanctions against Iran was, therefore, a Herculean business for the United States, requiring a large bundle of resources and significant coordination both internally and externally. In terms of domestic imperative, the job of interpreting and enforcing an encyclopedia of Iran sanctions involved many top American institutions, including the Department of Commerce, the Department of the Treasury, the Department of State, the Department of Defense or the Pentagon, the Department of Justice, the Central Intelligence Agency (CIA), the Federal Bureau of Investigation (FBI), etc.[5] Internationally, the United States simply needed to monitor the entire planet nonstop in order to make sure

13 THE WEST AND THE EAST ON THE LOOKOUT: TRACKING A TANGLED... 217

that Iranians themselves or any company and individual from other country did not violate sanctions. This elephantine and costly task required Americans to oversee incessantly what was really happening on the ground, on the high seas and oceans, in the skies, and on the cyberspace.[6] At the same time, Washington also had to resort to diplomacy and sometimes arm-twisting to force compliance among Iran's regional and international partners some of which were often hard to persuade and keep committed to the sanctions regimes in the long run.[7]

RELUCTANT TEAMMATES: EAST ASIAN STATES TOE THE LINE

After Europe, East Asia was perhaps the second most important regions in the world where the United States had to often use lots of political and economic pressures to buy the East Asian countries' acquiescence to its demands concerning Iran sanctions. Besides Taiwan as the most compliant and North Korea as the most disobedient players with regard to what Washington expected, other countries in the region normally required significant diplomacy laced with occasional threats to eventually submit to the diktats of the mostly US-devised sanctions against Iranians. The process of seeking compliance among East Asian states was hardly smooth as their ultimate yielding or resistance to some sanctions requests made by the United States sometimes greatly hinged on changing domestic and international factors. During the last decade of the Cold War, for instance, forcing China to comply with Iran sanctions proved to be problematic as compared to the time when American supremacy and unilateralism in international politics seemed to be the order of the day.

Out of the three big players in East Asia, Japan and South Korea were not very difficult to handle, though both countries were at times employing all means of horse-trading to maximize their benefits before giving up their sovereign rights of getting closer to Iran politically and economically in favor of the United States. Oil imports and exports markets were definitely the two most important issues related to Iran which always made Japan and the ROK very anxious whenever Washington asked them to get along with a new round of economic and financial sanctions against Tehran. Tokyo and Seoul had to be then assured that they could get as much as crude oil they required, while their economic loss from Iranian markets was to be partially made up through having more access to American and other Western markets. North Korea was also a hobbyhorse which the United States could bring up almost every time in order to

218   S. AZAD

persuade Japan and South Korea to comply with Iran sanctions in exchange for Washington's more punitive political and economic measures against the DPRK.

Unlike Japan and the ROK, however, China was expectedly and understandably a much tougher nut to crack. It was also among the few major world players which used to raise its voice publicly against Washington's Iran policies, including sanctions. China's stakes in Iran were certainly much more than only energy and markets because political and strategic factors were a driving force behind Beijing's policy toward Tehran as well. For all its political rhetoric and serious reservations with regard to Iran sanctions, however, China was still prepared to kowtow to Washington's demands most of the time when Beijing could manage to score a point concerning its simmering bilateral troubles with the United States. Since the mid-1990s onward, moreover, Americans made significant progress in terms of convincing China to fundamentally limit, if not abandon in total, its nuclear and missile cooperation with Iran. In the area of technology transfer to Iran, incessant US pressures obliged China to set up its own formal system of export control which was to regulate the scope and size of Beijing's technological cooperation with Iran, and the rest of the world in general.

Meanwhile, the deference of all East Asian countries, excluding North Korea, to persistent American advocacy for exerting sanctions against Iran had a lot to do with a number of other critical matters. The first important issue was East Asia's overdependence on the United States for exports markets and technology. In fact, the region's export-oriented industrialization and economic growth policies had little chance to succeed and thrive without benefiting greatly from huge US markets. In the same way, East Asian corporations and laboratories, including those located in Japan, had to always rely on importing American technologies to preserve their own international competitive edge. The more an East Asian company was at the mercy of Americans for market and technology, therefore, the more sway the United States enjoyed in prevailing over that business not to cooperate with Iranians. Even the threat of being excluded from American markets and technological ties was sometimes enough to persuade an East Asian corporation to relinquish all of its Iran interests.

The second critical issue was about East Asia's similarly large reliance on the US dollar, making businesses, especially banks and financial institutions, in the region more vulnerable to the threat of exclusion from the American banking system for sanctions violations. Although East Asian countries have recently tapped into local currencies for conducting some of their international commercial interactions with countries other than the United States, they are still doing a bulk of their extra regional trade, including crude oil imports, in the powerful American currency. Unlike the EU, the region also lacks a single common currency, leaving East Asian businesses and citizens with little option but to generally treat the US dollar as their most favorable foreign currency. All of these factors simply added to the so-called exorbitant privilege of the United States for its dollar supremacy in East Asia and beyond, making it very vital for the region's banks and financial corporations to maintain their nonstop connections to the American financial system in every possible way and refrain from any wrongdoing which may disrupt, even temporarily, such indispensable linkage.[8]

The third but not least important element was huge fines and punishments which the United States was prepared to mete out against East Asian businesses and individuals if they opted to defy some rules and regulations regarding Iran sanctions. Over the past several decades, a rather large number of court rulings across the United States exacted heavy financial penalties on many East Asian companies, including some top Japanese corporations and banks, for breaching some parts of Iran-related sanctions whether or not their acts were legal in their own home country. Likewise, many East Asian citizens, some of whom with a dual nationality, came under criminal investigations and punished severely by the American justice system because they had helped Iranians, either directly or indirectly, to evade sanctions. When the US sanctions diktats hanged over East Asian businesses and citizens like "the sword of Damocles," fewer companies and individuals from the region had the guts to face draconian American penalties and jail terms for ignoring what Iran sanctions stipulated clearly.

SLAPPED WITH HEFTY FINES: DISOBEDIENT COMPANIES PAY BACK

Over the past decade, most of the businesses which the United States sanctioned and fined for breaching Iran sanctions were active in banking and energy sectors. Washington also showed little leniency in punishing those companies regardless of their national affiliation. It seemed that some unruly Western banks and corporations got higher fines in comparison to the way the uncompliant Eastern businesses were treated. In late 2009, for instance, Credit Suisse, a Swiss bank, was fined $536 million for illegal banking transactions involving Iran and some other sanctioned countries. Later, Standard Chartered, a British bank, had to pay a $340 million fine for colluding with Iran by hiding from American banking regulators "60,000 transactions worth $250 billion" during a period of roughly one decade, while France's largest bank, BNP Paribas, reached a whopping $9 billion settlement because of ignoring financial sanctions against Iran, Cuba, and Sudan between 2004 and 2012.[9] A number of other European financial institutions, including HSBC and Commerzbank, also received handsome fines for facilitating international financial transactions with Iranian banks.[10]

Regarding East Asia, perhaps the most high-profile banking case involved one of Japan's top financial institutions, Bank of Tokyo-Mitsubishi UFJ. In June 2013, the Japanese bank agreed to pay $250 million to the state of New York for breaching Iran sanctions. The bank had been charged with handling 28,000 transactions worth around $100 billion by withholding some essential information which could identify the name of countries or individuals involved in the financial transactions.[11] Exactly one year earlier, moreover, the United States had sanctioned Bank of Kunlun which was partly owned by China National Petroleum Corporation. Accusing the Chinese bank of facilitating financial services for at least six Iranian banks, the United States was not able to fine Bank of Kunlun because it had little, if any, financial interactions with the American banking system.[12] Despite being sanctioned by Washington, the Chinese bank continued its business with Iran and played an instrumental role in sorting out various financial matters involving Sino–Iranian oil trade.

Beyond the peculiar world of banks and financial institutions, however, most of the Asian businesses which were sanctioned by the United States had something to do with oil trade or transportation. A big number of the sanctioned cases also took place in the final year of Trump's one-term presidency when his administration imposed sanctions incessantly on many Asian companies, especially those based in Hong Kong and China, for smoothing the way for Iran to bypass sanctions in energy and shipping sectors.[13] In January 2020, for instance, the Hong Kong-based Triliance Petrochemical was sanctioned for its role in selling Iranian crude oil and petrochemical products.[14] In September, the US Department of State also moved to punish several other companies which had facilitated Triliance's energy trade with Iran, including China-based Zhihang Ship Management,

New Far International Logistics LLC, and Sino Energy Shipping in addition to Hong Kong-based Jingho Technology Co. Limited, Dinrin Limited, and Dynapex Energy Limited. According to what Washington claimed then, part of that oil trade had been possible through some UAE-based companies all of which came under US sanctions too.[15]

In the same way, in December 2020 the Trump administration sanctioned four other companies, charging them with the sale of Iranian petrochemicals, including China-based Donghai International Ship Management Limited and Petrochem South East Limited as well as UAE-based Alpha Tech Trading FZE and Petroliance Trading FZE.[16] Vietnam Gas and Chemicals Transportation Corporation was also penalized for its role in facilitating the sale of Iran's petrochemical products.[17] Pretty similar to the energy sector, most of the transportation companies which came under US sanctions happened to be based in China and Hong Kong. Since June 2020, Washington under Executive Order 13382 had put IRISL and its Shanghai-based subsidiary, E-Sail Shipping Company Ltd. under sanctions for their alleged "proliferation-related conduct," sanctioning any foreign business that cooperated with Iran's shipping sector. In October 2020, therefore, at least six China and Hong Kong-based businesses and some of their executives were blacklisted by the United States for their cooperation with IRISL and E-Sail Shipping Company Ltd., sending a warning message to other companies in the world not to mess with Washington by assisting Iran to circumvent sanctions.[18]

In its round-the-clock crusade against rogue businesses and individuals that got the cojones to ignore Iran sanctions, however, the United States moved against two prominent Chinese companies whose major activities had little to do with finance, energy, and transportation. At least since 2012, some powerful political circles in Washington had also regarded both famous Chinese corporations as "potential security threat," asking Americans, sometimes implicitly and sometimes explicitly, to refrain from doing any serious business with those two companies. The first company was ZTE Corp. which came under technological restrictions in March 2016 after the United States charged it with exporting US technology to Iran through establishing front businesses to dodge American supervision on high-tech transfers to the Persian Gulf country.[19] As one of the world's largest producers of network switching gear and other critical telecoms products, the Chinese electronics company was temporarily teetering on the brink of failure after the United States blackballed it from purchasing certain American components vital for ZTE's survival in the long haul.[20]

US companies were reportedly supplying some 25 to 30 percent of the components which the giant Chinese firm was using in its equipment.[21] But unlike the case of ZTE Corp., the saga surrounding the second leading Chinese company, Huawei Technologies Inc., was more colorful and dragged for several years.

The Hungry Huawei in Hot Water

On December 1, 2018, Sabrina Meng Wanzhou, Huawei's Chief Financial Officer (CFO), was arrested at Vancouver International Airport by Canadian authorities at the request of the United States. Huawei and the Chinese government soon called Meng's detention a politically motivated act and demanded her immediate release. The US government also requested for Meng's extradition to face multiple charges mostly related to the violation of Iran sanctions.[22] As a consequence of her arrest, China's relationship with Canada soon sank to a lowest ebb, making many high-profile economic and political leaders in Canada to ask for Meng's swift release in the hope of mending fences with Beijing.[23] Some of those concerned individuals, including a former prime minister, doubted whether the allegations against Huawei's top executive and a daughter of its founder, Ren Zhengfei, really amounted to a serious Canadian offense for which Ottawa had to now jeopardize its significant vested interests in China.[24] But nothing serious happened then, and the contentious legal process in Canada as well as the relevant media coverage around the world were to continue with much fanfare for several years to come.

Deep down, the Chinese telecoms corporation was charged that it had breached US and EU sanctions against Iran by setting up fraudulently a front company named Skycom. "The crux of the fraud" was that Huawei had taken advantage of its "unofficial subsidiary" to engage in business with Iran between 2009 and 2014. In the process, Huawei could sell to Iran through Skycom a great deal of prohibited US goods and technologies, including "numerous computer servers, switches and other equipment made by HP, as well as software made by other American companies." Part of such sanctioned American items had apparently ended up being exploited by Mobile Telecommunication Company of Iran.[25] To better conceal its lucrative Iran business, Huawei had also reportedly taken advantage of another Chinese company, Panda International Information Technology Co., which enjoyed close connections with Huawei for many years. As part of its sanctions-busting collusion and misleading practices,

Huawei had frequently asked Panda International to send its goods and equipment to customers in the Iranian cities of Tehran, Shiraz, and Mashhad.[26]

The Chinese executive, moreover, had been charged with bank and wire frauds related to her surreptitious business deals with the Persian Gulf country. In 2013, for example, Meng herself represented to a number of banks that Huawei and Skycom were essentially separate, making it possible to "move money out of Iran by deceiving Western banks." Both Huawei and Meng rejected such accusations too, calling them politically motivated allegations.[27] As the case of ZTE had already proved, the deliberately protracted narrative of Meng's Canadian ordeal signified how much Huawei, as a major telecommunications-equipment maker in the world, had to rely on American technology and equipment to stay on the leading edge of business. Although the United States subsequently upped the ante by attempting to convince its close Western and Eastern partners not to apply Huawei's equipment in their "next generation 5G mobile telecommunication systems," the very lengthy legal process and all the relevant ruinous reports about Huawei's business conducts certainly cautioned many companies and individuals in China and other parts of the world to think twice before moving to engage in similar sanctions-busting practices.[28]

Disgraced or Ended in Jailhouse: Insatiable Individuals Dare Sanctions Diktats

Although the detention of Meng Wanzhou in Canada was the most high-profile case of nabbing East Asian citizens who had gone around Iran sanctions, both prior and after Meng's arrest a number of other individuals from the region were singled out by the United States or by their own governments for violating Iran-related international penalties and restrictions. Most of them turned out to be isolated cases involving the acquisition and shipment of some dual-use American goods and technologies to Iran either directly or through intermediaries. The early history of such types of sanctions-busting activities goes back to the 1980s and 1990s when some profit-seeking individuals from East Asia and other regions engaged in procuring certain sought-after sensitive goods and technologies for Iranians. But after Iran's nuclear and missile programs became highly controversial internationally and the country subsequently came under stringent UN and US sanctions, the United States and most of East Asian governments showed less patience with those individuals from the region who allegedly helped the Middle Eastern country to obtain some of its prohibited technological requirements.

In most cases, however, there happened to be hardly further news about those recalcitrant individuals after they were arrested or indicted. Perhaps they were let to walk away as soon as they could convince their relevant authorities that their conduct was quite legal and in full compliance with all the rules and regulations related to trade and international shipment. In other cases, the disobedient individuals who were sanctioned by the United States were simply residing somewhere in China, and the relevant American authorities were in no position to either lock them up or slap them with fines and penalties commensurate with their sanctions-busting offences committed beyond US borders.[29] In some cases, the very act of detention or the follow-up prosecution by an East Asian government could just be for the sake of showing-off to signify that the government was actually taking the relevant international and US sanctions against Iran very seriously in addition to sending a clear message to its citizens not to make similar troubles for their country by engaging in illegal business with the Persian Gulf country.

Chronologically, one of the first cases took place in October 2007 when Taiwan arrested three people in connection with sending "controlled electronic components" to Iran based on the speculation that those shipped items could be utilized for assembling some type of unconventional weapons. The trio, named Chang Hui-chuan, Chen Chung-yu, and Tang Yu-ling all of them from C-TEK Technology Corp., had been monitored for some six months with regard to supplying "12 sets of controlled electrical discharge machining systems" to Iran through Samoa.[30] In a similar case, moreover, in February 2010, the United States arrested a Taiwanese man, named Chen Yi-lan and known as Kevin Chen, in Guam charging him with procuring for Iran some dual-use American goods, including "P200 turbine engines, MIL-S-8516 sealing compound, glass-to-metal pin seals and circular hermetic connectors." Chen had allegedly sent those apparently military items from the United States to Taiwan and Hong Kong before being shipped to somewhere in Iran.[31] Like Chen's adventurous move, a Taiwanese woman was sentenced to a two-year prison term in October 2012 by the United States for her involvement in procuring lots of dual-use American technologies for Iran. Susan Yeh had been indicted that she had taken advantage of her serial companies in Taiwan and Hong

Kong to purchase and ship to Iran a whole array of goods and parts worth more than $2.6 million in close cooperation with at least two Iranian middlemen working from Dubai and other places in the period between October 2007 and June 2011. In the process, their transactions, which included some military-grade equipment, had involved at least 63 American companies in addition to many other businesses from around the world.[32]

Another less significant case involved three Japanese people who had wired 14 million yen (around $158,000) to a Singapore-based company apparently affiliated with IRISL in November 2011 and February 2012. In January 2013, Japan nabbed those three individuals, whose identities remained unknown, for their illegal transfer of funds to the Iranian beneficiary without getting the required financial approval from the Japanese government. In September 2010, Japan had blocked assets of IRISL and its subsidiaries in lockstep with some relevant UN sanctions against Iran, and the temporary detention of those three people in early 2013 was reportedly the country's first act of such law enforcement.[33] In sharp contrast to this case, in April 2014 the US Department of Justice filed criminal charges against a Chinese citizen named Li Fangwei for his role in shipping to Iran prohibited American goods and technologies worth millions of dollars. Li had to rely on several front businesses to manage his Iran trade, requiring him to also engage in some other crimes such as bank fraud and wire fraud. Since the fugitive Chinese man was not in the United States when he was indicted, the US government had to place a bounty of $5 million to get him handcuffed anywhere in the world.[34]

Somehow similar to the case of Li Fangwei, in March 2019 the United States arrested a 29-year-old Chinese woman named Liu Yang, who was on vacation in California, for helping to ship to Iran American electronics worth more than $870,000 over a period of six years. Liu was reportedly working for a Chinese technology company, but US authorities did not reveal much information about her affiliated business or the method she had used to send American goods to Iran.[35] Next year, however, when the US Department of Justice charged Huang Chin-hua a 42-year-old Taiwanese woman for her involvement in procuring American technologies for Iran, authorities in the United States were willing to provide more information about the case still under investigation.[36] As a sales agent for two Taiwanese companies, Huang had allegedly conspired to evade Iran sanctions by purchasing American goods and technologies without revealing anything about the final destination for those procured items which included "a power amplifier designed for use in electromechanical devices and cybersecurity software." Based on the US indictment, a government-controlled Iranian company was the end user for some of the sensitive American goods which Huang and her associates in Taiwan had shipped to Iran.[37]

Notes

1. Daniel W. Drezner, "Bargaining, Enforcement and Multilateral Sanctions: When is Cooperation Counterproductive?" *International Organization*, Vol. 54, No. 1 (2000), pp. 73–102.
2. Alexander, *Economic Sanctions*, p. 51.
3. Meghan L. O'Sullivan, "Iran and the Great Sanctions Debate," *The Washington Quarterly*, Vol. 33, No. 4 (October 2010), pp. 7–21.
4. "CIA Director Skeptical of *Iran Sanctions*," *The Washington Times*, June 27, 2010.
5. Bryan R. Early, "Sleeping with Your Friends' Enemies: An Explanation of Sanctions-Busting Trade," *International Studies Quarterly*, Vol. 53, No. 1 (2009), pp. 49–71.
6. "Norway Charges Professor with Violating Sanctions on Iran," *The Washington Post*, September 30, 2021.
7. "Persuading China to Put the Screws to Iran," *The Japan Times*, December 29, 2009; "US Delegation in Seoul to Discuss Iran Sanctions," *KBS*, January 16, 2012; and "A Role for China to Rein In Iran," *The Wall Street Journal*, November 17, 2015.
8. "Asia's Hidden Exposure to Iran Sanctions," *Nikkei Asia*, June 5, 2018.
9. "Prosecutors Link Money from China to Iran," *The New York Times*, August 29, 2012; and "Sanctions Eased but Japan Inc. Treads Warily in Return to Iran," *The Japan Times*, March 16, 2016.
10. Until 2008, banks and financial institutions could engage in financial transactions with Iranian banks, but such financial interactions were then suspended after the Middle Eastern country was accused of exploiting its banks and financial institutions to provide funds for its contentious nuclear and missile programs.
11. "Mitsubishi UFJ Fined $250 Mil in U.S. for Illegal Transfers to Iran, Sudan," *Japan Today*, June 21, 2013; and "MUFG to pay $250 Million to New York over Transfers to Sanctioned States," *The Japan Times*, June 21, 2013.
12. "Treasury Sanctions Kunlun Bank in China and Elaf Bank in Iraq for Business with Designated Iranian Banks," *U.S. Department of the Treasury, Press Center*, July 31, 2012.

13. Of course, the United States had previously punished some Western companies for engaging Iran in such areas. As a case in point, in March 2015 the Western Schlumberger Oilfield Holdings Ltd. was fined $232.7 million for facilitating oil trade with Iran and Sudan. "Schlumberger Oilfield Holdings Ltd. Agrees to Plead Guilty and Pay Over $232.7 Million for Violating US Sanctions by Facilitating Trade with Iran and Sudan," *Justice News* (US Department of Justice), March 25, 2015.
14. "Chinese, Emirati Companies Sanctioned for Exporting Iran Petrochemicals," *The Standard*, December 17, 2020.
15. "US Sanctions 11 Entities for Aiding Iran's Oil Sector," *Anadolu Agency*, September 3, 2020.
16. "US Sanctions Firms in China and UAE over Iran Petrochemical Sales," *South China Morning Post*, December 17, 2020.
17. "US Sanctions Companies in UAE, China over Iranian Petrochemical Sales," *Al-Monitor*, December 16, 2020.
18. Those six companies included Reach Holding Group (Shanghai) Company Ltd., Reach Shipping Lines, Gracious Shipping Co. Ltd., Noble Shipping Co. Ltd., Supreme Shipping Co. Ltd., and Delight Shipping Co. Ltd. For more details, see: "The United States Imposes Sanctions on Chinese and Hong Kong Persons for Activities Related to Supporting the Islamic Republic of Iran Shipping Lines," *U.S. Department of State*, October 19, 2020.
19. "U.S. Slaps Sanctions on Chinese Tech Supplier over Iran Ties," *The Japan Times*, March 8, 2016.
20. After the US Department of Commerce imposed a seven-year ban on sales by American suppliers to ZTE, the Chinese giant telecoms company had to close down its main operations after a couple of weeks, compelling the Chinese President, Xi Jinping, to intervene personally by asking Donald Trump to rescind the prohibition. When the ban was subsequently reversed, ZTE still had to pay a whopping fine of $1.2 billion in addition to replacing its board members and installing an American compliance officer. "Huawei CFO Sabrina Meng Wanzhou Fraudulently Represented Company to Skirt US and EU Sanctions on Iran, Court Told in Bail Hearing," *South China Morning Post*, December 8, 2018.
21. "Huawei, China Respond to Report of Probe," *China Daily*, April 27, 2018.
22. "Huawei CFO Sabrina Meng Wanzhou, Daughter of Founder, Arrested in Canada at Request of US Government 'for Violating Iran Sanctions'," *South China Morning Post*, December 6, 2018.
23. Lanteigne, *Chinese Foreign Policy*, p. 62.
24. "Don't Cave to Beijing's Demands, Taiwanese Foreign Minister Warns Canada," *The Globe and Mail*, January 9, 2020.

228 S. AZAD

25. "Huawei Found to Have Deep Links with Shell Companies in Iran, Syria: Report," *BGR India*, January 9, 2019.
26. "New Documents Show Huawei's Role in Violating U.S. Sanctions on Iran," *The Japan Times*, March 5, 2020.
27. "Chinese Tech Executive Lied to Evade Sanctions on Iran, US Charges," *The Seattle Times*, December 7, 2018; and "UK Court Hears Arguments from Huawei and HSBC over Iran Documents," *Financial Times*, February 12, 2021.
28. On September 24, 2021, Canada let Huawei's Meng walk away and fly to China after she reportedly reached an agreement with the United States. In fact, her release was based on a politically negotiated trilateral agreement between the United States, China, and Canada. As part of the agreement, the Chinese CFO accepted some of her wrongdoings with regard to violating American sanctions on Iran, the US Justice Department accepted to defer and drop wire and bank fraud charges against Meng, and the Chinese government released two Canadian prisoners who had been arrested soon after the Huawei executive was taken into custody in December 2018. "Huawei CFO Leaves Canada after U.S. Agreement on Fraud Charges, Detained Canadians Head Home," *Reuters*, September 24, 2021; and "Huawei CFO Meng Wanzhou Reaches Deal with Justice Department," *The Wall Street Journal*, September 25, 2021.
29. In October 2020, for instance, the US Department of State imposed sanctions on China-based New Far International Logistics LLC executive, Min Shi, and Sino Energy Shipping executive, Zuoyou Lin, for their role in assisting Iran to sell its sanctioned oil. In the same way, in October 2020 Eric Chen (Chen Guoping), Chief Executive Officer of Reach Holding Group (Shanghai) Company Ltd., and Daniel Y. He (He Yi), President of Reach Holding Group (Shanghai) Company Ltd. came under US sanctions for their involvement in helping IRISL and its subsidiaries to go around sanctions. "US Sanctions 11 Entities for Aiding Iran's Oil Sector," *Anadolu Agency*, September 3, 2020, and "The United States Imposes Sanctions on Chinese and Hong Kong Persons for Activities Related to Supporting the Islamic Republic of Iran Shipping Lines," *U.S. Department of State*, October 19, 2020.
30. "Three Arrested over Exports to Iran," *Taipei Times*, October 7, 2007, p. 1.
31. "Taiwanese Faces US Smuggling Charges," *Taipei Times*, February 6, 2010, p. 1.
32. "Taiwanese Jailed in US for Illegal Exports to Iran," *Taipei Times*, October 26, 2012, p. 1.
33. "Japan Arrests Three for Iran Sanctions Violations," *Global Times*, January 24, 2013.

13 THE WEST AND THE EAST ON THE LOOKOUT: TRACKING A TANGLED... 229

34. "Li Fangwei Charged in Manhattan Federal Court with Using a Web of Front Companies to Evade U.S. Sanctions," *U.S. Department of Justice*, April 29, 2014; and "Tehran's Chinese Missile Man," *The Daily Beast*, June 9, 2014.
35. "Chinese Woman's Secret Arrest in U.S. Hints that Sanctions Probe Goes beyond Just Huawei," *The Japan Times*, May 12, 2019.
36. In addition to Huang, the United States also charged two Taiwan-based companies, DES International Co., Ltd., and its subsidiary Soltech Industry Co., Ltd. for violating Iran sanctions; an offence which could cost each firm a fine of up to $500,000, while the punishment for the unruly woman could be incarceration of up to five years and a fine of up to $250,000. "Taiwanese Woman Charged in U.S. for Violating Iran Sanctions," *Focus Taiwan*, November 11, 2020.
37. "US Charges Taiwanese, Firms over Iran Sanctions," *Taipei Times*, November 12, 2020, p. 1.

CHAPTER 14

East Asia and Iran in Retrospective and Prospective: The Staying Power of Sanctions

There have been a lot of debates in the discipline of International Relations and some other academic fields with regard to effectiveness of international sanctions. In fact, sanctions scholars widely differ on whether sanctions can eventually achieve their intended objectives. They also disagree with each other that successful sanctions are worth enormous, and mostly unfair, costs they bring about. Such clash of opinions has a lot to do with the way sanctions worked in the twentieth century when some sanctions succeeded but most of them failed or produced tragic consequences. But the era of sanctions is far from over, and the early decades of the twenty-first century marked the continuation of sanctions politics. Iran happened to be the most prominent example targeted by sanctions in both periods, but despite its significance, the Iranian experience has, by and large, remained understudied. Being under incessant international sanctions for more than four decades, therefore, Iran is perhaps the perfect case, the study of which may help sanctions scholars and many other interested observers and activists to reappraise their academic conclusions and personal views about sanctions.

Besides their immense domestic repercussions which can be the subjects of numerous studies and investigations, Iran sanctions reshaped, in fundamental ways, the Persian Gulf country's relationship with the outside world. One of such cardinal and lasting implications was the emergence of East Asian states as major stakeholders in Iranian international affairs almost from the commencement of sanctions against Iran in late

© The Author(s), under exclusive license to Springer Nature Switzerland AG 2022
S. Azad, *East Asia and Iran Sanctions*,
https://doi.org/10.1007/978-3-030-97427-5_14

231

1979. As time went by, international sanctions against the Mideast country had something to offer to every political entity located in East Asia; from industrialized Japan and South Korea to communist China and North Korea and from sandwiched Taiwan to rudderless Hong Kong all could benefit, one way or the other, by playing their expected role in a politically isolated and economically penalized Iran. At the same time, Iran had to rely, sometimes critically, on its partners in East Asia to acquire a great deal of its requirements and muddle through. As a corollary, international sanctions turned out to be truly instrumental in determining the contours of rather multifaceted relationship between Iran and East Asian players in the past as well as for the foreseeable future.

Politically, the US-led international sanctions overhauled the previous pattern of interactions between East Asian countries and Iran. The United States needed to take advantage of its Japanese and South Korean allies to further isolate the Middle Eastern country by driving a diplomatic wedge between them. Washington also required the expected "yes vote" of both East Asian countries to push ahead its incessantly drafted resolutions of sanctions against Iran at the UN, though the subsequent implementation of those sanctions equally hinged on a cooperative political will of top authorities in Tokyo and Seoul. For all their close security alliance and political coordination with the United States, however, both Japan and South Korea never severed their diplomatic and political relationship with Iran even in the heydays of their sanctions-induced collusion with Washington at the cost of Tehran. Sustainable diplomatic ties were vital for South Korea to vouchsafe its vested interests in Iran, while Japan considered political relationship more than *modus operandi* for securing its sedimented interests in the Middle Eastern country. That was no coincidence why Japanese leaders were often willing to play a mediating role between Washington and Tehran sometimes only for the sake of mitigating some painful effects of international sanctions against Iranians.

Meanwhile, sanctions gave birth to another set of political alliance-making as the politically isolated and militarily embargoed Islamic Republic rushed to befriend the communist regimes of North Korea and China in the early 1980s in spite of its visionary "neither the East, nor the West" rhetoric at home. In the following years and decades, moreover, Tehran's political relationship with Pyongyang and Beijing grew by leaps and bounds, turning both communist East Asian countries into some of close international partners of Iran to go around sanctions. In particular, China emerged over time as one of the most critical companions for the Persian

Gulf country, and cozy bilateral cooperation between the two countries was extended into other areas as the US-led West continued to heap Iran with new rounds of crippling sanctions under one pretext after another. And despite the fact that China had to occasionally side with the United States regarding Iran sanctions, its political capital and strategic weight remained relatively intact in the corridors of power in Tehran, making the rising Asian power a linchpin of Iranian foreign policy orientation toward the outside world in the long run.

Beyond the realm of diplomacy and politics, energy trade was one of the most important areas which sanctions could affect substantially. As a mainstay of the Iranian national economy, crude oil had for decades become a building block of generating foreign exchange before being targeted by a more stringent set of international sanctions. By this time, East Asian countries had also become major buyers of Iranian crude oil partly because of their growing thirst for energy resources and partly because of the sanctions levied against Tehran. International sanctions forced Iran to engage in more commercial interactions with East Asian nations, selling them more cargoes of crude oil in exchange for importing a larger volume of goods and products manufactured by East Asian companies. Apart from purchasing Iranian crude oil, moreover, East Asians, especially Chinese companies, were among few foreign investors willing to throw their capital and technology into Iran's energy projects amid its growing financial and technological troubles in the wake of sanctions.

When sanctions drew a bead on Iran's oil exports, East Asian countries turned out to be far more instrumental in the Middle Eastern country's energy trade with the outside world. For some time, China as well as Japan and South Korea could take advantage of their US-granted waivers to import significant volumes of Iranian crude oil. Even North Korea could bring in some oil from Iran through China, no matter if Taiwan had decided to forgo its waiver and give up buying Iranian oil in favor of receiving more supplies from Saudi Arabia and other oil-exporting countries in the Persian Gulf. At the same time, sanctions had forced Iran to increasingly tap into a bartering system through which it was importing manufactured products from its East Asian partners for exporting crude oil to those countries. There were also reports about supplying concessional crude oil to China long before Trump's reinstated international sanctions effectively dwindled the flow of Iranian crude exports to a trickle. From now on, Iran's problem was not only about dodging sanctions to sell more cargoes of crude oil; Tehran was simultaneously desperate to bring back its oil revenues which had already been piled up in East Asia and some other regions because of international financial sanctions.

Basically, the history of freezing Iranian assets abroad was much older, harkening back to the very 1979 when the Carter administration resorted to blocking assets of Iran as one of the first American acts to settle the so-called hostage crisis. Later, moreover, the government of Ahmadinejad moved some of the Iranian assets from Europe to China in the run-up to the UN sanctions against Tehran over its contentious nuclear program. Those Iranian euros transferred to China remained frozen after the Iranian central bank itself came under sanctions, while the nuclear-related international penalties and restrictions were to prevent Iran from bringing back its additional oil revenues for many years to come. In the wake of nonexistent financial transactions between Iran and foreign banks, therefore, a hefty sum of funds earned from the export of Iranian crude oil to East Asia had to remain blocked. Such unfortunate development had taken place several years before other rounds of stringent sanctions pushed by the United States under Trump made it virtually impossible for Iran to import goods and products from East Asian countries for its oil incomes frozen by those Asian states.

When push came to shove, however, Iran had to react, and the easiest target among its East Asian trading partners was South Korea which had blocked at least $7 billion of Iranian oil money. Japan had already provided Iran with a lot of financial services, and it was not a good idea to provoke Tokyo unnecessarily at this point over some $3 billion Iranian assets frozen by the Japanese government. China was also too important to piss off, though many top Iranian officials denied publicly that Iran had any assets frozen by an order dictated somewhere within the corridors of power in Zhongnanhai in the first place. Iran, therefore, resorted to a gunboat diplomacy of sorts, seizing a Korean oil tanker in the Persian Gulf by its powerful IRGC in order to put additional pressures on the ROK to release at least part of the Iranian frozen assets in Seoul. After dispatching a number of its top officials, including Prime Minister Chung Sye-kyun, to Tehran to negotiate for releasing the captured vessel and for settling the blocked funds, South Korea announced that it was simply hapless to do anything about Iran's frozen assets unless the United States permits Seoul to unblock them. Sanctions had already ground to a halt South Korean–Iranian commercial interactions, including oil trade, and any lasting solution for releasing the ROK-based frozen assets probably hinged on settling the ongoing disputes between Tehran and Washington concerning the nuclear deal tossed by Trump.

Still, international sanctions created financial troubles for Iran more than met the eye. The problem was not about the impossibility of bringing back oil revenues alone; any type of international financial transactions for Iranians just became unfeasible. As the country's sources of earning foreign exchange were tightened substantially, the government moved to devalue stupendously the Iranian currency, rial, to be able to manage the state of affairs under constant sanctions and financial constraints. Iranian citizens also panicked and quickly engaged in hoarding foreign currencies and gold to fight against the swiftly nosediving value of their hard-earned savings and assets. At a time of "dollar drought," foreign currencies as well as golds and jewelries worth tens of billions of dollars were hoarded unproductively aside from the billions of dollars which left the country to purchase properties in Turkey and other places. Stagflation and social despondency were some immediate outcomes, and there seemed to be no short-fix and remedy in East Asia either as long as Iran was not allowed to tap into its vast frozen assets abroad to overcome such dire socio-economic problems.

Those economic and social upheavals were simmering in Iran against a backdrop of international financial promises part of which were supposed to be delivered by East Asian countries. Basically, after Iran and the 5+1 group agreed about the JCPOA in June 2015, the Middle Eastern country signed optimistically dozens of financial agreements with East Asian states, particularly South Korea and China, in order to ratchet up bilateral financial interactions with those countries. Part of such deals involved setting up joint banks and offering more banking services for Iranian citizens, including their access to MasterCard-esque international banking cards issued by a credible financial institution headquartered somewhere in East Asia. More important, some of those financial accords required East Asian countries, especially China, to finance a whole array of Iranian projects, ranging from infrastructure to energy undertakings. Such measures were to ultimately benefit Iran and its citizenry, one way or other, no matter if some of those financing packages promised by East Asian countries were going to be bankrolled by Iran's own frozen assets blocked in the wake of international financial sanctions.

More than a decade and half before Iran encountered international banking impediments unprecedentedly, however, the country had been hit with a paucity of foreign investments. In lockstep with the Clinton administration's "dual containment" policy, the United States had created a whole host of barriers, discouraging international investors and entrepreneurs to throw their capital into Iranian projects. Many foreign companies, particularly Western and Japanese businesses, which had already invested significantly in Iran had to also scrape their Iranian deals and depart the country in total. But Iran was a big and bankable market, tempting ambitious companies from South Korea and later China to move in and take on many projects which had previously been carried out by more sophisticated and resourceful European and Japanese investors. Although more Korean companies rushed to invest in "the world's largest emerging market" after the conclusion of the nuclear deal in 2015, nonetheless, Trump's withdrawal from the nuclear deal in 2018 and the follow-up reinstated sanctions forced Koreans to give up their Iran agreements, including some joint projects with Iranian companies, and leave the active Chinese businesses in the Mideast country almost unrivaled.

Two additional developments, moreover, had influenced China's growing attention to Iran as an up-and-coming market for investments, though international sanctions and limitations were at the same time curbing Chinese options in the Persian Gulf country. The first important development was China's own BRI which had become a main plank of Xi Jinping's foreign policy since 2013. Situated "at the heart of BRI" undertakings, Iran was thereby going to be part and parcel of the Chinese lavish investments appropriated for the greater Middle East region alone. The other development, which was partly related to the Chinese ground-breaking BRI, was the 25-year strategic agreement between China and Iran. Signed ultimately in March 2021, the contentious deal had been a subject of bilateral talks and negotiations since early 2016 when Xi Jinping broached the topic while paying a state visit to Tehran. According to the agreement, China promised to invest in Iran a whopping $400 billion out of which roughly $280 billion will be allocated to Iranian energy projects.

By and large, Iran's attraction for East Asian investments, whether by Chinese or Japanese and Koreans, had a lot to do with its rather huge consumption markets. Since the first oil shock in the 1970s, Iran had been turned into one of the Middle East's top destinations for foreign goods and products. The Islamic Republic's unrealistic industrial and economic policies simply made things worse and increased the populous country's overdependence on foreign products. By the time most of Western goods and brands had to leave Iran because of international sanctions, therefore, the Middle Eastern country had become a gravy train of sorts for a number of East Asian companies, especially those from South Korea, as a result of Tehran's disproportionate and unwarranted imports which some observers called "worse than the Mongol invasion." Larger volumes of imports also signified that the energy-dependent East Asian exporters could enjoy a more favorable trade balance with Iran in sharp contrast with their often negative trade balance with other oil-exporting countries in the Persian Gulf region.

The Iranian nuclear controversy and the ensuing UN and US sanctions, moreover, compounded the situation because Iran was no longer able to bring back its oil revenues and had to buy more cargoes of East Asian products for the crude oil it was exporting. Escalated and accelerated by the so-called oil for goods bartering schemes, the scope and size of importing goods from East Asian countries, China in particular, were so unrestrained that led to the total bankruptcy of some well-established and famous Iranian brands and products. The problem was not about omnipresent Chinese goods alone; certain traditional businesses had now been handed over to Chinese nationals. The most prominent example was the large presence of Chinese fishers in Iranian southern waters. The government first denied that there was any Chinese fishing boat in Iranian waters at all, but later it tried to justify their arrival by announcing that the Chinese fishers had actually hired themselves out to Iranians—a dubious explanation which could hardly convince many skeptics in Iran several years after they had heard some similar excuses for the influx of Chinese workers to carry out Iranian infrastructure projects.

Iran's reliance on foreign technology and technical knowhow was, additionally, a critical factor behind its elephantine imports one decade after another. At least since the mid-1990s, the United States' extraterritorial sanctions had practically intimidated many interested foreign companies to transfer their advanced technologies to the Middle Eastern country by investing in some critical industrial projects which required sophisticated expertise and newfangled equipment countries like Iran essentially lacked. After the Iranian nuclear program became a hot-button international issue, transfer of foreign technology to Iran came under more serious impediments. In particular, various UN and US sanctions compelled industrialized and developed countries, including East Asian nations, to subsequently place more stringent restrictions with regard to transfer of certain dual-use technologies and components which were suspected to be exploited by Iran for its contentious nuclear and missile programs. As a consequence, procuring such dual-use items for Iran in every possible way became a new obsession and profession of some East Asian companies and individuals that wished to quickly make a huge fortune primarily by risking their business and personal reputation.

Long before the flow of foreign technology to Iran dwindled to a trickle because of crippling sanctions, however, technology transfer was an integral part of Iranian cooperation with East Asian countries. In fact, technology transfer was the raison d'être behind their bilateral partnership involving industrial projects in the energy sector as well as in some other non-oil sectors such as the auto industry. More important, transfer of technology could facilitate business ties and pave the ground for larger presence of a willing East Asian company in Iranian consumption markets. As experienced by a number of Korean automobile and electronic companies, East Asian investors could be given generously a larger share of Iran's profitable markets in exchange for sharing with Iranians part of their expertise and technical knowhow. Iran preferred joint ventures as a *modus operandi* to bring in foreign technology, but certain East Asian companies opted for setting up their own factory and work independently of Iranians as long as they faced few, if any, serious foreign competitors in the Persian Gulf country.

Militarily, East Asia's collaboration with a sanctioned Iran is older than many other areas. Its history dates back to the early 1980s when North Korea and China engaged in substantial arms deals with Iran that had been embargoed militarily by the West. The Persian Gulf country had to fight its neighboring Iraq for eight years, and the internecine conflict provided the ground for a bustling arms market in the Middle East. Aside from North Korea and China, South Korea and Taiwan could also supply arms to the region, though probably they were simultaneously playing the role of a middleman selling American armaments to the warring parties in the Middle East somehow similar to what the DPRK was doing for China in the early years of the Iran–Iraq War of 1980–1988. After the conclusion of the war, North Korean and Chinese military and defense cooperation with Iranians continued in both conventional and unconventional weapons. By the late 1990s, however, China came under tremendous American arm-twisting, and Sino–Iranian military collaboration, at least in the field of nuclear and missile programs, was inevitably and officially shelved.

In the twenty-first century, China and Iran were persuaded to rekindle their military and defense synergy in the wake of "rising new security challenges," ranging from terrorism to cyber security. By the time the UN arms embargoes against Iran were lifted and the signed 25-year strategic agreement promised enhanced military and defense cooperation between China and Iran, the two countries had already planned and carried out many relevant initiatives, including conducting several joint naval drills, some of which involved active participation of Russia. This "emerging Eastern coalition" did not go unnoticed as the United States under Trump moved to put together its own naval coalition in the Persian Gulf in order to put additional pressures on Iran after a number of top Iranian officials vowed to make troubles for the flow of oil from the region if Tehran was not allowed to export its own crude oil. Despite a strong American lobby, Japan and South Korea did not join the US-led naval coalition, but both Tokyo and Seoul dispatched their own small and independent naval force to the region aiming to further augment their own international security profile without antagonizing gratuitously either Washington or Tehran.

Meanwhile, Iran sanctions were not about the hard fields of military as well as politics and economy alone; culture and the broader cultural realm, including the cloistered world of academia, had been affected gravely by international sanctions and restrictions. Discouraged and disappointed by the visionary system of the Islamic Republic, a growing crowd of Iranian talents and experts left the country often permanently from the early 1979 onward. Coupled with myriad domestic economic and social restraints and barriers brought about by the ruling Islamists, the ensuing regimes of sanctions and international limitations only exacerbated the situation and prompted more capable graduates and talents to join the unstoppable wave of Iranian brain drain. Most of them opted for studying or working in the industrialized and developed Western countries located in North America or Europe, but a growing number of Iranians also decided to move to East Asia and gradually lay the foundations of larger academic and cultural interactions between Iran and East Asian societies.

As successive conservative and reformist governments in Tehran had to double down their looking-East policies partly because of unceasing sanctions and international constraints, the Persian Gulf country realized the importance of fostering stronger academic and cultural relationship with East Asian countries almost several decades after those Eastern states, especially Japan and South Korea, had carved out some similar initiatives in the aftermath of the first oil shock of 1973–1974. Thus, a number of Tehran-based Iranian universities belatedly commenced their East Asian programs with a particular focus on Japanese and Chinese studies. A few relevant institutes and think tanks were also set up in Tehran in order to produce more sophisticated and up-to-date research and analysis about

East Asian countries and the dynamics of their contemporary societies. In spite of such late measures, Iranians still needed to do a lot in the realm of public diplomacy in East Asia at a time when some East Asian cultural phenomena, particularly the Korean wave or *Hallyu*, were already mesmerizing both hearts and minds of impressionable and unsuspecting youngsters in some Middle Eastern countries, including Iran.

Concerning the general public, sanctions were inevitably influencing the average citizenry's cultural understanding of and opinions about endless international penalties and how those detrimental restrictions were shaping their country's overall orientation toward the outside world, including its looking-East proclivities. There happened to be this sobering realization among many people that international sanctions, and especially their high-sounding version of "smart sanctions" or "targeted sanctions," were not really what they all were cracked up to be as far as the declared objectives of those penalties entailed. Thanks to international sanctions and restrictions, the ruling elites as well as their stalwarts had become more powerful politically and enormously opulent economically. Quite to the contrary, sanctions had turned the average Iranian citizens into pulverized paupers many of whom had little options but to sell their kidneys and other vital organs to survive in a rich land endowed with a cornucopia of natural resources. Many other frustrated and discontented Iranians, moreover, knew that their historically polyglot and proud country had literally being sold down the river, and international sanctions and constraints had further trapped them between the devil and the deep blue sea.

Likewise, there were disenchanted views among many Iranians regarding the looking-East policy which had long aimed to partially make up for the troubles and limitations rendered by sanctions. Opponents asserted that looking-East had only deepened Iran's dependence on a number of Eastern countries which had strived to only cash in from international sanctions and the Western animosity toward Iran over the past several decades without serving as a cushion against the Middle Eastern country's political troubles with the West and economic difficulties at home. Proponents of the looking-East orientation, however, had certain sanguine opinions that were diametrically opposite to what the critics thought. In their views, Eastern nations were among the true friends of Iran that had helped the country during its tough times of military conflict and economic sanctions. They were also claiming that international sanctions and restrictions, especially those constraints pushed by the United States, were not going to disappear anytime soon, and Iran thus could better win over their crippling repercussions in close cooperation with some Eastern countries, China in particular.

As far as sanctions-busting was concerned, those zealous advocates of the looking-East approach were right on target. Almost from the early days when the United States slapped Iran with sanctions and restrictions, the Persian Gulf country had to tap into both conventional and peculiar methods to go around sanctions. As time went by and the country was levied with more stringent sets of international sanctions and limitations, Iranians also became more experienced and sophisticated in terms of coming up with new measures and finding additionally willing foreign partners to dodge sanctions and muddle through. They established virtually an empire of a sanctions-busting network whose far-reaching and twisted tentacles spread into every continent. Easily accessible cities and ports as well as greedy companies and insatiable individuals from East Asia were certainly part of this rather complicated web of circumventing sanctions, enabling Iranians to acquire a great deal of their required technologies and products denied to them by international sanctions and restrictions.

Domestically, the labyrinthine system of sanctions-busting encompassed three core groups aside from what the Iranian government and its affiliated institutions were doing here and there to bypass sanctions and limitations. The first powerful group was the shadowy mafia or what Ahmadinejad once called "smuggling brothers" with their own special docks and strong lobby in the Islamic Republic's key centers of power and wealth. The second group consisted of certain influential families and hand-picked individuals that could benefit from a whole host of state privileges and nepotism, including easy access to subsidized foreign currency. The final group was, by and large, ordinary citizens who were themselves often among major casualties of sanctions. Porters epitomized this group, but many families and individuals from this group were smuggling foreign goods and products by motor ferry and some other means instead of using their own physical power as porters used to do. Unlike the other two favored and privileged groups, members of the third group were like sitting ducks and a prime target of the government's random campaigns against the so-called commodity smugglers.

Externally, however, sanctions-busting was not always an easy burden as far as the United States was concerned. As the chief architect and the main guardian behind sundry international sanctions against Iran, the United States had to allocate a great deal of time and resources monitoring whether or not foreign countries were implementing Iran sanctions. It was simply a Herculean task because the business of sanctions oversight required Americans to know uninterruptedly what was actually going on in every serviceable and useful domain (land, sea, air, and cyberspace). Despite their fluctuating policy approaches toward Tehran, successive American administrations across the political spectrum were committed to supervising sanctions implementation by both US allies and competitors. After all, carrying out sanctions diktats was not optional at all; nation-states as well as their businesses and individuals could face significant penalties just in case they ignored what sanctions required them by daring to provide Iran with any type of goods and services prohibited by sanctions.

As it turned out, draconian punishment meted out by the United States was a powerful tool to bludgeon unruly companies and individuals into compliance with Iran sanctions. In doing so, American authorities behaved indiscriminately whencesoever sanctions violation came. That was no coincidence why some Western banks had to pay whopping fines for facilitating certain international financial transactions for Iran. In the same way, a slew of East Asian companies and individuals were penalized by the United States for helping Iranians evade sanctions. A number of giant Chinese companies, ZTE and particularly Huawei, were among the prominent cases from East Asia which aroused the wrath of Americans for going around Iran sanctions by procuring prohibited American goods and technologies for Iranians and their front companies registered here and there. Uncompliant individuals from the region, no matter they were from Taiwan or mainland China, were similarly punished with exorbitant fines and imprisonment for doing the same service for the sanctioned Iran.

All in all, sanctions functioned as a sinews of East Asian success in the Middle Eastern country almost in all diplomatic, political, military, economic, financial, technological, and cultural areas. A sanctioned Iran was where the old maxim horses for courses signified because if international sanctions and restrictions had prevented some East Asian players to perform better in certain areas, they would have definitely achieved much beyond what they could imagine in other fields. Iranian connections to East Asia in all sectors were equally affected by sanctions as the Persian Gulf country had to readjust a great deal of Tehran's conventional foreign and economic policies *pari passu* with its growing vested interests in East Asian countries. Sanctions, or at least some of them, will not go away any time soon, making it imperative for Iran to rely as usual on its partners in East Asia to acquire part of what was denied to Iranians. Just in case Iran sanctions were unbelievably lifted all together for good, they have already played their substantive role in molding certain dynamics of Iranian–East Asian interactions for the foreseeable future.

BIBLIOGRAPHY

Alexander, Kern. 2002. United States Financial Sanctions and International Terrorism. *Butterworths Journal of International Banking and Financial Law* 17 (5): 212–223.
———. 2009. *Economic Sanctions: Law and Public Policy*. New York: Palgrave Macmillan.
Alikhani, Hossein. 2000. *Sanctioning Iran: Anatomy of a Failed Policy*. London and New York: I.B. Tauris Publishers.
Amuzegar, Jahangir. 2008. Iran's Oil as a Blessing and a Curse. *Brown Journal of World Affairs* 15 (1): 47–61.
Azad, Shirzad. 2019. *East Asian Politico-Economic Ties with the Middle East: Newcomers, Trailblazers, and Unsung Stakeholders*. New York: Algora Publishing.
———. 2020. *Looking East: A Changing Middle East Realigns with a Rising Asia*. New York: Algora Publishing.
———. 2021. *East Asia's Strategic Advantage in the Middle East*. Lanham, MD: Lexington Books.
Baldwin, David A. 1971. The Power of Positive Sanctions. *World Politics* 24 (1): 19–38.
———. 1999. The Sanctions Debate and the Logic of Choice. *International Security* 24 (3): 80–107.
Baldwin, David A., and Robert A. Pape. 1998. Evaluating Economic Sanctions. *International Security* 23 (2): 189–198.

© The Author(s), under exclusive license to Springer Nature
Switzerland AG 2022
S. Azad, *East Asia and Iran Sanctions*,
https://doi.org/10.1007/978-3-030-97427-5

244 BIBLIOGRAPHY

Barber, James. 1979. Economic Sanctions as a Policy Instrument. *International Affairs* 55 (3): 367–384.

Berger, Bernt, and Phillip Schell. 2013. Toeing the Line, Drawing the Line: China and Iran's Nuclear Ambitions. *China Report* 49 (1): 89–101.

Bermudez, Joseph S., Jr. 1998. *North Korean Special Forces.* Annapolis, MD: Naval Institute Press.

Bianchi, Robert R. 2013. China–Middle East Relations in Light of Obama's Pivot to the Pacific. *China Report* 49 (1): 103–118.

Blackwill, Robert D., and Jennifer M. Harris. 2016. *War by Other Means: Geoeconomics and Statecraft.* New York: The Belknap Press of Harvard University Press.

Bolton, John R. 2007. *Surrender Is Not an Option: Defending America at the United Nations and Abroad.* New York: Threshold Editions.

———. 2020. *The Room Where It Happened: A White House Memoir.* New York: Simon & Schuster.

Borszik, Oliver. 2016. International Sanctions against Iran and Tehran's Responses: Political Effects on the Targeted Regime. *Contemporary Politics* 22 (1): 20–39.

Brewer, Jonathan. 2016. UN Financial Sanctions on Iran. *The RUSI Journal* 161 (4): 22–26.

Brzoska, Michael. 1987. Profiteering on the Iran–Iraq War. *Bulletin of the Atomic Scientists* 43 (5): 42–45.

Burns, William J. 2019. *The Back Channel: A Memoir of American Diplomacy and the Case for Its Renewal.* New York: Random House.

Caisova, Lenka. 2019. *North Korea's Foreign Policy: The DPRK's Part on the International Scene and Its Audiences.* Abingdon and New York: Routledge.

Calabrese, John. 1999. China and Iraq: A Stake in Stability. In *China and the Middle East: The Quest for Influence,* ed. P.R. Kumaraswamy, 52–67. New Delhi: Sage Publications.

Carbonnier, Gilles. 2015. *Humanitarian Economics: War, Disaster and the Global Aid Market.* New York: Oxford University Press.

Carswell, Robert. 1981. Economic Sanctions and the Iran Experience. *Foreign Affairs* 60 (2): 247–265.

Carter, Barry E. 1988. *International Economic Sanctions: Improving the Haphazard U.S. Legal Regime.* Cambridge: Cambridge University Press.

Carter, Stephen G. 2014. Iran, Natural Gas and Asia's Energy Needs: A Spoiler for Sanctions? *Middle East Policy* 21 (1): 41–61.

Chan, Steve, and A. Cooper Drury. 2000. Sanctions as Economic Statecraft: An Overview. In *Sanctions as Economic Statecraft: Theory and Practice,* ed. Steve Chan and A. Cooper Drury, 1–16. New York: Palgrave.

Christiansen, Drew, and Gerard F. Powers. 1995. Economic Sanctions and the Just-War Doctrine. In *Economic Sanctions: Panacea or Peacebuilding in a*

Post-Cold War World? ed. David Cortright and George A. Lopez, 97–117. Boulder, CO: Westview Press.

Clinton, Hillary R. 2014. *Hard Choices: A Memoir.* New York: Simon & Schuster.

Cohen, David S., and Zachary K. Goldman. 2019. Like it or Not, Unilateral Sanctions Are Here to Stay. *AJIL Unbound* 113: 146–151.

Cole, Bernard D. 2016. *China's Quest for Great Power: Ships, Oil, and Foreign Policy.* Annapolis, MD: Naval Institute Press.

Cooney, Kevin J. 2002. *Japan's Foreign Policy Maturation: A Quest for Normalcy.* London and New York: Routledge.

Craven, Mathew. 2002. Humanitarianism and the Quest for Smarter Sanctions. *European Journal of International Law* 13 (1): 43–61.

Cumings, Bruce. 2010. Rapprochement in Postwar History: Implications for North Korea. In *New Challenges of North Korean Foreign Policy,* ed. Kyung-Ae Park, 205–222. New York: Palgrave Macmillan.

Dobson, Alan P. 2002. *US Economic Statecraft for Survival 1933–1991: Of Sanctions, Embargoes and Economic Warfare.* London and New York: Routledge.

Dorraj, Manochehr, and James English. 2013. The Dragon Nests: China's Energy Engagement of the Middle East. *China Report* 49 (1): 43–67.

Dowty, Alan. 1994. Sanctioning Iraq: The Limits of the New World Order. *The Washington Quarterly* 17 (3): 179–198.

Doxey, Margaret P. 1980. *Economic Sanctions and International Enforcement.* 2nd ed. London: Macmillan for the Royal Institute of International Affairs.

———. 1983. International Sanctions: Trials of Strength or Tests of Weakness? *Millennium: Journal of International Studies* 12 (1): 79–87.

———. 1996. *International Sanctions in Contemporary Perspective.* 2nd ed. London: Macmillan Press LTD.

Drezner, Daniel W. 2000a. Bargaining, Enforcement and Multilateral Sanctions: When is Cooperation Counterproductive? *International Organization* 54 (1): 73–102.

———. 2000b. The Complex Causation of Sanction Outcomes. In *Sanctions as Economic Statecraft: Theory and Practice,* ed. Steve Chan and A. Cooper Drury, 212–230. New York: Palgrave.

Drifte, Reinhard. 1996. *Japan's Foreign Policy in the 1990s: From Economic Superpower to What Power?* London: Macmillan Press LTD.

Drury, A. Cooper. 2005. *Economic Sanctions and Presidential Decisions: Models of Political Rationality.* New York: Palgrave Macmillan.

Early, Bryan R. 2009. Sleeping with Your Friends' Enemies: An Explanation of Sanctions-Busting Trade. *International Studies Quarterly* 53 (1): 49–71.

Eaton, Jonathan, and Maxim Engers. 1992. Sanctions. *Journal of Political Economy* 100 (5): 899–928.

246 BIBLIOGRAPHY

Elliott, Kimberly A. 1998. The Sanctions Glass: Half Full or Completely Empty. *International Security* 23 (1): 50–65.

———. 2005. Trends in Economic Sanctions Policy: Challenges to Conventional Wisdom. In *International Sanctions: Between Words and Wars in the Global System*, ed. Peter Wallensteen and Carina Staibano, 3–14. Abingdon and New York: Routledge.

Eyler, Robert. 2007. *Economic Sanctions: International Policy and Political Economy at Work*. New York: Palgrave Macmillan.

Farrall, Jeremy M. 2007. *United Nations Sanctions and the Rule of Law*. New York: Cambridge University Press.

Farrar, Marjorie M. 1974. *Conflict and Compromise: The Strategy, Politics and Diplomacy of the French Blockade, 1914–1918*. The Hague, Netherlands: Martinus Nijhoff.

Fayazmanesh, Sasan. 2008. *The United States and Iran: Sanctions, Wars and the Policy of Dual Containment*. Abingdon and New York: Routledge.

Feder, Toni. 2010. Sanctions on Iran Slow Science, Slam a Scientist. *Physics Today* 63 (8): 22–25.

Fitzpatrick, Mark. 2020. Sanctioning Pandemic-plagued Iran. *Survival* 62 (3): 93–102.

Galtung, Johan. 1967. On the Effects of International Economic Sanctions, With Examples from the Case of Rhodesia. *World Politics* 19 (3): 378–416.

Garver, John. 2013. China–Iran Relations: Cautious Friendship with America's Nemesis. *China Report* 49 (1): 69–88.

Gates, Robert M. 2014. *Duty: Memoirs of a Secretary at War*. New York: Alfred A. Knopf.

Gill, Bates. 1998. Chinese Arms Exports to Iran. *Middle East Review of International Affairs* 2 (2): 55–70.

Gordon, Joy. 2011. Smart Sanctions Revisited. *Ethics & International Affairs* 25 (3): 315–335.

———. 2019a. The Not So Targeted Instrument of Asset Freezes. *Ethics & International Affairs* 33 (3): 303–314.

———. 2019b. The Hidden Power of the New Economic Sanctions. *Current History* 118 (804): 3–10.

Gordon, Philip H. 2020. *Losing the Long Game: The False Promise of Regime Change in the Middle East*. New York: St. Martin's Press.

Green, Michael J. 2001. *Japan's Reluctant Realism: Foreign Policy Challenges in an Era of Uncertain Power*. New York: Palgrave.

Grimmett, Richard F. 1988. *CRS Report for Congress: Trends in Conventional Arms Transfers to the Third World by Major Supplier, 1980–1987*. Washington, DC: Congressional Research Service, Library of Congress.

Haass, Richard N. 1997. Sanctioning Madness. *Foreign Affairs* 76 (6): 74–85.

BIBLIOGRAPHY   247

Haley, Nikki R. 2019. *With All Due Respect: Defending America with Grit and Grace*. New York: St. Martin's Press.

Hatipoglu, Emre, and Dursun Peksen. 2016. Economic Sanctions and Banking Crises in Target Economies. *Defence and Peace Economics* 29 (2): 171–189.

Heiss, Mary A. 2004. The International Boycott of Iranian Oil and the Anti-Mosaddeq Coup of 1953. In *Mohammad Mosaddeq and the 1953 Coup in Iran*, ed. Malcolm Byrne and Mark J. Gasiorowski, 178–200. Syracuse, NY: Syracuse University Press.

Hirsch, Andrew von. 1996. *Censure and Sanctions*. New York: Oxford University Press.

Hufbauer, Gary C., Jeffrey J. Schott, Kimberly A. Elliott, and Barbara Oegg. 2007. *Economic Sanctions Reconsidered*. 3rd ed. Washington, DC: Peterson Institute for International Economics.

Huntington, Samuel P. 1970. Foreign Aid for What and for Whom. *Foreign Policy* 1 (1): 161–189.

Hyakuta, Naoki. 2014. *Kaizoku to yobareta otoko* [A Man Called Pirate]. Tokyo: Kodansha.

Jacobson, Michael. 2008. Sanctions against Iran: A Promising Struggle. *The Washington Quarterly* 31 (3): 69–88.

Jones, Lee. 2015. *Societies Under Siege: Exploring How International Economic Sanctions (Do Not) Work*. Oxford and New York: Oxford University Press.

Joyner, Christopher C. 2003. United Nations Sanctions after Iraq: Looking Back to See Ahead. *Chicago Journal of International Law* 4 (2): 329–332.

Juneau, Thomas. 2019. The Enduring Constraints on Iran's Power after the Nuclear Deal. *Political Science Quarterly* 134 (1): 39–61.

Kaempfer, William H., and Anton D. Lowenberg. 1988. The Theory of International Economic Sanctions: A Public Choice Approach. *The American Economic Review* 78 (4): 786–793.

———. 1999. Unilateral Versus Multilateral International Sanctions: A Public Choice Perspective. *International Studies Quarterly* 43 (1): 37–58.

Kawashima, Yutaka. 2003. *Japanese Foreign Policy at the Crossroads: Challenges and Options for the Twenty-First Century*. Washington, DC: Brookings Institution Press.

Kemenade, Willem van. 2010. China vs. the Western Campaign for Iran Sanctions. *The Washington Quarterly* 33 (3): 99–114.

Kerry, John. 2018. *Every Day Is Extra*. New York: Simon & Schuster.

Kilpatrick, Richard L., Jr. 2019. North Korea's Sanctions-Busting Maritime Practices: Implications for Commercial Shipping. *Chinese (Taiwan) Yearbook of International Law and Affairs* 37: 199–220.

Knorr, Klaus. 1975. *The Power of Nations: The Political Economy of International Relations*. New York: Basic Books.

Koike, Masanari. 2006. Japan Looks for Oil in the Wrong Places. *Far Eastern Economic Review* 169 (8): 44–47.

Lacy, Dean, and Emerson M.S. Niou. 2004. A Theory of Economic Sanctions and Issue Linkage: The Roles of Preferences, Information, and Threats. *The Journal of Politics* 66 (1): 25–42.

Lamrani, Salim. 2013. *The Economic War against Cuba: A Historical and Legal Perspective on the U.S. Blockade.* New York: Monthly Review Press.

Lanteigne, Marc. 2008. China's Maritime Security and the 'Malacca Dilemma'. *Asian Security* 4 (2): 143–161.

———. 2020. *Chinese Foreign Policy: An Introduction.* 4th ed. Abingdon and New York: Routledge.

Lewis, George, and Frank von Hippel. 2018. Limitations on Ballistic Missile Defense—Past and Possibly Future. *Bulletin of the Atomic Scientists* 74 (4): 199–209.

Lindsay, James M. 1986. Trade Sanctions as Policy Instruments: A Reexamination. *International Studies Quarterly* 30 (2): 153–173.

Maloney, Suzanne. 2010. Sanctioning Iran: If Only It Were So Simple. *The Washington Quarterly* 33 (1): 131–147.

Matthee, Rudi. 2020. 'Neither Eastern nor Western, Iranian': How the Quest for Self-Sufficiency Helped Shape Iran's Modern Nationalism. *Journal of Persianate Studies* 13 (1): 59–104.

Medeiros, Evan S. 2007. *Reluctant Restraint: The Evolution of China's Nonproliferation Policies and Practices, 1980–2004.* Palo Alto, CA: Stanford University Press.

Miller, Nicholas L. 2014. The Secret Success of Nonproliferation Sanctions. *International Organization* 68 (4): 913–944.

Ministry of Foreign Affairs of Japan. 2020. *Diplomatic Bluebook 2020.* Tokyo: Ministry of Foreign Affairs of Japan.

Miyagawa, Makio. 1992. *Do Economic Sanctions Work?* London and New York: Palgrave Macmillan.

Miyata, Osamu. 1997. Coping with the 'Iranian Threat': A View from Japan. *Silk Road* 1 (2): 30–41.

Moret, Erica S. 2015. Humanitarian Impacts of Economic Sanctions on Iran and Syria. *European Security* 24 (1): 120–140.

Mori, Hiromasa. 1995. Foreign Migrant Workers in Japan: Trends and Policies. *Asian and Pacific Migration Journal* 4 (2–3): 411–427.

Neff, Stephen C. 1989 [1988]. Boycott and the Law of Nations: Economic Warfare and Modern International Law in Historical Perspective. In *The British Yearbook of International Law*, ed. Ian Brownlie and D. W. Bowett, 135–145. Oxford: Oxford University Press.

Nephew, Richard. 2018. *The Art of Sanctions: A View from the Field.* New York: Columbia University Press.

BIBLIOGRAPHY   249

Newnham, Randall. 2002. *Deutsche Mark Diplomacy: Positive Economic Sanctions in German–Russian Relations*. University Park, PA: The Pennsylvania State University Press.

Nukii, Mari. 2018. Japan–Iran Relations since the 2015 Iran Nuclear Deal. *Contemporary Review of the Middle East* 5 (3): 215–231.

O'Sullivan, Meghan L. 2003. *Shrewd Sanctions: Statecraft and State Sponsors of Terrorism*. Washington, DC: Brookings Institution Press.

———. 2010. Iran and the Great Sanctions Debate. *The Washington Quarterly* 33 (4): 7–21.

Olson, Richard S. 1979. Economic Coercion in World Politics: With a Focus on North–South Relations. *World Politics* 31 (4): 471–494.

Orakhelashvili, Alexander. 2011. *Collective Security*. New York: Oxford University Press.

Palgrave, David W.H. 1991. *Western Trade Pressure on the Soviet Union: An Interdependence Perspective on Sanctions*. New York: Palgrave Macmillan.

Pape, Robert A. 1998. Why Economic Sanctions Still Do Not Work. *International Security* 23 (1): 66–77.

Parasiliti, Andrew. 2010. After Sanctions, Deter and Engage Iran. *Survival: Global Politics and Strategy* 52 (5): 13–20.

Peksen, Dursun. 2019a. Political Effectiveness, Negative Externalities, and the Ethics of Economic Sanctions. *Ethics & International Affairs* 33 (3): 279–289.

———. 2019b. When Do Imposed Economic Sanctions Work? A Critical Review of the Sanctions Effectiveness Literature. *Defence and Peace Economics* 30 (6): 635–647.

Peksen, Dursun, and A. Cooper Drury. 2009. Economic Sanctions and Political Repression: Assessing the Impact of Coercive Diplomacy on Political Freedoms. *Human Rights Review* 10 (3): 393–411.

Penn, Michael. 2014. *Japan and the War on Terror: Military Force and Political Pressure in the US–Japanese Alliance*. London and New York: I.B. Tauris Publishers.

Pham, J. Peter. 2010. Iran's Threat to the Strait of Hormuz: A Realist Assessment. *American Foreign Policy Interests: The Journal of the National Committee on American Foreign Policy* 32 (2): 64–74.

Pieper, Moritz. 2013. Dragon Dance or Panda Trot? China's Position towards the Iranian Nuclear Programme and Its Perception of EU Unilateral Iran Sanctions. *European Journal of East Asian Studies* 12 (2): 295–316.

Pillar, Paul R. 2016. The Role of Villain: Iran and U.S. Foreign Policy. *Political Science Quarterly* 131 (2): 365–385.

Portela, Clara. 2010. *European Union Sanctions and Foreign Policy: When and Why Do They Work?* Abingdon and New York: Routledge.

Rodman, Kenneth A. 2001. *Sanctions beyond Borders: Multinational Corporations and U.S. Economic Statecraft*. Lanham, MD: Rowman & Littlefield Publishers.

250 BIBLIOGRAPHY

Rubin, Barry. 1980. *Paved with Good Intentions: The American Experience and Iran*. New York: Oxford University Press.

Ryan, Greg. 2018. *US Foreign Policy towards China, Cuba and Iran: The Politics of Recognition*. Abingdon and New York: Routledge.

Salisbury, Daniel, and David Lowrie. 2013. Targeted: A Case Study in Iranian Illicit Missile Procurement. *Bulletin of the Atomic Scientists* 69 (3): 23–30.

Salitskii, A.I., Zhao Xin, and V.I. Yurtaev. 2017. Sanctions and Import Substitution as Exemplified by the Experience of Iran and China. *Herald of the Russian Academy of Sciences* 87 (2): 205–212.

Schwebach, Valerie L. 2000. Sanctions as Signals: A Line in the Sand or a Lack of Resolve? In *Sanctions as Economic Statecraft: Theory and Practice*, ed. Steve Chan and A. Cooper Drury, 187–211. New York: Palgrave.

Shawcross, William. 1989. *The Shah's Last Ride: The Story of the Exile, Misadventures and Death of the Emperor*. New York: Touchstone.

Shehadi, Philip. 1981. Economic Sanctions and Iranian Trade. *MERIP Reports* 98: 15–16.

Shen, Simon. 2015. Hong Kong–Middle East Relations: Chinese Diplomacy and Urban Development. *Israel Journal of Foreign Affairs* 9 (2): 253–266.

Simon, Steven. 2018. Iran and President Trump: What Is the Endgame? *Survival* 60 (4): 7–20.

Simons, Geoff. 1998. *The Scourging of Iraq: Sanctions, Law and Natural Justice*. 2nd ed. London and New York: Palgrave Macmillan.

———. 1999. *Imposing Economic Sanctions: Legal Remedy or Genocidal Tool?* London and Sterling, VA: Pluto Press.

Spindler, Zane H. 1995. The Public Choice of Superior Sanctions. *Public Choice* 85 (3/4): 205–226.

Stone, Richard. 2018. Renewed Sanctions Strangle Science in Iran. *Science* 361 (6406): 961.

Takeyh, Ray, and Suzanne Maloney. 2011. The Self-limiting Success of Iran Sanctions. *International Affairs* 87 (6): 1297–1312.

Tankel, Stephen. 2018. *With Us and Against Us: How America's Partners Help and Hinder the War on Terror*. Cambridge, MA: Columbia University Press.

Tarock, Adam. 1998. *The Superpowers' Involvement in the Iran–Iraq War*. Commack, NY: Nova Science Publishers.

Taylor, Brendan. 2009. Chapter Three: Sanctioning Iran. *The Adelphi Papers* 49 (411): 59–100.

The Financial Times. 1983. *Financial Times Oil and Gas International Year Book*. London: Longman.

Togo, Kazuhiko. 2005. *Japan's Foreign Policy, 1945–2003: The Quest for a Proactive Policy*. 2nd ed. Leiden and Boston: Brill.

Tzanakopoulos, Antonios. 2011. *Disobeying the Security Council: Countermeasures against Wrongful Sanctions*. New York: Oxford University Press.

BIBLIOGRAPHY   251

United Nations Educational, Scientific and Cultural Organization (UNESCO). 2001. *Dialogue among Civilizations: The Round Table on the Eve of the United Nations Millennium Summit.* Paris: UNESCO.

Walzer, Michael. 1977. *Just and Unjust Wars: A Moral Argument with Historical Illustrations.* New York: Basic Books.

Watanabe, Tetsuya. 2019. *Sekai to nihon keizaidai yosoku 2020* [The World and Japanese Economic Forecast 2020]. Tokyo: PHP kenkyūjo [PHP Institute].

Weiss, Thomas G. 1999. Sanctions as a Foreign Policy Tool: Weighing Humanitarian Impulses. *Journal of Peace Research* 36 (5): 499–510.

Weiss, Thomas G., David Cortright, George A. Lopez, and Larry Minear. 1997. Toward a Framework for Analysis. In *Political Gain and Civilian Pain: Humanitarian Impacts of Economic Sanctions,* ed. David Cortright, George A. Lopez, Thomas G. Weiss, and Larry Minear, 35–53. Lanham, MD: Rowman & Littlefield.

Wintrobe, Ronald. 1990. The Tinpot and the Totalitarian: An Economic Theory of Dictatorship. *The American Political Science Review* 84 (3): 849–872.

Wood, David. 2007. Iran's Strong Case for Nuclear Power is Obscured by UN Sanctions and Geopolitics. *Atoms for Peace: An International Journal* 1 (4): 287–300.

Yoder, Robert S. 2011. *Deviance and Inequality in Japan: Japanese Youth and Foreign Migrants.* Bristol, UK: The Policy Press.

Zarate, Juan C. 2013. *Treasury's War: The Unleashing of a New Era of Financial Warfare.* New York: Public Affairs.

Index[1]

NUMBERS AND SYMBOLS

25-year Iran–China agreement, 32, 51, 116–118, 142, 159, 192, 238

A

Abadan, 50, 112
Abe, Shintaro, 35
Abe, Shinzo, 34, 40n56, 41n65, 61, 113, 162
Afghanistan, 108, 133
Africa, 69n83, 115
Ahmadinejad, Mahmoud, 57, 77, 118, 130, 205–209, 234, 241
Akhondi, Abbas, 200
Alliance, 25, 28, 33, 232
alliance spirit, 80–84
Alpha Tech Trading FZE, 221
Ambulance, 85
Arabian Sea, 162
Arms

embargo, 6, 25, 29, 151–153, 155, 160, 238
intermediary role, 31, 154
Iran–Contra, 152, 153
Aseman Air, 145
Asset freeze, *see* Blocked funds
Atomic Energy Organization, 156
Austerity, 28
Australia, 172, 185
Automatic identification system (AIS), 202
Axis of evil, 106
Azadegan, 108, 113

B

Ba'ath Party, 50, 62
Balance of power, 14
Bandar Abbas, 84, 112, 121n40, 161
Bangladesh, 53, 202
Bank Mellat, 80

---

[1] Note: Page numbers followed by 'n' refer to notes.

© The Author(s), under exclusive license to Springer Nature Switzerland AG 2022
S. Azad, *East Asia and Iran Sanctions*,
https://doi.org/10.1007/978-3-030-97427-5

253

254 INDEX

Bank Melli, 76
Bank of Kunlun, 59, 77, 100,
  202, 220
Bank of Tokyo-Mitsubishi UFJ, 79
Bankruptcy, 106, 128, 183
Barter, 45, 55–56, 73–76, 85, 177,
  203, 237
  Barter Committee, 127
Beirut, 79
Belgium, 43
Biden, Joe, 85
Bin Salman, Mohammad, 41n63
Birth rate, 13
Blinken, Antony, 86
Blocked funds
  China, 73–78, 99, 234
  East Asia, 145, 235
  gunboat diplomacy, 80–87
  history of, 71–73
  India, 74
  International Court of Justice
    (ICJ), 83
  Iraq, 75
  Italy, 75
  Japan, 76–79
  Luxembourg, 75
  sanctions, 71–76
  South Korea, 78–84, 188, 234
  Turkey, 74
Bolton, John, 41n63, 184
Bombay, 185
Brain drain, 96, 128, 169–171,
  184, 239
  Sharif University of Technology, 172
Brexit, 25
Brilliance Auto, 144
Britain
  5+1 group, 23
  arms exports, 153
  INSTEX, 75
  Iran policy, 25
  oil nationalization of Iran, 50

sanctions-busting, 204
Standard Chartered, 220
trade with Iran, 43, 123
UN resolution, 25
Brzezinski, Zbigniew, 148n3
Bush, George H., 106
Bush, George W., 40n56, 44
Byzantine bureaucracy, 26

C
California, 225
Canada, 9, 23, 172, 185
  Huawei, 222, 228n28
Capitalism, 123
Captain, 86
Carpet, 132
Carter, Jimmy, 25, 43, 71, 105,
  148n3, 151, 234
Caspian Sea, 216
Central Asia, 115, 202
Central Bank of Iran (CBI), 24, 71,
  78, 81, 94, 99, 153
Central Intelligence Agency
  (CIA), 216
CF Crystal, 53
Chaebol, 81, 125
Changan, 129
Chang, Hui-chuan, 224
Chang Hwa Bank, 164n12
Chen, Chung-yu, 224
Chen, Yi-lan, 224
  Chen, Kevin, 224
Cheonghae Unit, 163
Chery, 129, 144
Chief Financial Officer (CFO), 222
China National Petroleum
  Corporation, 59, 220
Chinese Communist Party (CCP), 115
Chinese energy strategy (*zhongguo
  nengyuan zhanlue*), 47
Choi, Jong-kun, 85

INDEX   255

Choi, Kyung-soo, 103n27
Chung, Sye-kyun, 86, 234
CISCO Shipping Company, 80
Clinton, Bill, 22, 25, 57, 105, 106, 156, 235
Cold War, 201, 217
Collateral damage, 2, 7, 11
Comparable to war, 183
Comprehensive Iran Sanctions, Accountability and Divestment Act (CISADA), 57, 67n53
Comprehensive sanctions, 5
Comprehensive strategic partnership, 116
Concessional oil, *see* Discounted oil
Condensate, 53, 60, 65n31, 69n85, 81
Confucius Institute, 176
Conoco, 106
Continental power, 161
Conventional sanctions theory, 4–7
Coronavirus, *see* COVID-19
COVID-19, 70n96, 82, 188–189
  AstraZeneca, 188
  COVAX, 189
  Sinopharm, 189
  SK Bioscience, 188
C-TEK Technology Corp., 224
Cuba, 8, 71, 216, 220
Currency coup, 95
Cyber security, 142, 159, 238

D
Daelim, 109
Daewoo Electronics, 144
Dialogue among civilizations, 177
Diet (Japanese parliament), 52
Dinrin Limited, 221
Discounted oil, 46–51, 117
Diversification, 185
Doha, 85

Donghai International Ship Management Limited, 221
Doosan, 109
Drug addiction, 128
Dual containment, 22, 105, 108, 142, 152, 236
Dual-track policy, 25
Dubai, 56, 74, 203, 206, 225
Dynapex Energy Limited, 221

E
East China Sea, 53
Eastern century, 191
Eastern Europe, 124
Eastern triangle, 161
Economic war room, 75
Economic warfare, 2
Einhorn, Robert, 80
Eldorado, 127
Embargo, *see* Comprehensive sanctions
Emerging market, 112–115, 236
Encyclopedia, 8
Enemy of the year, 22
Energy security, 47–49, 54
Entekhab Industrial Group, 144
European Union (EU), 9, 45, 52, 125, 172, 195n34, 219
  euro, 77, 96, 100, 118, 208
Excess transportation costs, 69n83
Executive Order (EO), 9, 43, 71, 107, 204, 221
Exim Bank, 114
Exorbitant privilege, 219

F
Facebook, 159
Federal Bureau of Investigation (FBI), 216
Financial Action Task Force (FATF), 101, 117

256 INDEX

Financial Supervisory Service
   (FSS), 80
Financing, 72, 106
   China, 78, 98–99, 235
First Middle East boom, 114
Foroughi, Javad, 187
Forward defense, 22
France
   5+1 group, 23
   BNP Paribas, 220
   INSTEX, 75
   Iran policy, 25
   nuclear deal with South Korea, 156
   trade with Iran, 43, 123, 131
   UN resolution, 25
Free trade, 123

G
Galtung, Johan, 4
Gas and Chemicals Transportation
   Corporation, 221
Gates, Robert, 49, 182
Gazprom, 118n3
Genocide, 12
Geopolitics, 28
Germany
   5+1 group, 23
   brain drain, 170
   Germany of the Middle East, 145
   INSTEX, 75
   Iran policy, 25
   Nazi Germany, 46, 201
   trade with Iran, 126, 131
   UN resolution, 25
   West Germany, 43
Glass ceiling, 185
Globalization, 3, 93
Going-out strategy (*zouchuqu
   zhanlue*), 48
Golden loan, 98
Greece, 45, 58

GS, 109
Guam, 224
Gulf of Aden, 162
Gun lobby, 9

H
Hana Bank, 81
Hanwha Total, 60
Hemmati, Abdolnaser, 83
Hezbollah, 22
Hong Kong Monetary Authority, 76
Hostage crisis, 9, 29, 43, 72, 78, 183
Huang, Chin-hua, 225
Huawei, 77, 129, 221–223, 242
Humanitarian trade, 188
Human rights, 9, 23, 182, 216
Hussein, Saddam, 49, 54, 62, 72, 97,
   152, 207
Hyundai, 109, 128, 129, 135n21,
   141, 144
   Hyundai Oilbank, 60
   Hyundai Samho Heavy
      Industries, 53

I
Idemitsu, 50
Imperial Japan, 46
India, 58, 124, 141, 208
Indonesia, 84
Industrial Bank of Korea (IBK), 81
Industrialization, 32, 47, 139, 140,
   191, 218
Inpex Corporation, 108
INSTEX, 75, 90n54
Interdependence, 3, 93
Intermediary, 85, 154, 202, 223
Internationalization, 9, 146, 185
International law, 21, 72, 83
International Maritime Security
   Construct (IMSC), 162

INDEX   257

International Olympic Committee (IOC), 187
Internet, 8, 142, 147, 159
Interview, 33, 78, 83
Ira-Ira Gaikou (Iran–Iraq diplomacy), 35
Iranian plateau, 27
Iran–Iraq Arms Non-Proliferation Act, 152
Iran–Iraq War, 29, 72, 105, 118, 144, 152, 238
Iran–Japan Petrochemical Complex (IJPC), 108, 143
Iran–Libya Sanctions Act (ILSA), 23, 142
Iran Petrochemical Commercial Company, 80
Iran Sanctions Act (ISA), 106, 142
Iran Threat Reduction and Syrian Human Rights Act, 73
Iraq, 8, 44, 108, 182, 204, 211n26, 238
Iraq War, 34, 162
Isfahan, 112
Islamic Republic of Iran Shipping Lines (IRISL), 205, 221, 225
E-Sail Shipping Company Ltd., 221
Islamic Revolutionary Guard Corps (IRGC), 62–63, 152
China, 206
Foreign Terrorist Organization (FTO), 94, 153
Imam Housein University, 165n26
Quds Force, 94, 153, 206
Rezai, Mohsen, 165n26
Tokyo Summer Olympics, 187
Islamization, 173
Isolation, 16, 63, 127
Israel, 31, 47, 165n26
Italy, 45, 58

J
Jahangiri, Eshaq, 206, 208, 213n42
Japan Bank for International Cooperation (JBIC), 113
Jewish lobby, 9, 31
Jiang, Zemin, 152, 156
Jingho Technology Co. Limited, 221
Jin, Jong-oh, 187
Joint bank, 99, 117, 235
Joint Comprehensive Plan of Action (JCPOA), 23, 34, 58, 112, 118, 157, 235
5+1 group, 74, 76, 86, 98, 131, 157, 235
Geneva, 45, 76, 114, 146
withdrawal from, 44, 79, 109, 132, 151, 162, 190
Joint naval drill, 160–161
Jurisdiction, 79

K
Kan, Naoto, 78
Kazakhstan, 121n40, 202
Khatami, Mohammad, 177
Kia, 128, 129
Kim, Seung-ho, 114
Kish, 117
Koizumi, Junichiro, 34, 40n56, 108
Korea International Cooperation Agency (KOICA), 82–83
Korea National Oil Corporation (KNOC), 65n31
Korean wave (*Hallyu*), 177, 240
Kuwait, 44, 59, 72, 97, 152, 202

L
Lavan, 112
Lebanon, 22, 79, 183
Lee, Myung-bak, 27, 80

258 INDEX

LG, 128, 130
Lifan, 144
Li, Fangwei, 225
Lion, 27
Liu, Yang, 225

M
Macao, 13
Mafia, 186, 205–206, 241
Malacca, 49
  Malacca Dilemma, 115
Malaysia, 55, 60, 118n3, 202, 208
Malek Ashtar University, 172
Maoism, 61
Maritime sleight of hand, 55
Mashhad, 223
MasterCard, 99–101
Mattis, James, 24
Mazaheri, Tahmasb, 78
McMaster, H.R., 24
Middleman, 45, 154, 157, 200,
  225, 238
Migration, see Brain drain
Militia, 22
Ministry of Knowledge Economy
  (MKE), 52
Missile
  ICBM, 158
  No-dong, 158
  Scud-B, 158
  Scud-C, 158
  Shahab-1, 158
  Shahab-2, 158
  Shahab-3, 158
Mitsubishi Heavy Industries, 145
Mitsui, 108, 144
Mobile Telecommunication
  Company, 222
Modernization, 124, 139, 160
Mongolia, 45
Moon, Jae-in, 27, 82, 163

Most biting sanctions ever, 24, 151
MT Hankuk Chemi, 84, 163
Multilateralism, 3
Muscat, 163
MVM, 145
Myanmar, 84

N
Narcotic-trafficking, 9, 37n6, 159
National Defense Authorization Act
  (NDAA), 57
National Iranian Oil Corporation
  (NIOC), 24, 106, 143
National Iranian Tanker Company, 53
Nationalization, 43, 50
Neither the East, nor the
  West, 28, 232
Netherlands, the, 43
New Far International Logistics
  LLC, 221
New York, 79, 220
New Zealand, 185
Nippon Export and Investment
  Insurance, 113
Nissho Maru, 50, 65n30
Non-Aligned Movement (NAM), 124
Nonproliferation, 156, 216
North Atlantic Treaty Organization
  (NATO), 192
Northeast Asia, 13
Nuclear deal, see Joint Comprehensive
  Plan of Action (JCPOA)
Nuclear Iran, 152

O
Obama, Barack, 30, 34, 37n11, 44,
  74, 80, 106
  singular foreign-policy initiative, 24
Oil discount, see Discounted oil
Oil-for-food program, 50

INDEX   259

Oil for gasoline, 54–56
Oil for gold, 54–56
Oil for goods, 54–56, 127, 237
Oil shock, 46, 52, 54, 114, 186,
    236, 239
Oil waiver, *see* Significant Reduction
    Exceptions (SREs)
Old friend, 79
Olympics, 187
Oman, 163
Operation Desert Storm, 22, 162
Opposition, 12, 182
Organization of Petroleum Exporting
    Countries (OPEC), 47,
    59, 62, 202
Ottawa, 222

P
Pacific Bravo, 59
Pahlavi monarchy, 14, 29, 45, 97,
    108, 139, 143
Panda International Information
    Technology Co., 222
Park, Geun-hye, 27, 114
Parliament, 83, 118, 142
People's Liberation Army, 157
Perl Harbor, 46
Petrochem South East Limited, 221
Petroliance Trading FZE, 221
Petronas, 118n3
Peugeot, 131, 144
Piracy, 159
    anti-piracy mission, 162
Pistachio, 132
Port of Kawasaki, 50
Powerhouse, 31
Privatization, 62
Propaganda, 11
Proxy, 22
Public diplomacy, 176–178
Putin, Vladimir, 30
Pyeongchang, 187

Q
Qatar, 85, 133
Quiet combat, 2

R
Rabiei, Ali, 85
Racial homogeneity, 185
Reform and opening-up (*gaige
    kaifang*), 30
Regional economic superpower, 112
Renault, 131
Ren, Zhengfei, 222
Resistance economy, 28, 132, 140
Resource diplomacy, 46–49
Responsible stakeholder, 31, 156
Rhetoric, 12, 21, 28, 75, 152,
    218, 232
Rhodesia (Zimbabwe), 4
Romney, Mitt, 163n5
Rouhani, Hasan, 130, 170, 206
Rubio, Marco, 148n14
Russia, 15, 55, 60, 101, 133, 161, 192
    5+1 group, 23
    arms exports, 154
    Iran ties, 29–30, 33, 62, 75, 190
    joint naval drills, 161, 239
    North Korea, 45
Russo–Persian War, 118

S
Saffron, 132
Saipa Corporation, 144
Saito, Mitsucho, 33, 61
Samoa, 224
Samsung, 128, 130
    gift ban, 187
Sanchi, 49–51
Sanctions-busting, 30, 50, 117, 241
    arms, 151–155
    Bank of Kunlun, 220
    Bank of Tokyo-Mitsubishi UFJ, 220

260 INDEX

Sanctions-busting (*cont.*)
BNP Paribas, 220
by any way, 201–203
Commerzbank, 220
Sanctions-busting (*cont.*)
cost of, 200
Credit Suisse, 220
doctorate in, 199
Dubai, 201–205
East Asian individuals, 223–226
East Asian states, 217–219
economic paramilitary, 205–208
greedy companies, 217–222
Hong Kong, 201–205
HP, 222
HSBC, 220
Huawei, 219–223
Meng Wanzhou, Sabrina,
222, 228n28
Panda International, 223
porters, 207–209
Skycom, 222
smuggling brothers, 203–206, 241
South Korean embassy, 203
Standard Chartered, 220
Triliance Petrochemical, 220
United States, 215–217, 242
Zanjani, Babak, 207
Zarrab, Reza, 207
ZTE, 221, 227n20
Saudi Arabia, 41n63, 44, 59, 62, 110,
141, 233
Schlumberger Oilfield Holdings
Ltd., 227n13
Sea of Oman, 161
Secondary sanctions, 9, 105–107, 142,
148n14, 215
Second Japan, 139
Second Middle East boom, 114
Security threat, 30
potential security threat, 221
Shahid Beheshti University, 172, 175

Shah of Iran, 139, 152, 156,
169, 190
Shanghai, 53, 121n40
Shanghai Cooperation Organization
(SCO), 192
Shanghai University of International
Studies, 175
Shiraz, 223
Sideline support, 86
Siege, 1, 5, 11
Significant Reduction Exceptions
(SREs), 56–61, 82
Silk Road, 121n40
Belt and Road Initiative (BRI),
115–116, 191
Singapore, 204, 208, 225
Sino Energy Shipping, 221
Sirri, 106
SK Incheon Petrochem, 60
Smart sanctions, 6, 183–185, 240
Smuggling, 49, 203–209, 241
Society for Worldwide Interbank
Financial Telecommunication
(SWIFT), 76, 87n10, 95,
100, 107
Soft power, 160
Song, Wong-yup, 82
South Asia, 74, 202
Southeast Asia, 202
Sovereignty, 21, 204, 215
Soviet Union, 29, 45, 124, 154, 190
Spain, 45
Spinach treatment, 31
Sri Lanka, 202
Ssangyang, 128, 143
Statecraft, 1, 54
Stock exchange, 99–101, 103n27
Straits of Hormuz, 23, 49, 63, 162
Strongest sanctions in history, 24, 182
Swiss, 220
Sword of Damocles, 105–107, 219
Syria, 183

INDEX 261

T

Tang, Yu-ling, 224
Targeted sanctions, 6, 181, 240
Technology
  dependence on, 218
  dual-use, 142–143, 157, 223, 237
  exchange center, 145
  transfer of, 139–147, 238
Tehran, 223
Tehran University, 175
Terminology, 9
Terrorism, 9, 22, 72, 159, 182,
    216, 238
  sponsor of, 22
Tillerson, Rex, 24
Total, 118n3
Toughest sanctions ever, 59
Toyota, 141, 144
Trade war, 207
Treaty of Turkmenchay, 118
Trump, Donald, 24, 36, 44, 61, 75,
    162, 235
  maximum pressure, 95
  travel ban, 172
  Western unreliability, 190
Turkey, 56, 58, 126, 133, 208
Turkmenistan, 121n40

U

Unforgettable loyalty, 52
Unilateralism, 3, 21
United Arab Emirates (UAE), 44, 60,
    81, 126, 129, 203, 208
United Nations (UN)
  Resolution 598, 35
  Resolution 1929, 23, 73
  Resolution 1737, 73
  Resolution 2231, 23
  sanctions, 23, 57, 94, 106, 116,
    152, 225
  Security Council, 23, 29, 73, 78

  veto, 29
  yes vote, 232
United States
  5+1 group, 23
  alliance, 24–27
  arms exports, 153
  Congress, 9, 23, 72, 107, 216
  Democrat, 80, 216
  Department of Commerce, 216
  Department of Defense, 216
  Department of Justice, 216,
    225, 228n28
  Department of State, 8, 22, 216,
    220, 228n29
  Department of the Treasury,
    8, 75, 216
  dollar, 21, 75, 81, 85, 95–96,
    171, 219
  Huawei, 222, 242
  IMSC, 162
  Iran–Contra, 152, 153
  IRGC, 94, 152
  Japanese mediation, 35, 41n65
  National Security Advisor,
    24, 41n63
  oil imports, 43
  Republican, 148n14, 163n5, 216
  sanctions against Iran, 8–10,
    21–24, 71, 183, 204,
    215, 234
  secondary sanctions, 105, 142
  Secretary of Defense, 24
  Secretary of State, 24
  Significant Reduction Exceptions
    (SREs), 57
  visa, 171
  ZTE, 221, 242

V

Vaezi, Mahmoud, 95
Vancouver International Airport, 222

262 INDEX

Venezuela, 56
Vienna, 202
Vietnam, 84, 202, 221
Visa, 171, 186
Visa (card), 100
Volkswagen, 131

W
War by other means, 2
War on terror, 108
Washington, *see* United States
Weapons of mass destruction
  (WMD), 12, 23
White House, 9, 23, 72, 77,
  107, 191
Wilson, Woodrow, 21, 36n1, 183
Woori Bank, 81, 84, 100
World Bank, 72, 97, 183
World War II, 46, 201
World War III, 24
Worse than the Mongol invasion,
  127–129, 237

X
Xi, Jinping, 32, 115–116,
  227n20, 236
Xiaomi, 129

Y
Yakuza, 186
Yeh, Susan, 224
Yiwu, 121n40
Yom Kippur War, 47

Z
Zanganeh, Bijan Namdar, 46,
  202, 207
Zarif, Mohammad Javad, 79,
  199, 206
Zhangjiangang, 161
Zhejiang, 121n40
Zhihang Ship Management, 220
Zhongnanhai, 32, 234
ZTE, 221, 227n20, 242

Printed in the United States
by Baker & Taylor Publisher Services